ALBERTA

PRI

VANCOUVER
NEW WESTMINSTER

U. S. A.

VICTORIA

BRITISH COLUMBIA
RIDES A STAR

Books by VERA KELSEY

Nonfiction:

BRITISH COLUMBIA RIDES A STAR

RED RIVER RUNS NORTH!

BRAZIL IN CAPITALS

SEVEN KEYS TO BRAZIL

FOUR KEYS TO GUATEMALA

With L. de J. Osborne

For Younger Readers:

YOUNG MEN SO DARING

TOMORROW IS FOR YOU!

SIX GREAT MEN OF BRAZIL

MARIA ROSA

Novels:

WHISPER MURDER

FEAR CAME FIRST

THE BRIDE DINED ALONE

SATAN HAS SIX FINGERS

THE OWL SANG THREE TIMES

BRITISH COLUMBIA
RIDES A STAR

by Vera Kelsey

Illustrated

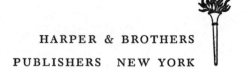

HARPER & BROTHERS
PUBLISHERS NEW YORK

CONTENTS

CONTENTS

vi

List of Illustrations

The following photographs appear in a group after page 76:

Alpine meadow, Mt. Revelstoke National Park

Earlscourt Ranch in the Cariboo-Nicola area, Canada's "Last Great West"

Anarchist Mountain rising above the Cascade Mountains, Okanagan Valley

Interlocked islands wall Howe Sound

British Columbia's fruit basket, the Okanagan

Abandoned gold mine in Coast Mountains

The Upper Columbia flows through Revelstoke

The Alaska Highway crosses Coal River

Thompson River canyon

The wild, lone Northwest

Mt. Cathedral in the Rockies of Yoho Valley

Tunnel Bluff on the Trans-Canada Highway

The *S.S. Moyie* on Kootenay Lake (from a painting by Alec J. Garner)

"Old and New Forest" by Emily Carr

"Mountain and Lake" by Dr. Lawren Harris

Victoria, the capital

Vancouver, on Burrard Inlet

Chemainus, Vancouver Island

Powell River

South Pender, Gulf Island

Trail, on the Columbia

vii

ACKNOWLEDGEMENTS

So many men, women and children contributed wittingly or otherwise to *British Columbia Rides a Star* that a second volume might be needed to list them all. Of scores, perhaps hundreds, with whom I talked in the friendly casual way of fellow travellers, I do not know the names. To them must be added whole groups of men and women all over the Province who gave generously of their time, experience and knowledge. Provincial and municipal officials, newspaper publishers and editors, librarians, executive secretaries or members of Boards of Trade and Chambers of Commerce, the personnel of ships, trains and hotels, bus and taxi drivers, specialists in every field, writers, artists—to them all, I am grateful.

To one man and one group I am deeply indebted: Mr. Edgar S. Robinson, Director of the Vancouver Public Library, and the tirelessly patient and able members of the various reference departments. They never failed me.

Specifically, I am grateful to others who, as one way of expressing it, went far beyond the call of duty to help a stranger to know, understand and enjoy the life of their community in particular, of the Province in general:

Campbell River ....Mr. and Mrs. Roderick Haig-Brown
Caulfeild ....Mr. and Mrs. Hugh Davidson
Dawson Creek ......Mr. and Mrs. D. R. S. Bell, Mr. C. S. Kitchen, Mr. and Mrs. Arthur McLellan
Fort St. John ......Mrs. George Murray, Mr. and Mrs. W. J. Powell
Kamloops ....Mr. G. A. Luyat, Supervisory District Agriculturist; Mrs. Editha McLennan, Mr. and Mrs. A. J. Millward
Kelowna ....Mr. Ian F. Greenwood, Assistant to General Manager, British Columbia Fruit Processors; Mr. F. M. Magee, Despatcher, British Columbia Interior Vegetable Marketing Board; Mr. Harry Van Ackeren, Manager, British Columbia Fruits, Ltd.

ix

ACKNOWLEDGEMENTS

Nanaimo .... Miss Anne Mossman, Director, Yellow Point
Little Theatre

Nelson .... Mr. E. W. Florendine, Secretary-Treasurer,
Chamber of Mines for Eastern British
Columbia; Mr. and Mrs. M. T. Harris, Mr.
R. R. McCandless, Mrs. Frederick Niven,
Mr. and Mrs. C. D. Pearson, Mr. Al Steele,
Mr. and Mrs. Gordon Webb

Penticton .... Mrs. George Kingsley, Mr. Wallace Mutch,
Mr. and Mrs. Howard Patton, Mr. J. W.
Watson, Penticton Co-operative Growers

Port Alberni .... Mr. and Mrs. M. E. Trebett

Prince Rupert ...... Mrs. Jocelyn Bolton, Curator, Museum of
Northern British Columbia; Mrs. J. T.
Harvey, Dr. R. Geddes Large

Proctor .... Captain Norman MacLeod, S. S. *Moyie*

Quesnel .... Mr. Arthur Downs, Managing Editor, *North-
west Digest*; Mr. Alvin Johnston, President,
Quesnel Historical Society; Mr. A. R. Traves,
District Agriculturist

Revelstoke .... Mrs. Earle Dickey

Terrace .... Mrs. Thomas Fraser

Toronto .... Mr. Roy Ransom, Geologist, Rio Canadian
Exploration Company, Ltd.

Vancouver .... Professor F. C. Boyes, University of British
Columbia; Mr. George J. Fox, Passenger
Traffic Representative, Canadian Pacific
Railway Company; Mr. and Mrs. Robert
Francis, Miss Marjorie Greig, Captain
Donald J. MacKillop, *Princess Alberni*;
Captain Angus MacNeill, S. S. *Coquitlam*;
Mr. E. R. MacPherson, Public Relations
Officer, Canadian Pacific Railway Company;
Mr. and Mrs. John Magor, Miss Mae Oxen-
dale, Mr. and Mrs. T. C. Rankine, Dr. Olive
Sadler, Dr. and Mrs. S. E. C. Turvey, Mr.
and Mrs. James Wallace, Mr. Roland Wild

Victoria .... Mrs. Gwen Cash, Mrs. Stella E. Gummow,
Superintendent of Women's Institutes; Mr.
A. H. Plows, Director, Division of Elementary Correspondence Instruction, Department of Education

Winnipeg .... Miss Clara Holmes

Acknowledgements

White Rock .... Mr. and Mrs. Melville M. Greig

From first to last both *British Columbia Rides a Star* and I owe more than can be said in words to Miss Doris Milligan and Mrs. Cassandra McClelland for friendship that included everything from loaning me their apartment to offering wit, wisdom and understanding, as needed.

VERA KELSEY

NECESSARY WORDS

British Columbia has many able writers. For this book, however, the publishers sought someone with little or no knowledge, preconceived impressions or opinions about the Province. Above all, no trace of the rooted loyalty, characteristic of British Columbians, for the particular corner in which they dwell. What would such an innocent see, hear, find significant, interesting, amusing, beautiful?

Without pride, I must admit they made the perfect choice. I did not even know that in size—366,255 square miles—British Columbia is larger than Texas. Larger than the United Kingdom and many other countries. Up and down and across it I travelled before I learned that in size—and lack of information about it—the Province is only comparable to Pakistan.

Horizontally, that is. As part of the great American Cordillera which margins the western Americas from Alaska to Cape Horn, it is ribbed from north to south with mountains. Some peaks rise from the bed of the sea to an average height of eight thousand feet. Some lift from the Mainland to heights of thirteen thousand, fifteen thousand and over. Together, they give the Province a maximum relief of almost twenty-five thousand feet and an area that, if ironed out, would double or triple its square miles.

Between the ranges lie a vast central plateau and long, shallow valleys or "trenches." To the north, the plateau is about two hundred miles wide, two thousand to four thousand feet in height. To the south it tapers to thirty or forty miles in width while it mounts to four thousand and six thousand feet. The valleys vary from a few hundred miles to the thousand-mile length of Rocky Mountain Trench. Mighty rivers or 40- to 130-mile-long lakes drain them all.

Lying between the 49th and 60th Parallels, British Columbia knows a climate as varied as its terrain. In the north, summers are short, winters long and rugged. In the interior, the warm and cold seasons achieve a balance except in the extreme south where, or so I was assured, four-month winters are the rule. The southern coast or Lower Mainland also claims a short winter. I found it a scrambled if often delightful jigsaw locally described as "All weather and no climate." Summer sometimes arrives full blown in April or May. Spring, a bittersweet thing, may follow to linger into mid-July.

With a general idea that I should wend my way back and forth from south to north, from the known to the unknown sections of the Province, I arrived in Vancouver on a what-is-so-rare morning in late May. Shortly and willy-nilly, because of the travel routes and climates, I found myself bound north "to take advantage of its summer season."

I not only took advantage of it there. I took it with me everywhere. Rains, cloudbursts, gales or cold might occur before I arrived, after I departed, or even during a night I remained at some destination. With one exception, none touched or hindered me. Secret of my success, I suspect, is that I never stayed long enough in one place to wear out the elements' patience. In Victoria and in Vancouver, where I did remain some months, I encountered everything they could devise.

For electoral, taxation and such purposes, British Columbia is divided into districts. During the past century, however, popular usage has defined and named, sometimes characteristically, sometimes illogically, eight different regions with more or less fluid boundaries. These are presented here in the order I visited them, an order not necessarily logical either.

Above all, I did not realize that lack of a Panama Canal or natural equivalent gave the entire Pacific Northwest the fortunate or unfortunate distinction of being one of the very last regions on this planet to know western civilization. Nor did I realize that, since the end of World War II, British Columbia's economy had been enjoying a tremendous boom, particularly in the north.

The first made it difficult, the second simple, to understand why I found myself writing again and again that one development or another was the largest in Canada, in the Commonwealth or the world.

And that reminds me to say here that all figures, statistics and early dates in these pages should be taken as suggestive or approximate. Population figures of one date might almost have doubled a few months later. Statistics have a way of dragging their feet for a year or more before coming to light. Pioneer dates often are controversial.

Because I did not travel as a scalpel to probe the depths of the Province's life and scene, but as a mirror to reflect them, the economic rather than the cultural picture may seem to be overaccented here. Other reasons, local and national, however, account for the fact that the economic picture *is* larger than the cultural. Here, too, I am reflecting the thinking of British Columbians.

Since the first white men crossed the Rockies, the Province has been frontier country. Hardly had the fur trade established its frontier than a gold rush overran it. As the gold rush tapered to a close, everywhere and naturally in a land carpeted with forests, loggers and sawmill operators took over and, in appropriate areas, fishermen, cattle raisers, fruit growers, mining interests. Today *their* frontiers are giving way before the impact of modern industry. Frontier life basically is an economic struggle.

As a British Colony and as a Dominion, Canada has been overshadowed, if not dominated by the United Kingdom on one side, by the United States on the other. Only now is an independent Canada emerging and a people conscious of their own nationality and of the culture inherent in their own soil.

Cut off from the rest of the Dominion by the Rockies, linked immediately by land, sea and air with the United States, British Columbia has been peculiarly vulnerable. Not only continental travellers but many British Columbians recognize in their tastes and ways of living, working, thinking, a closer kinship with the people of the American Pacific states than with those of eastern Canada.

By nature, their own, their climate's and the terrain's, British Columbians are sun worshippers and, in a land of mountains, lakes, rivers, sea, sports-minded the year round. Long, cold months or long, grey, wet months of winter behind them, they pour out of homes, offices, schools, to revel in summer sports and outdoor recreation. Under both heads, they cultivate gardens.

Travelling most of the Province from spring to late autumn, I thus had closer contact with their summer activities than with their cultural. And when I did not observe for myself that arenas, gymnasiums and other sports facilities were well provided for while theatres, auditoriums and other cultural facilities were not, someone always pointed!

Neither British Columbians whom I have quoted nor I mean to imply, of course, that the Province lacks cultivated men and women or appreciation of beauty in nature and the arts. On the contrary.

In a single winter, the little theatre groups, supported by almost every community, large or small, present everything from Aeschylus to modern London or Broadway successes. One or two, notably in Fort St. John, write many of their own plays. Almost every community sponsors an Artists Series. Though lacking facilities and population to attract the world's great artists, they do hear the best in music, performed many times by young artists who will be the celebrities of tomorrow.

Physically and psychologically, the Province is made to order for the artist with pen or brush, professional and amateur. Like Prince Rupert, various communities arrange summer art classes to which amateurs and professionals of every age and national origin flock to study under Canada's foremost painters. No one is out of range of a library, local branch of the Provincial Regional Library, or both. Play-reading and book clubs, art and music groups, orchestras, bands, choral organizations, are legion.

The number of British Columbians who have made or are making names for themselves in England, Europe and the United States is the best testimony to the stimulus they derived from their home background. As actors, dancers, musicians, vocalists, writers, to say nothing of radio and television personalities, they first tried their talents on Provincial audiences.

Perhaps British Columbians underestimate themselves and their accomplishments to date. Forgetting that at the earliest their Province did not find its feet until the twentieth century, they yearn to equal if not surpass within a decade or two all that other regions and countries have achieved cumulatively through centuries. And they forget or do not appreciate that most of the responsibility and vision for the direction and growth of every phase of their Province's life rests on but 56 per cent of a population of less than one and a half million. The remaining 44 per cent is under nineteen years of age or is sixty years and over.

Often as I listened, I remembered a woman I had noticed on the very first evening of my travels. Beneath the unblinking stare of a deck light and in the lee of an air vent, she sat apart from the passengers gathered along the rails of the ship about to sail.

Dark curls, fresh from a permanent wave machine, coiled tightly about her head. A faded sweater looped about her shoulders. Comfortable old slippers dangled from her weary feet. Plainly she had had only a few hours' notice to make that sailing and many things to do before she could. Now she was absorbed in extracting and organizing the contents of a handbag of such huge proportions and age that it once must have been known as a reticule.

Letters and documents. Small, bulging purses. Checkbooks. Cosmetics. Bits of wrapped packages. Rings and earrings. All manner of possessions piled up on the arms of her chair and on the deck about her feet. She continued to delve while the ship pulled away. She still was plumbing the apparently inexhaustible depths when I sought my cabin.

The next time I saw her she was smart in tweeds. As she walked briskly, purposefully down the gangplank, a group of official-looking gentlemen on the pier moved to welcome her.

Had I glimpsed then what I would know after thousands of miles of travelling the Province, I never need have written *British Columbia Rides a Star*. I could have clapped that woman between book covers. She was, in essence and in symbol, British Columbia as I saw it.

VERA KELSEY

BRITISH COLUMBIA
RIDES A STAR

1

EIGHT O'CLOCK, SAILING TIME

Bound for Prince Rupert and the Queen Charlotte Islands, the S. S. *Coquitlam* would travel at least fifteen hundred miles before returning to Vancouver. Yet, with every cabin filled, only an occasional passenger drifted out from "A" deck's horseshoe lounge and as silently drifted away. No one, not even a member of the crew, was to be seen on the dock. Except when the single enormous smokestack tossed a black feather into the air, nothing moved.

All around the warehouse-walled crescent of the waterfront, other ships, white or grey, and dark freighters, motionless at their berths, had steam up. Only here and there on them, too, a shadow moved.

If the purser had not taken my ticket and a steward my bags, I could have imagined myself aboard the painted ship that sailed the painted ocean. Instead, spared the prolonged banalities, din and confusion of transoceanic sailings, I was free to enjoy the cool, mother-of-pearl evening and the scene.

Beyond the warehouses, the towers of the Marine, Shell Oil and Vancouver *Sun* buildings rose like fence pickets above the darkening wall of the commercial district. Behind them a distant, silhouetted cluster of Coast Mountains thrust snow-powdered heads into clouds. About city and waterfront, Burrard Inlet faithfully reproduced the pale, merging greys of the sky, save low in the west where a sickle of sun cut through haze. The only positive notes in the whole muted scene were a few scouting gulls, a self-sufficient little coot riding the ripples like an old cowhand and, across the harbour, the snub, fir-tipped nose of Stanley Park sniffing shadowed waters.

Suddenly, up the stern stairwell darted a flock of young Indian boys. Neat as penguins in grey wool trousers and white shirts, their straight black hair so smooth and shining it might

1

have been lacquered on their heads, their dark eyes as quick as their soundless feet, they scurried about, not out of curiosity apparently but to check accustomed terrain. Satisfied that all was as it should be, they darted away.

Replacing them came a quartet of high-school girls, Indian also, in grey wool skirts, white blouses and dark-blue naval jackets, their curled black bobs framing youthfully pretty faces. Still no one said a word.

Forward now, however, the dock was alive with stevedores, the freight deck with crew. Obedient to their hand signals, a crane transferred great red nets of grapefruit, white balls of garlic, dozens—hundreds—of crates of soft drinks from warehouse to yawning hatch. Crates of "Grade A, Large Size" eggs, of sauerkraut, lettuce and catsup followed.

Nine o'clock! Lights came on in the office buildings and one by one the ships became golden glows in the dimming light. Passengers in husband-and-wife pairs or small family groups gathered along the rails. All practised so assiduously the traditional British custom of keeping themselves to themselves that they did not even speak to one another.

Ten o'clock! The ship's whistle blasted hoarsely and somewhere a man said, "Every time I make this trip, I think, 'There goes two days out of my life.'" Another answered, "Not me! I could ride these boats forever."

And beside me a carefully correct male voice murmured, "The delay in getting away is due, I imagine, to the fact that now June is here, fishing camps and resorts are opening up. All those eggs, fruit, et cetera, are going to them."

A smallish man stood there, with iron-grey hair, weatherbitten face, and four-foot shoulders or made so by a stunning white sweater, hand-knit from what must be the hawsers of the yarn industry. Exactly and perfectly woven into it, fore and aft, were totem poles in red and black. Without changing tone, he asked, "Notice the Indian kids? Forty-three of them aboard. Students from a residential school on Vancouver Island, returning to Prince Rupert and nearby villages for the long vacation."

While I visualized the ship as a shambles within twenty-four hours, he told me that before World War II he had been an Australian electrician. Now a Canadian, he worked for the British Columbia Fisheries "up north." Already he was so loyal to his northern home that he could not find a kind word for Vancouver or any part of the Lower Mainland.

As just one instance of its myriad superiorities, he assured me the tails of northern oolichan, or candlefish, were so oily that, touch a match to them and they'd burn, "actually give off the light of one candlepower per fish. You can't do that with Fraser River oolichan."

By that time we had crossed the harbour to round Stanley Park's nose into the First Narrows. Behind us, against a navy-blue sky, the lighted towers of Vancouver glittered like Walt Disney castles. Overhead, the long, slender span of Lions Gate Bridge, twinkling with lights and headlights of many cars, framed the cliff-walled passage to Howe Sound.

"Once the Sound is behind us, you can say good-bye to clear days," the new Canadian promised me. "To really warm ones, too. Rain, rain, rain, mist, fog—"

Those warning words I had heard so often in Vancouver that my bags bulged with umbrella, raincoat, rain boots, warm wool suits, and a powerful mosquito killer. I had rebelled at including a hot-water bottle, but now, lest this coastal authority convince me of my error, I waited for a semicolon in his proud listing of the rigours to come, and said good night.

3

"THE COAST"

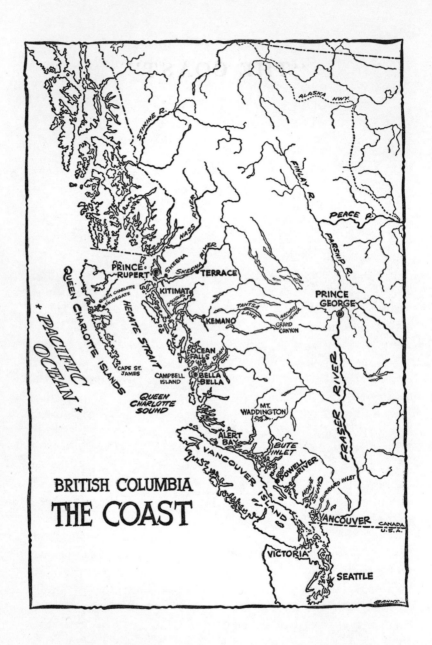

PACIFIC OCEAN

Queen Charlotte Islands

HECATE STRAIT

STIKINE R.

NASS RIVER

SKEENA RIVER

PRINCE RUPERT

KITIMAT

TERRACE

QUEEN CHARLOTTE SKIDEGATE

CAPE ST. JAMES

QUEEN CHARLOTTE SOUND

CAMPBELL ISLAND

OCEAN FALLS

BELLA BELLA

KEMANO

TANTSA LAKE

GRAND CANYON

PRINCE GEORGE

ALASKA HWY.

FINLAY R.

PEACE R.

PARSNIP R.

FRASER RIVER

MT. WADDINGTON

ALERT BAY

BUTE INLET

VANCOUVER ISLAND

POWELL RIVER

HOWE SOUND

BURRARD INLET

VANCOUVER

CANADA
U.S.A.

VICTORIA

SEATTLE

BRITISH COLUMBIA
THE COAST

2

IN SEA COUNTRY, HOMES ARE
FLOATS AND NEIGHBOURS A
COUPLE OF FJORDS AWAY

In a mother-of-pearl morning I stationed myself at "A"
deck's starboard rail for a long look at the famous Inside
Passage which, with those along the coasts of Norway and
Chile, provide the only three such vistas of alpine and marine
scenery in the world. During the night we had left the Gulf
of Georgia, one of its main features, behind. Now we were
unravelling the snarl of narrow channels between islands that
crowd like stepping-stones from Mainland to Vancouver Island.

When I pried myself loose an hour later, one thing I knew.
Whoever named this complexity of mountains, islands, waters,
forests, is a master of oversimplification.

Inside Passage is a vast "drowned" coastal trench, created
when some mighty volcanic upheaval sucked down the north
Pacific seaboard and the ocean rushed in. Beginning at the
south with Puget Sound and a sizable bite out of the Strait of
Juan de Fuca, continuing through the Gulf of Georgia and this
warren of waters, to end with Hecate Strait, water roofs it.
Submerged mountains and valleys floor it. The Cascade-Coast
Mountains wall it on the east. And on the west the snow-
capped Olympics, the Insular Mountains of Vancouver Island,
and the Queen Charlottes, separated by rolling seas, stand
like an eroded sea wall between Passage and Pacific.

Mountains, mountains, mountains! Rising straight up from
the sea, outer ranks of the Coast Mountains, now worn down
to foothills, form an irregular rampart of solid granite. Two
thousand to four thousand feet high, they are as solidly
napped with one of the finest rain forests on earth. Behind
them others rise, tier on tier, until clouds neatly guillotine
their heads.

7

But for the continental ice sheet of Pleistocene times and its modern heir, the Fraser River, the Coast Mountains would be recognized as a major part of one of the longest mountain systems in the Americas. In their drive to the Pacific, ice sheet and river gouged an immense valley through them.

South of that valley, as the well-known Cascades, they roll through northern California, Oregon, and Washington for more than seven hundred miles. North of it, as the little-known Coast Mountains, they continue on a northwest diagonal for more than a thousand miles. In those Canadian miles, they arch from four thousand feet at the south to a crown studded with peaks of ten thousand feet and over, then diminish again to four thousand feet in the Skeena River Valley. (Purists distinguish between the Coast Mountains, which follow the coast into Alaska, and the Coast Range, which, separated from them by a wide valley, rise behind them, to end in the southwest corner of the Yukon.)

For this lack of information about them, the Coast Mountains themselves are to blame. Because interior peaks veil their heads in clouds, only on very clear days are more than the coastal foothills visible. Masses of rocks hurled every which way by the ice sheet, deep crevasses and steep precipices discourage climbers interested in exploration or sport.

In addition, the mountains lack water. And this is strange because each year the coastal ranks are deluged with a hundred inches or more of rain and drizzle. In winter, heavy, wet snows fall so steadily over the inland ranges that sometimes by March they are buried thirty feet deep.

Their snow-white summits, not unnaturally, have created a great illusion—that it must be cold up there. On the contrary! The Northwest Drift, modern name for a branch of the Japanese Current, mellows the climate of the entire British Columbia seaboard. Average temperatures range from just above zero in January to 60 degrees in July, even though an occasional heat wave in the 70's or 80's may be included.

Not cold, but sea winds, heavy with moisture from the Pacific, sculpture granite crests into rounded, marble-white

8

beauty. Forced to climb thousands of feet to cross the mountains, they sooner or later must release their increasingly heavy cargoes—to fall as snow. Local mountain climbers complain that their chief problem is not how to keep warm, but dry.

Watching mile after mile of this panorama unfold, I kept one eye futilely cocked for the mysterious peak that literally and figuratively tops the geologic and scenic features of the coast. This elusive summit existed merely as rumour until 1922 when a surveyor sixty miles away both saw and photographed it. Named Mt. Waddington to honor the man who lost a fortune in the 1860's trying to build a wagon road from the head of neighbouring Bute Inlet to the interior, it is a small range in itself.

A score or two of lesser peaks rise from just under ten thousand feet to more than twelve thousand around a summit that looks like nothing so much as a thermometer thrust into a writhing patient's mouth. By means of this glassy, perpendicular tube. Mt. Waddington soars 13,260 feet to stardom as the highest mountain within British Columbia's borders. And one of the most difficult to climb. Not until 1936 was anyone victorious, and that was the sixteenth attempt.

Islands, islands, islands—thousands of islands! Flat-topped, undulating, cone-shaped, saw-toothed. Of every height from a few feet above sea level to three thousand or more. Of every size from a two-minute walk in circumference to Vancouver Island's 12,408 square miles. Those known as the Gulf (of Georgia) Islands are monadnocks which existed as islands way back in the heyday of the post-glacial sea. The rest are submerged mountains. Large islands are their peaks; little ones, their spurs.

Water, water, water! Inside Passage does more than embrace such substantial bodies as Puget Sound, Gulf of Georgia and Hecate Strait. Sea-filled valleys between island mountaintops and spurs filigree the seaboard with sounds, straits, channels, passages, passes, that look from the air to be a 100-mile-wide border of silver lace. Still more! In a south-north line, the mainland coast is 541 miles long. But to follow all the ins and outs of its inlets or fjords, bays, coves, a ship would have to travel more than eight times that distance.

Narrower than the fjords of Norway and Scotland, with higher and more nearly parallel walls, these inlets (according to Don Munday, Canada's well-known mountaineer) can be compared in size and intricacy only with those of Greenland. Rarely more than three miles wide, seldom less than a mile, they wind inland round snow-crested and glaciered peaks as much as ninety miles to endow British Columbia with a scenic wonderland.

One of them endows the coast with a phenomenon known as *Skookum-Chuck*—Strong Waters. A 20-foot tide pouring through its narrow mouth has about the same effect as a fire-hose forcing its way into a bottle. In retreat, especially when canyon walls pinch it or high winds excite it, it creates whirlpools that can suck down a Douglas fir or boil up in 12-foot-high caves into which its own waters crash in foaming cataracts. Residents on its shores must time their goings and comings to one of its four brief periods of slack water.

Above all, there are the forests. They climb every mountain slope—to about five thousand feet in the south, four thousand in the north. They carpet every valley. They wind round and round every island from waterline to summit.

Western red cedar and western hemlock dominate them. In the south they may grow to a height of 150 feet, with a diameter of two or three. A towering favourite is the Douglas fir, which averages two hundred feet in height and five in diameter. Here and there where fire or loggers have cleared a patch— about the size of a man's hand, comparatively—fresh greens of poplars highlight the sombre conifers. Up near the timberline are mountain hemlock and alpine fir.

I'm quoting, of course. To my untutored eyes they all were fir and should have been spelled f-u-r. From the level of a ship's deck they resembled the thick down of a beaver's inner coat. Quite truly, one can't see the trees for the forest.

From time to time glistening white threads twist down from mountaintop or shoulder to disappear and reappear until, as recognizable waterfalls, they plunge into the sea. Everywhere among the green, slim white skeletons remain rigidly erect. These cedar rampikes or "grisly spearmen with spikes uplifted in salute to death," as some depressed viewer described them, result largely from the thin and sterile soil in which the forests stand.

Stand! So shallow are their roots that each tree is held in place by its neighbours and by undergrowth as dense. Tall ferns, bracken and salal. Vines. Bushes, large and small. And that "most diabolical plant in North America," devil's club. Engaging to see, with its broad, rounded leaves set like petals about a spike of scarlet berries, it bristles with sharp, semi-poisonous thorns.

While my imagination creaked to picture this Amazon of green as merely a swatch of the great coniferous belt that runs from northern California to southern Alaska, a sawmill super-intendent, pausing to toss a cigarette overboard, asked, "Enjoying the bush?"

Bush! "Bush," to me, meant a vast unpeopled and undeveloped wilderness, like the African veldt. Yet, looking again at that unbroken façade of forest, I realized that bush was the word. Except for the odd slant of a roof among the living green, nothing suggested that since 1744 Europeans had known this coast. Or that for centuries, if not millenniums, before the first Spanish navigators viewed it, Indians had called it home.

To the Spaniards its temperate summers and rainy winters may have been too unlike sunny Spain or sunny Mexico. After taking possession here and there for the Crown, they sailed south. With one of them, the pinch of "official colonists" deposited on Vancouver Island's west coast insisted on sailing, too. Captain James Cook had been concerned to find a Pacific entrance to a Northwest Passage that would give British trade access from the Atlantic to the treasure of the Orient. Captain George Vancouver kept one eye open for it while he explored and surveyed the coastline.

Russia was the first power to have ideas about peopling it and, of all things, with Americans. In 1844, afraid that the British-French entente was growing too powerful, she offered to *give* what is now British Columbia to the United States. On one condition: that the States bar Great Britain from the Pacific.

Not until 1858 did England establish the Crown Colony of British Columbia. Another half century passed before British Columbians themselves recognized this coastal region as more than a bottomless reservoir of forest and fish to be exploited seasonally and ignored the rest of the year. Today, only 3 per cent—about forty-five thousand—of the Province's approximately a million and a half population live on "The Coast."

(Here, I should insert that the coast of British Columbia and "The Coast" are birds of two different feathers. The coast extends from the International Boundary to Prince Rupert, more than five hundred miles north. "The Coast," according to popular British Columbian geography, begins with Point Atkinson at the junction of the northwest waters of Burrard Inlet and Gulf of Georgia. The southern fragment, including Vancouver, is known as Lower Mainland. This is only the first of many confusions.)

My sawmill friend held a different view. Waving a hand to embrace thirty to fifty thousand square miles of land and sea, he complained, "People all over the place. Too many of them. And more coming all the time."

Fishing villages and logging camps account for a large share of the forty-five thousand. In bays and inlets, colonies of retired couples live on minute pensions or savings. In others, small farmers and ranchers, artists and writers have taken root. On hundreds of boats and floats (rafts), anchored in sheltered waters, still others live alone or in small groups from spring to fall or the year around.

As he talked, "Inside Passage" and "Coastal Trench" rapidly shrank to academic titles, useful to geographers, historians, mapmakers and others of that ilk. The coastal region came alive as a vast unintegrated community, with a way of life as characteristic and colourful as that of the Polynesians in warmer waters.

The scattered and mobile population depends on water for everything from dooryard and food to livelihood, transportation, communication and recreation. Their tens of thousand miles of super and secondary highways, streets and lanes are paved with water. Their comings and goings are regulated by the inexorable law of the tides. Hundreds of Provincial, local and personal signals, from lighthouses, flashing lights and buoys, to splashes of white, orange or black paint on rocks, serve as traffic lights and direction signs.

From family garages built over water, by flivver rowboat or fast, sleek cruiser convertible, men and women go to work, to church, to store and post office, to dance or visit with the neighbours. Stores provide floats as parking lots for their customers. In some places children drive to and from school in a "school bus" which picks them up at their own dock or gangplank every morning and delivers them to a school float in a village harbour. To serve them all, floating filling stations, complete with bright oil pumps and mechanics, anchor in accessible bay or cove.

In really out-of-the-way sea country, a privately owned float village may arrive by tugboat tow. Chains and cables anchor it offshore. Logs or boomsticks are interposed between it and beach or rocky cliff to ward off danger from violent tides or winter winds. That done, owner and partner—i.e., usually husband and wife—to be ready for business need only open the doors of general store, post office, restaurant, gas station, warehouse, bunkhouse, their own home, and sometimes of a portable sawmill.

Then, whether a steamer calls weekly, fortnightly or by chance, morning, afternoon or evening, "boat night" begins. Launches, rowboats, canoes, rented seiners or other holiday craft tie up all round the townsite, thick as cowponies at the hitching rails of cowtowns on Saturday night. Loggers, fishermen and their families, tourists and Indians, swarm aboard to divide up the fresh fruit, vegetables, meats. Each keeps his own record, pays what he owes to the penny. Meantime the owner, as postmaster, sorts the mail—if any. And in the restaurant, his wife prepares and serves steak dinners until she or the supply is exhausted.

What water does not give water brings. The farther north we sailed, the more small craft we saw. Strung out in broken packs like beagles hot on the scent of a rabbit, they appeared and disappeared between islands as they hugged the Mainland shore.

"Our swallows of Capistrano," my companion said. "When you see them heading north, it's spring."

As "float" houses, shops and services, they were hurrying to chosen locations from which they move about more readily than trailers on land to logging camps, fishing villages, farms and ranches. Among them were "general stores" whose stock included staples from shoes to hats for men, women and children and a few folderols like fancy kerchiefs and chocolates to please sweetheart or sweet tooth. A jewelry store, well supplied with engagement and wedding rings to meet the perennial demand after a long, grey winter. Hardware. Books and magazines. Drugs and cosmetics. Groceries. Fishing supplies. Lithographed Bible scenes, Testaments, rosaries. . . .

Dentists, doctors, opticians, insurance salesmen, radio repairmen tie up at each settlement for their annual one- to three-day visits. So do various combinations—barber and beauty operator, barber and tailor—to give impatiently waiting loggers manicures, shampoos, permanent waves, and to refurbish "store suits" for a brief fling among the bright lights of Vancouver.

Church and medical profession also join, by way of mission boats, to bring spiritual and physical aid to the coast. From spring to fall, small craft visit lone families in remote waters to make sure all is well, to translate or write letters for immigrants, to pass on tips about new job openings, deliver purchases made during the winter in Vancouver. Larger boats, like the small steamers the Columbia Coast Mission has operated since 1905, ply deeper waters the year round.

A combination hospital-chapel-movie-theatre-library, the Columbia Mission boat annually serves some five thousand people in 225 settlements and answers SOS calls from land or sea. Anyone, anywhere may signal for help, with a red shirt or a sheet with a lower corner turned back. Usually the captain receives calls when he listens in daily at a regular hour to the radiophone's clutter of conversations between fishing boats, logging outfits or coastal vessels.

If the call is urgent, no matter how far south or north the ship may be, she heads for it immediately—sometimes to travel day and night for a hundred miles or more, in snow and ice of winter, rains and fog of summer.

Distant freighters and fishing boats revealed men of this cold-water world at work. So seldom, however, was anyone to be seen on deck that they might have been operated by radar from some distant port.

One freighter had what looked like the hull of a nineteenth-century sailing vessel, with derricks replacing masts; engines, sails. Another was the unpainted shell of a small ship designed for war service but not completed in time. The majority were motor-powered barges, equipped with boxlike living quarters, breezeway, woodpile, and clothesline.

Bouncing over the swells came a fantastic craft—with twin prows hardly larger than a rowboat's, twin cabins, and on two small, raised rear decks enormous wooden spools, one a violent blue, the other glassily varnished. From one stubby mast fluttered a faded blue flag; from the other, a blue-and-orange.

"Gillnetters," another rail-gazer told me. "They often tie up like that, side by side. So one fisherman can run both boats while the other sleeps, eats, or mends his gear. For company's sake, too. Fishing in these parts is a hard and lonely life."

They were not fishing now. Too early in the season, he said, though they might be on their way to river or bay location. There, by means of the spools, or rollers, the fishermen pay out long, small-meshed webs with lead weights along their lower edge, cork floats on the upper, across likely stretches of water.

This they do again and again, "as fussy as some fool woman about the hang of her skirt," until the net drifts just right with the current. For salmon, they add a large-mesh web or trammel. Into them swim the fish, confident they have the right of way, until their heads are caught by the gills.

Soon we passed an ungainly craft as long and wide as a barge, with a two-storey structure forward, a deep well midships. Aft, on a raised deck, an enormous seine was coiled so precisely that its cork floats described a perfect new moon across its middle. This was a "seiner," aristocrat of the coastal fishing fleets (but not of the deep sea!), manned by a skipper and crew of two or three. Battered and clumsy though it may look, such a boat with its equipment can represent an investment of $100,000.

Hard as the life of gillnetter and seine fisherman may be, it is a foam-rubber existence compared with that of the proletariat of the fishing profession—the handliner. All alone in a rowboat, this "two-bit" fisherman trolls promising waters of sea or river from dawn until late afternoon, his eye alert to sundry poles rigged with lines, bait, weights, fixed to both sides of his craft. When a fish strikes, he ships his oars to haul in the plunging line. If the strike is a 40-70-pound salmon, the battle to boat it usually ends when both are exhausted.

This the handliner does over and over—if lucky!—until, since he carries no ice, he must stop in time to row to the nearest fish buyer. Catch sold, he rows again to some deserted beach, to unpack his gear, wash the boat and haul it above tidewater for the night. Then he is free to set up his tent, build a fire, cook his supper, wash up and, at long last, turn in for the few hours remaining before dawn comes round again.

At my starboard-rail salon, and thereafter during the voyage, I learned of other hardy souls whose love of sea and boats had lured them from more gainful areas to pioneer Mainland seaboard or island, on hope and a shoestring. Tales of young and able men, of married couples who, with boatyards, floating trading posts, floating filling stations, fishing camps and summer resorts, had built better mousetraps were so numerous that if the trend continues this coastal region one day may be as webbed as a fishnet with beaten paths.

3

"WHERE WOULD YOU BE TONIGHT?"

Mountaintop Cormorant Island lies off the northeast coast of Vancouver Island, just where crowding islands end and Queen Charlotte Sound begins. From the forested ridge above an open harbour, Alert Bay rises in a broken arch from its brief business street. About 125 miles due north, Bella Bella rises in the same pattern from the forested ridge of Campbell Island, one of the welter of islands off the Mainland coast. Like sturdy bookends, they enclose volumes of varied interest.

As our ship approached Alert Bay, two signals should have warned me that times had changed for the one-time village, known for its cormorants, large Indian population, and totem poles. First a cloud of knowing gulls took off from rocks and rotted piles to scout the ship's wake for a midmorning snack while, with bitter cries, a lone and rusty cormorant lumbered away to a small cemetery. Then the cemetery came into clear focus.

An Indian cemetery, now only a few feet from the lip of the ridge which the sea has been eating away, it was so much closer to its past than to its present that its graveposts and gravehouses, sunken and crumbling, were lost in tall, wild grass. A ragged line of grey posts only faintly suggested the brilliantly carved and painted totems which once honoured the Great Spirit and tribal heroes.

Though I knew that today's port is a growing distribution, fishing and logging centre and headquarters for many regional services, I was totally unprepared to see and hear how fast times had changed.

Because we remained but twenty minutes, no passengers could go ashore. But as we neared the dock, a bevy of Indian

17

high school girls in the standard grey, white and blue uniforms rushed to lean perilously forward over open water. Our passenger equivalents climbed the ship's rail to do the same. There, almost meeting in mid-air, they exchanged greetings and chitchat that rivalled the excitement and decibels of a teen-age Vancouver audience dissolving at the feet of the current crooner sensation.

They shrieked with laughter, groaned with despair. They slapped palms to forehead, swooned, stood rigid, mouths and eyes wide open. They stamped their feet, lifted arms to heaven, whirled round in circles. Their native idiom was no more difficult to understand than which reaction indicated delight, which shock or horror.

With literary memories of the impassive, taciturn Indian fixed in my mind, the impression they generated that life in these remote waters was an unbroken series of emotional crises seemed amusing. At first. As it became plain that they were repeating themselves over and over, I wondered if—subconsciously, of course—these young things could be staging a modern version of the powwow from which their ancestors drew pride and strength and unity of purpose. If, using their curled bobs, modern dress, extravagant speech and gestures as weapons, they were not fighting for a secure place in the very way of life their ancestors had fought to reject.

As the ship pulled away and the laughter and screaming died, I was sure of it. Both the girls and the boys who had stood wordless but shining-eyed in the background visibly exuded satisfaction and pride in that synthetic demonstration.

Hardly had Cormorant Island fallen behind than the sun burned partially through the overhead haze to silver the sound's low, slow swells and unveil on the west a wall of midnight-blue mountains whose crests and upper slopes were planed with snow. The Insular Mountains of Vancouver Island! And on the east, the Coast Mountains, now on their northwest diagonal drawing closer to the sea, finally to form the coastline itself, displayed several ermined peaks.

Within that handsome frame, a changing scene appeared.

Lower, rounded hills replaced the coned or peaked coastal foothills. Hemlock and spruce replaced Douglas fir. The forests in general were of visibly poorer quality. Islands became lower and broke up into groups of smaller islands, some almost denuded of trees, their shores a mass of black and grey rocks, softened by golden lichen.

One could watch the sea at work, undermining trees, rank by rank, even in the act of carrying them away. Watch white-fanged breakers gnawing large islands into smaller ones, small ones down to their basic rocks.

If Inside Passage's changing scene was varied, often dramatic, equally so were the insights provided by the passengers into the calibre of the men who have built and are building British Columbia.

There was Commander, a snowy-haired gentleman of impressive dignity and charm. Seated at a window table in the lounge, he daily poured over scientific tomes written in such technical language that few people could read them. Yet, born in Lancashire, England, seventy-two years before, he had started to work "in the mill" when he was only ten and so small he had to stand on a box to operate the machines. After three years of working mornings, going to school in the afternoon, he ended his formal education to settle down as a full-time millworker for the rest of his life.

Fourteen years later a daring fellow worker proposed that they try their luck in western Canada, then at the last moment backed out. Though Commander never had been outside Lancashire, knew only the name of one town in Canada's west, Saskatoon, he set out alone.

Working on a Saskatoon farm, he heard about Victoria, on the very rim of the Pacific. There, the flash and dash of fire apparatus filled him with desire to join the city's Fire Department. He did, to rise steadily through the years to the title of Chief. When he retired at sixty-five, he knew so much about fire fighting and fire prevention that the Canadian Navy made him a reserve officer and consultant to the Admiral who heads Canada's fire-prevention program in time of war.

19

There was the Russian I'll call Salamander. In 1922, as a teen-ager, he had fled from Communist Russia to China. During the thirty years before he fled from Communist China to Canada he became a man of standing and property. Both were lost, of course, when the Communists confiscated all privately owned wealth, Chinese and foreign.

Even so, as the Communists replaced every foreigner with a Chinese, the nationals of European and American countries could claim protection from their home governments, eventually be assisted to leave. Refugees from Russia's Communism, though good citizens of China for thirty years, had no country. Unless Chinese friends risked their lives to help them secretly, they starved. And many did.

Aided by Chinese friends and his knowledge of Chinese custom and languages, Salamander managed to remain alive though twice the Secret Police threw him into prison for long periods. By the second time he knew all the answers, especially the answer to a key question embedded in an endless questionnaire.

"What work did your father do?" it asked. Salamander's father had been a successful fur merchant in Czarist Russia, but he wrote, "Labourer. Very poor man."

For no good reason, I said, "You could have said farmer, couldn't you?"

"No, no! Oh, no! Farmer, he is very bad capitalist. He owns land. He pays two-three other mans to work for him."

Over and over, as he talked, he interrupted himself to whisper, "Oh, I am so happy, so happy, so lucky." Once, pulling out an almost empty bag of smoking tobacco and a few cigarette papers, he said, "When these finish, I smoke no more. Before time I smoke because I am so afraid something must go wrong. Now I walk close by soldier or policemans and fear nothing. No man can touch me. I am Canadian."

Also with us were "Kitimat characters"—assorted young men who remained in their cabins to polish up their poker game in anticipation of the cutthroat competition that thousands of men isolated in a wilderness make standard practice.

And Indians, adult and juvenile. Never by glance, word or gesture did they voluntarily indicate their awareness that any non-Indian was aboard.

My fear that, with forty-three grade and high school youngsters at large, the ship would be a shambles, died early on the vine. Except that the boys' sleek hair became more dishevelled daily as they wrestled over checkerboards and other games, and in "C" deck corridors girlish giggles flowed like running water, they all might have missed the boat.

Not until the evening before we reached Prince Rupert did they express their collective presence. Gathering somewhere below decks, they set the whole ship athrob with the unique beat their clear young voices gave to school songs, hymns, chants, popular favourites old and new. Then it was passengers and crew who were silent.

The teacher in charge of the girls and the young sports instructor in charge of the boys laughed when I spoke of the students' model behaviour and becoming uniforms. The children did want to do the right thing, they agreed, and by June, after nine months of school life far from home, their goodness did reach a peak. September ships which carry them back to school after a long, undisciplined summer sometimes reach Vancouver slightly the worse for wear. As for the "uniforms" —they were the students' own idea, a fad of the moment.

The Alberni Indian Reservation School from which they came is one of several such elementary schools maintained by the United, Anglican and Catholic Churches in British Columbia. All follow the curriculum and standards of Canadian schools everywhere and the children work hard to meet them, are very proud when they can. In 1954, this Alberni school added a High School Residential Plan, to enable girls and boys to live at the school and attend the city high school in Port Alberni.

After hours when only Queen Charlotte Sound's rollers, accompanied by grey skies and a cold breeze from the open Pacific, had filled our view, we entered a wild and lonely world. Mountaintop islands forming Inside Passage's western sea wall

21

closed round us again. And to the east, snow-heavy peaks rose six to eight thousand feet from the succession of fjordlike passes that add up to Dean Channel.

Even when the ship moved between a leaden sea and a tumbled sky of small white clouds and long grey windrows that threatened to engulf us all in gloom, the scene was impressive. With sunset it became spectacular.

On the dot of nine, the sun, a blazing ball, burned through the clouds above the mountaintops. The windrows fled south. The white clouds scattered in filmy sprays. Then as we unwound mile after mile of silver-blue waters, the reflected mountain crests, advancing, withdrawing, engaged in a stately minuet. And the sun, in an ecstasy of light, flung itself among them.

Soon it was gone and the snow-capped peaks, flushing gold and crimson, stood out in three-dimensioned beauty. Gradually they faded to orange, burnt sienna and rose, pale lemon and shell pink, while their headlands and slopes melded every shade of blue against a sky that now curved from tourmaline to turquoise.

In that "celestial light," as coastal residents describe it, we rounded the last island to see Bella Bella ahead. Some sixty years ago a colony of Norwegian immigrants crossed Canada to find here the site that most nearly resembled the forested mountains and fjords from which they came. Here they planted orchards and gardens, fished and logged a little. Now they are gone and the orchards are going. Sons and grandsons prefer to fish and log full time.

Round them has grown a village, largely peopled by Indian fishermen and their families. A substantial fish cannery and several small ones logically are the leading industry. But dominating village and inlet is the big white Mission Hospital of the United Church.

Again no passengers could go ashore, but there was no need. Bella Bella came to us. Before we arrived, while we remained, even as we drew away, Indians of every type, age, size, dress, wealth or lack of it had come or were coming down the long pier across the tidal flats. Among them were a dozen white men and women.

Unable to see any reason for such a gathering, a passenger waylaid a local resident wandering happily about with an assortment of magazines from the ship's newsstand under his arm, to ask for one.

"Madame," he said, "once every two weeks a coastal steamer makes its way in here. If you lived in Bella Bella, where would you be tonight?"

4

PIONEERS WITH PICTURE WINDOWS

Heavy green mountains, their feet in sparkling emerald waters, their snow-splashed rock crests sharp against blazing blue sky, were filing past the *Coquitlam* to port and starboard the next morning. We were ascending Douglas Channel, the 75-mile fjord at whose head stands Kitimat.

Kitimat (People of the Snow) and Kemano (Men of the Rock) are old Indian names for the youngest of the three great industrial communities now taking advantage of the hydro-electric power this coastal watershed affords. With Powell River and Ocean Falls, they are, in fact, three of Canada's largest industrial enterprises.

Because industry is not, to my garden variety of mind at least, an absorbing or even a comprehensible subject, I had thought that to see one of these communities would be to see them all. But now, remembering the hundreds of miles of green, varied so rarely by small villages, I had reviewed the day before, I was sorry Powell River and Ocean Falls lay behind us. One must see at first hand the distances and wilderness involved to appreciate the dynamic imagination and grand-scale planning, the skills and effort that have gone into making this trio celebrated realities.

Powell River and Ocean Falls are the sites of giant paper and pulp mills. Both are beautifully situated. Powell River, eighty-five miles north of Vancouver, looks across the Gulf of Georgia to Vancouver Island. Ocean Falls, almost 350 miles north, overlooks Cousins Inlet. Freight boats from all the world arrive at their long piers. Bag booms filled with millions of feet of logs pattern their harbours.

For different reasons, their company towns are especially interesting. Powell River's, because in the forty-four years of its existence so many employees have bought their homes that it now has lost its title of company town. And, because of the improvements they have made, of neighbouring lakes, sandy ocean beaches, good hunting and fishing, the mill one day may find itself merely a bread-and-butter feature of a popular summer resort.

Ocean Falls, a youth in comparison and, with thirty-five hundred people, only a third as large, is a modern town whose white homes, apartment houses and shops cling like swallows' nests to the face of a mountain. It still is a company town though here, too, employees have begun to buy their homes. On a glorious sunny day, Cousins Inlet and mountain walls provide a setting frequently compared with the Riviera's.

The catch is that with an annual rainfall of 180 inches not many days are clear and sunny. And with access by sea and air only, the workers, particularly young, unmarried men, often are overcome by a sense of being cut off from what is known as Life. The result is one of the highest labour turnovers in the Province.

Others, to whom high wages and low living costs spell security, make a determined effort to cope with "life under a waterfall." With more than eighty recreational clubs, a whirling social round, regular and healthy deposits with their Credit Union, they keep themselves too busy to think about weather and isolation.

Kitimat also was born on a bed of blueprints, and its rearing repeats in some degree the experience of the older enterprises. Its different purpose, however, and the much grander scale on which it was conceived make it unique among all Canadian industries.

Its origin dates back to a summer day in 1874 and a high pass behind the Coast Mountains, four hundred miles north of Vancouver. Then Charles Horetsky looked down on Lake Tahtsa, one of a chain of long lakes that lie like bright, light-blue canoes on a sea of lesser mountains, rippled with forest and shadowed by black-rock, white-capped crests. But viewing it all with the eye of a surveyor searching out a route for what

25

is now the Canadian National Railways, the wretched man wrote, "A terrible silence, broken only by the crash of some falling avalanche, reigned over this scene of desolation," and went away.

Fifty-four years later the Provincial government, increasingly restive about the vast waste of hydroelectric power draining from these high lakes into the Nechako River, sent in surveyors. But, despite the exciting possibilities their reports revealed, no Canadian industry was so desperate at that time for power that it would spend the half billion dollars required to develop it here.

Came World War II, to uncover uses for metals unneeded by the pre-war world and to multiply the demand for those already in use. Aluminum was one of the metals already in use. And the eastern plants of the Aluminum Company of Canada —"Alcan," for short—were approaching the limits of expansion. They sought a western site capable of continuous industrial development, large enough to accommodate a city of fifty thousand people, and accessible by air, sea and land.

In this wilderness, a windsock-shaped area met all their specifications. From a 50-mile-wide mouth, bounded on the south by what is now Kemano, on the north by Kitimat, it tapers east for 150 miles. Obviously under the influence of Horetsky, they titled the six-part saga they were to write here *Kitimat Project*.

In 1948, Alcan surveyors came in. In 1951, construction began. In 1954, a closing switch signalled completion of the "first phase" of the project.

To merge a dozen of the high lakes in a 358-mile reservoir, they sealed the Grand Canyon of the Nechako River with Kenney Dam, largest rock-fill dam in the Commonwealth. But now, between the lakes forever barred from their self-chosen outlet to the sea and sea-level Kemano, their new, man-determined outlet, Mt. Dubose intervened.

To induce their waters to drop sixteen times the height of Niagara Falls to the turbines they were to turn, Alcan workers drove a 10-mile-long tunnel into the mountain's granite heart.

And there, in a bedlam of din and darkness, they blasted out a cavern, large enough to house the S.S. *Queen Mary*. In the cavern they installed the largest impulse electric generators in the world.

Dam, tunnel and generating station were routine, however, compared with Kitimat Project's fourth undertaking—the 50-mile transmission line from Kemano to Kitimat. It not only had to contend with muskeg, forests, glaciers, snowfields, precipices, crevasses and 80-mile gales, but with iceloads thicker and heavier than any existing cable could support. So, laboratories devised one.

Meantime, muskeg and snowfields had blocked the men trying to lay out a route for the line up and over mile-high Mt. Kildala. To save months, possibly years, Canadian airmen first developed new techniques to overcome thin air, treacherous downdrafts, and other local hazards. Then helicopter-borne surveyors mapped out a course—in weeks.

But when six windy winter months later, a 4-mile road edged up Kildala, the pass still remained six steep miles away. To blast out miles of "switchbacks" in the face of snowslides and avalanches again threatened to take both lives and years. To the rescue this time came a fearless French Canadian and his helper. In seven days they piloted a huge crawler tractor up a snowfield 150 feet deep at the base to the Pass. Even so, and with helicopters carrying everything from Band-Aids to girders, three and a half years passed before fifty miles of 80- to 110-foot towers were ready to carry the heavy cable to Kitimat.

Kitimat Smelter began on the cold, grey April day in 1951 when six carpenters stepped from a small boat onto the snow-deep tidal flats at the head of Douglas Channel. But again three and a half years passed before the "first phase" of the smelter was ready to produce annually ninety thousand tons of aluminum.

Men, machines and time were the only tools required to clear Kitimat River's odiferous 2-mile-wide delta of mud and decaying bush, to dredge gravel from the harbour bottom and more from a neighbouring gravel mountain, to pack the gravel

27

deep enough to insure firm footing for the involved 12-acre web of block-long aluminum buildings, towers, tanks, chutes and cable that today functions upon it.

At last, like the old nursery rhyme about the rat that began to gnaw the rope, the waters of the reservoir began to turn the turbines, the turbines began to drive the Kemano generators, the generators began to feed power over the transmission line. And at Kitimat on August 3, 1954, the Duke of Edinburgh figuratively "tapped" the first 50-pound aluminum ingot.

Within three years the smelter's annual production had more than doubled. When Kemano's generators reach their total 1.2 million h.p. capacity, a few additions and constructions again will double its capacity to give Kitimat Smelter an ultimate annual production of 550,000 tons. IF—

Because the future of Kitimat Project depends on a permanent supply of thousands of trained, experienced men, young, vigorous and for the most part married men, the Municipality of Kitimat was designed to be a "model workingman's city." Before a nail was driven, three years of study by the foremost city planners in North America were invested in blueprinting an independent, self-governing community that would attract and hold young, able and responsible citizens.

The plan calls for an 80-acre City Centre where all main roads meet and all shops, banks, hotels and other features essential to a downtown district will be located. About it, ten individual neighbourhoods, each with its own shopping centre, eventually will circle.

With the safety and well-being of young families its primary concern, this "suburb without a metropolis" is six miles from the noisy smelter area where docks, wholesale houses and industries are or will be located. Two miles distant is the service area where auto repair shops, laundries, dairies, bakeries, the Canadian National Railways depot, can operate without anyone in Kitimat losing sleep.

The townsite itself is so laid out that every home will face parkways whose winding paths lead to schools, playgrounds, churches, shopping centres. With streets running behind the

28

homes, backyards, alleyways and sidewalks were eliminated. And to cope with an annual 93-inch fall of rains and snows, covered terraces, breezeways and wide eaves permit children to play outdoors in bad weather.

While some two thousand men, women and children still lived in the construction camp, Alcan requested the Provincial Legislature to establish the Municipality of Kitimat. This was done in March, 1953. One month later, 70 per cent of the men and women eligible to vote splashed through rain and knee-deep mud to elect their own municipal council and reeve.

On that August afternoon when the Duke of Edinburgh formally inaugurated the smelter, fifteen miles of paved and gravelled roads led to and through three hundred acres of cleared townsite. A million-dollar bridge crossed Kitimat River. Electricity had been brought in from Kemano. Water mains and storage tanks for eight hundred homes had been installed.

Within another year, deep-sea freighters were bringing bauxite to Kitimat's smelter from Jamaica sixty-five hundred miles away and coastal freighters and steamships made it a regular port of call. Commercial and private planes dropped down to its airport. The Canadian National, via a branch line from Terrace on the Skeena, linked it with the transcontinental line. A highway to travel the same forty miles to the Prince Rupert-Prince George Highway was under construction. And with seven thousand people in residence, Kitimat was on its way.

A few more years and Kitimat may be difficult to distinguish from industrial cities all over Canada and the United States. Already the population has doubled, as have the miles of streets and highways. Soil excavated from the Kitimat River bed and more freighted down from Terrace frame "Neighbourhood A," the first residence section in lawns.

On the sunny June morning in the last months of its pioneer period when I first glimpsed it, it appeared that its modern era had arrived. Across the head of the channel, the smelter's acres of aluminum and steel shone like a silver web. From it, tall towers of the transmission line marched past the grey and white village of Kit-a-maat Indians, across the feet of south shore mountains, up and over Kildala with the precision of Seaforth Highlanders. The dock bustled with people, taxis, trucks, private cars.

As I stood at the crowded rail watching Vancouver's lettuce and eggs wing ashore, a small ramshackle bus rattled to a stop beside the gangplank. "That's for sightseers," my neighbour said. "Shall we take it?"

Two hours later we returned, not only physically exhausted, but depressed. We were not alone. In cabins or in deck chairs all about us, fellow passengers sagged in the same discomfited state.

Many reasons are given for Kitimat's wearing impact on the stranger within its gates. A local Adam declared that women are responsible, specifically the "third woman." Two, it seems, are enough; they will stick together through thick and thin. With the third, "naturally," distinctions and prejudices begin. As proof he recalled the good old days of 1951-54 when men of all walks and levels lived and worked together without regard to economic, professional or social backgrounds. As Kitimat took form, however, more and more women, as wives, secretaries or clerks, arrived with complete sets of conventions and preconceived ideas.

But, naturally, also, the types of men who conceived and built Kitimat Project now are engaged in high adventure elsewhere. Men and women—who work with time and precedent, not against them—are filling in the design its creators merely sketched.

Above all, or so it seemed to me, pioneering in a wilderness, whether with covered wagon, axe and candle or with all of today's techniques and conveniences, is still pioneering. Possibly even more so.

These pioneers arrive to find approximately $15,000 homes —the minimum value—complete with electricity, telephone, plumbing, picture windows and carports waiting to be bought —or built—"on easy terms." Shops and services provide all the necessities, many luxuries. Kitimat's blueprints indicate parks, playgrounds, leave the way open for the pioneers to add them and all the equivalents of food, clothing and shelter for mind and spirit.

They start without the challenges and perils Canadian and American frontiersmen knew during the past three centuries. They come from all corners of the world, speak a babel of foreign languages, represent every background. The Kitimat of tomorrow, I thought often as we drove about, would be much more interesting than today.

Today, though enclosing mountains, green from root to summit, invited the eye, they repelled desire and foot. So there was no escape from the stark, metallic grey gravel which covered the valley floor. Without grass, shrubbery, trees, the straight-lined, flat-surfaced, "modern utilitarian" homes, shops, industries appeared to stare into space like eyes devoid of lashes and brows.

On this hot, sunny day, every truck moved in a cloud of gritty grey dust. Every man who walked did also. Even a small, once-white dog that sat down to scratch a flea was lost in a miniature fog. Against dust and glare, all doors and windows were closed.

Not a woman or child was visible as the bus sped between the grey buildings and installations of the smelter and shops and factories of the industrial district. Beyond them drab, temporary dormitories, kitchens, commissaries of the construction camp and the small, prefabricated homes, schools and other buildings of smelter employees covered more acres. And beyond a blur of gravel mountain, a hotel, motel, the Kitimat *Northern Sentinel*, and the million-dollar bridge, lay "Neighbourhood A."

Here, about a large, one-day-to-be-landscaped commons, one-to-four-unit homes and the first block-long units of its shopping district were centred. Their inviting displays brought wails of anguish from the passengers, each with lists of lost or forgotten articles, souvenirs, fruit, to purchase. This was Closing Day observed by every store in Kitimat!

On once more—between acres of levelled, gravelled land

waiting for more homes, shopping centres, and acre after acre of felled trees and undergrowth, piled and smouldering beneath billows of white smoke. Constantly we met trucks loaded with more gravel. At regular bus stops, we passed small, silent groups of men, suitcases or duffel bags at their feet, waiting to be carried to the *Coquitlam* or the Canadian National depot and away.

Though the labour turnover still is high, said the elderly Kitimat gentleman who had joined us, it does not reach the 100 per cent it sometimes did when the project was under construction. Then, as six hundred men came in six hundred went out. The magic of fabulous wages was not enough to overcome isolation, lack of recreation, including "just the sight of young women moving about."

At that point a dark, youngish man, who never before or later in my hearing opened his mouth, interrupted to say, "Know what Alcan should have done? Before they touched stick or stone for the smelter, they should have put up a candy factory and a dime store and filled them with nice, no-fooling, good-looking girls."

From the driver's seat came a fervent "Hear! Hear!"

As a reward for that suggestion, the driver whirled us past what he called the "dee-lux homes of the big shots" and their splendid mountain view and back to the hotel. As my companion and I belatedly entered the lobby, a forbidding chill greeted us. Small wonder! An early-bird passenger was concluding his strolling appraisal of décor, personnel and guests with "I say, not *bad*. Not bad at all!"

Hastily we departed to try our luck at the "ladies'" beer parlour next door. No sooner had we stepped inside the dim, well-filled room than an even more penetrating chill froze us to the threshold. Later—too late for our pride—we learned that Kitimat's wives and secretaries view with restraint each new feminine arrival until she has proved her virtue.

Pioneers! Oh, Pioneers!

My impression of Kitimat represents, of course, only one point of view. There are others.

32

Just before we sailed, a young couple who had left a tearful, homeward-bound Ontario grandmother in her cabin, stopped near my deck chair to assure their loudly alarmed small son that *they* were not leaving Kitimat. "It's a rough life," the wife told me, "but, as you see, we like it."

A few minutes later, while water widened between wharf and ship, the grandmother herself appeared. After a long look landward, she said softly but clearly, "Behold, I will do a new thing; now it shall spring forth; shall ye not know it? I will even make a way in the wilderness."

Turning to find me within earshot, she explained, "I was quoting Isaiah and thinking of all those young people in Kitimat. *They* are doing a new thing in this wilderness, but they don't know it, poor dears. They make everything a matter of course."

5

JUST EAST OF SUNDOWN

On my map the Queen Charlotte Islands looked like the partially assembled jigsaw of a seahorse, abandoned when the pieces forming the head and curled-tail tip were missing. Actually, as the peaks and spurs of a submerged mountain chain, they are a 156-mile-long archipelago, divided by a thread of water and Skidegate Inlet into two immense islands whose eastern shores are thickly beaded with small islands and islets.

The two main islands are as unlike as Jack Sprat and his wife. Graham (2,485 square miles) lifts from beach level to a plateau circled to south and west by hills. Moresby (1,060) bulges with forested mountains that rise to four thousand feet.

Their physical difference is picayune compared with the contrast between Kitimat's modernity and their old-fashioned villages and logging camps. One feels as though he had stepped from a blazing July noon into the long, cool shadows of an October twilight.

That contrast begins far out at sea where a sandbar crooks a beckoning, bone-white finger into Hecate Strait. The gesture is futile; the waters are empty. Yet though this 80-mile-wide strait and 150 miles of Queen Charlotte Sound isolate the islands from the rest of British Columbia, they were known to five nations on three continents long before the white man had any interest in the north Pacific mainland.

A few glossy sea-otter pelts set their ball rolling. Vitus Bering's ill-starred expedition of 1728 got no closer to the archipelago than to sight Mt. Elias' snowy cone, four hundred miles north. But the pelts its survivors carried back to Russia created such a demand that the Russians hastened to build trading posts along the Alaskan coast.

Some forty years passed before word of this disturbed the ears of European powers. Spain then sped navigators to claim

34

for the Crown everything up to the 60th Parallel. Britain and France despatched others to find an entrance to Northwest Passage before Russian or Spaniard stumbled upon it.

None of these valiant sea explorers completed his assignment. By 1788, however, they had sighted, finally identified as islands, and named the archipelago in honour of Britain's Queen Charlotte. At that point, Boston's Captain Robert Gray sighted a land mass here and, unaware that anyone had preceded him, named it Washington Isle in honour of "the great American general."

By another of history's vagaries, the man who did not even sight the islands focussed world attention upon them. In 1788, also, Captain Cook's *Voyage to the Pacific Ocean* was published. Its descriptions of the thousands of sea otters he had seen while scouring the coast from Puget Sound into Bering Strait for the Northwest Passage set off a maritime fur rush comparable to the gold rushes of the next century. So furious was the competition that within forty years the mammal that grew the golden fur was extinct.

Within these same years the islands were ringed with a motley of names. Indian titles now replace many, but enough remain to recall that cosmopolitan era. Juan Perez Sound, San Chrystoval Mountains (Spanish). Kerouart Islands (French). Cape St. James, Graham and Moresby Islands (British). Ingraham and McIntyre Bays (American). *Haikoon,* or Long Nose, the Indian name so appropriately applied to the sandbar we were following, early was renamed Rose Point to honour a British statesman.

Eventually Rose Point merged with the curve of Graham Island's north shore to lead us to Masset Inlet, an 18-mile throat which winds inland to an immense bay. Just within the inlet's mouth lies Old Masset, one of the islands' two Indian reservations. Three miles beyond is Masset, pioneer white settlement, founded in 1876. Inland on the bay, Port Clements is the northern terminus of the islands' one highway. Forty miles south, Queen Charlotte City, as its southern terminal, overlooks the clear green waters of Skidegate Inlet. Aside from a few logging camps and farms, the islands' population centres in or about these three villages.

Though young in years, all three are reminiscent of aging pioneer prairie settlements which railroad, highway and modern utility passed by as progress raced along the shortest routes from Atlantic to Pacific. In them, at last, I found men and women of venerable years. Some had grown up with their village. Others had retired to these picturesque spots from various parts of Canada and the British Isles.

Masset's streets were pooled with water from a morning deluge when in noon sunshine everyone flocked ashore to visit the clam and crab cannery that is its main industry. The clam season had ended; the crab season just begun. As I stood at the seaside door, two boats came in, one to report ten thousand crabs and the other fourteen thousand. "Going to be a good year," the foreman said.

Good indeed, I thought as I watched a young man sort live crabs for boiling. The perfect ones came out a rich red, to be sorted again by sizes for freezing and shipment to American markets. Broken or missing bits went from boiling vats to canning room, where Indian women in aprons and caps removed every bone before the ivory meat was weighed, packed and sealed.

Then, to celebrate "the finest afternoon Masset has had in two years," two California women and I extracted Harold, a local taximan, from his garden for a drive through miles of fir, cedar and hemlock stillness flooded with an eerie, green-gold radiance. At one point we ran out into tidal meadows where beef cattle grazed among scores of Canada geese and long-legged herons.

"Should see deer, too," said Harold. "So many hundreds of them in these woods, we can hunt them the year round. And birds! So many different kinds a man here collects them for museums."

Neither deer nor bird did we see, but beyond more green stillness we came upon a most unexpected view. On one side, across a rough clearing, sparkling blue combers rolled high on a beach, so wide, hard and white that cars can race upon it for almost thirty miles without leaving a trace. On the other, tall firs and a brisk dark-green trout stream enclosed grassy lawns and cabins of a $100,000 resort, closed during its third season to await more frequent transportation than the *Coquitlam's* fortnightly calls.

Harold had refused flatly to drive us to Old Masset. The halibut boats, he declared, had returned the day before from Prince Rupert, loaded with whisky, "and to put it plainly, ladies, those Indians are celebrating." But about an hour before we sailed for Port Clements, I found a taximan willing to make a quick round trip.

Lo, though smoke sauntered from a few chimneys and here and there dishes clinked or voices murmured, only two things distinguished the irregular rows of frame cottages from an old and badly run-down lake colony after the summer ends. The towered white Anglican church. And what looked to be headstones, two to seven feet high, standing on or in front of several porches.

Headstones they were! As modern substitute for the totem pole, they one day will be placed with great ceremony over the graves of recently or long-departed husband or eldest son. That day will come, though perhaps not for years, when the bereaved family has saved enough money to give the community a lavish funeral feast. Meantime, as a form of standing invitation, the stone is displayed.

Jabbing a thumb at the worn cottages, the driver told me, "They were as nice as you'd hope to see when the Indian Department built them. These Indians won't take care of them. Not because they don't have the money! Wasn't so long ago that a young fisherman got married. According to their custom, he should have taken his wife to his father's home. But it already was so full of married children and grandchildren that the Indian agent said no, he must have his own. And the son had $700, enough to start work on it. When the father complained that that was 'against the custom' and the agent still

37

said no, what did the old chap do? He says, 'This man is my oldest son and when I die I must give my house to him. So now you give him back his $700 and I will give you the $700. You build his house, but I will be the one to give it to my son.' "

Where had my wits been? Not until I heard about that proud father twisting Indian Department regulations to conform to tribal law did I realize that these "Indians" were Haida, once one of the most colourful and powerful peoples in all the Americas.

With the Tlingit of Alaska and the Tsimshian of the north-central British Columbia mainland, the Haida are believed to have crossed Bering Strait during the eighth, and last, millennium of the great Asiatic migration to settle and dominate the north Pacific coast. There, hundreds of miles of mountain ranges walled them off from eastern North America even after the white man occupied the rest of the continent. There, dense forests confined them to narrow sea and river beaches. Undaunted, they became formidable mariners and fishermen, warriors and traders, with a culture based on cedar and salmon.

In the isolated Queen Charlotte Islands, the Haida found a domain made to order for their vigorous, aggressive, arrogant natures. Steep, rocky cliffs and headlands, abetted by swift tide rips, treacherous currents, hidden reefs, provided an almost invulnerable defence for their villages. To mariners of Haida prowess, however, they were no obstacle to expeditions for trade or conquest on mainland or island.

There, in 1774, Juan Perez, the first European known to enter these northern seas, came upon them. Well, nearly there. Though an enraged Hecate Strait kept his sailing vessel miles offshore, it did not prevent tall, dark and handsome Haida from paddling out in canoes filled with dried fish and rush hats to trade. From then on, mariners and traders recorded in journals or logs their amazement and admiration for these sea-going canoes and the men who built them.

Unfortunately, they did not convey that impression to the Haida, who, though still in the Stone Age, had reached a peak of physical and cultural skills. European ridicule of their customs and arts contributed much toward their moral and physical decline.

But while they were their own masters they used steam to split and mould great cedars into everything from fishhooks to totems, cradles to coffins. They raised huge perpendicular planks to build communal homes, 40 by 55 feet long, 30 by 50 wide, 12 by 19 high, and added three to six feet to this height by excavating the floor in three terraces. Before these lodges they erected carved and painted totems fifty-five feet high, and behind the lodge of a great chief they raised another.

From single cedars they shaped canoes, 35 to 65 feet long, 6 to 8 feet in the beam, with flaring gunwale, fixed seats, and long projecting spurs at bow and stern to make them more seaworthy. In them, thirty-five warriors or traders and five tons of freight travelled hundreds of sea miles to terrorize the coast, trade with Tlingit and Tsimshian, or range for days far out of sight of land, hunting whales, seals and fish in the Pacific.

Of fine physique and feature, both men and women dressed proudly in well-woven and dyed fibre clothing that reached almost to their heels. In winter they wrapped themselves in sea-otter, seal or other furs. Instead of feathers, they wore cone-like hats, woven of spruce root or cedar fibre and painted with stylized designs.

Their arrogance carried over into their arts. Scorning the geometric designs of many primitive peoples, they used birds, fish, animals, people. If necessary to preserve symmetry or balance, they rearranged wings, fins, legs and arms to conform to the surface they wished to cover. Just as boldly, they scorned unity to combine the symbolic, realistic and grotesque.

One art is original with them. From argillite, a slate whose only known source is Graham Island, they sculptured plaques, statuettes, and miniature totems which today's collectors and museums value as beautiful examples of primitive art.

During the years of the sea-otter trade, the Haida prospered. Afterwards, with no new commerce to replace it, they steadily grew poorer and fewer. Smallpox, measles and other white man's diseases killed hundreds, if not thousands. The taste they acquired for his viciously doctored rum killed even more. From the six to eight thousand Haida the first navigators found on the islands, their numbers had dwindled to less than seven hundred by 1928. Then the Federal Indian Department gathered them into reservations at Old Masset and Skidegate. With a higher standard of living, with fishing, logging and other means of earning their way, they now have increased to about a thousand.

From its high perch on one of the rounded hills that circle Masset Inlet's vast bay, Port Clements still basked in the warmth of a high sun when we docked at nine-thirty. A fishing hamlet of one rambling street, it looked—and was—the answer to the poet's cry for time to turn backward.

At the head of the street, a frame hotel, almost hidden by trees, was dark except for a naked bulb dimly burning behind one dusty window. On the opposite corner, a general store, locked for the night hours before, was guarded on the inside by a mayhem-minded dog. Outside another bulb dangling between huge display windows lighted tin tops and coiled skipping ropes. Hand-lettered signs announced a white elephant sale and a school picnic—"weather permitting."

Here ended the public utilities, for the minute post office, though defended by a very easily irritated dog, had only a small glass lamp burning in its window. In each heavily curtained "front" window of the cottages, too, a parlour lamp, its bulbous globe embellished with floral designs, further obstructed the sweeping view of bay and hills.

Either the late hour or reluctance to remain on view while wide-eyed passengers strolled about held all but two residents indoors. A woman pulled her sunbonnet closer about her face while she pumped a pail of water. And from the doorstep of his pint-sized home, a convivial, pint-sized character introduced himself as "Mike—an old codger living like a king." But on our return to the ship we found the officers still shaken by the speed with which change was coming to Port Clements.

Not only was the Federal government about to build a $300,000 breakwater across the harbour for the protection of the fishing boats. Until that night, two seventy-ish sisters had been so notoriously shy that if a stranger approached their garden they scurried into the house to wait behind closed doors until he passed. What impulse impelled them that night to brave the long pier and gangplank to drink a bottle of pop together at the ship's newsstand?

In bright morning sunshine, Queen Charlotte City was a most engaging sight. Its yellow and white cottages and stores, its lawns and rainbow-hued flower borders, curved like a gay, young moon between tall green hills at its back and a harbour so nearly enclosed by others that it resembled a lake. Until two drowsy, grey-haired women appeared, however, none of its residents were abroad to appreciate it.

Asked what time the stores opened, they replied in thick, Scotch brogue, "Oh, we're in no hurry here. Maybe ten, ten-thirty." One of them had come "out" thirty-four years ago, never gone "home," never expected to. The other, with her husband, had arrived fifteen years before for a visit that prolonged into permanent residence.

"Taxi, miss?" another Scotch voice asked. "Skidegate Mission's only a few miles and your ship won't be sailing for an hour, two maybe. Nice drive along the sea."

That "nice drive" decided me. Though not a mission, Skidegate is so called locally to distinguish it from White Skidegate, a small settlement three miles from Queen Charlotte City. I assumed it would be a smaller Old Masset, set in an odd but much more beautiful background. Tucked into the extreme southeast corner of Graham Island, almost hidden by two small, forested islands offshore, Skidegate had appeared from the sea to be an oasis of green in a desolation of logged-off mountains.

The neat and ordered village centred about a United Church and Community Hall came as a surprise. So did the explanation for its odd setting. After long deliberation the village council had leased the forest rights to their lands to a logging

41

company on one condition. A wreath of trees, broad enough to shut out all view of the despoiled slopes, must be left standing from shoreline to mountain summit. With the "lease money" they had installed electricity in every home and building.

Such enterprise was not the only difference between these southern Haida and their northern kinsmen. In fact, Skidegate's three hundred residents consider Old Masset's seven hundred as "country cousins" whose superstitions, customs and ideas are too old-fashioned for words. They not only have electricity in their homes, but plumbing and modern furniture, including electric washing machines, deep-freeze units, and "fridges." Many own cars in which to drive to Queen Charlotte City or Port Clements on business or pleasure. Passionately eager for education, they maintain a six-grade school; for junior and senior high school, they send their children elsewhere.

From the two teachers I learned that all Skidegate residents know English, but prefer to speak their own language. All are active members of the church and of various church and community organizations. The men are very intelligent and civic-minded. Of the old Haida who has served as counsellor for thirty-two years, the Indian agent said, "If I come to one decision and he to another, I take his."

The women follow the fashions more closely than most of the women in the white villages. Proud of their skill as "modern cooks," they delight in preparing elaborate luncheons or teas. For formal receptions and dinners following a wedding complete with all the ritual the United Church affords, they really let themselves go.

What with the Women's Association, Sons of Skidegate and other organizations staging various events, the weekly motion picture in the Community Hall, and numerous social affairs, Skidegate has few dull days. Somehow, around the edges, the older women manage to enjoy at least one or two afternoons a week of their favourite pastime—auction bridge.

Over a recent event the village still was in a high state of excitement. Just across a mountain is the argillite mine from which comes the slate for their carvings, but Haida sculptors now are few and old. Two years ago, in the hope of saving this native art from extinction, a course in argillite carving was added to the school curriculum and each pupil required to submit an example of his work before the spring term ended. This June an 11-year-old boy had designed and carved a miniature totem of such promise the Haida now feel sure that succeeding years will develop others.

Neither Cumshewa Inlet's green waters nor the heavily frosted and forested mountains through which they wind into northeast Moresby Island are the beautiful innocents they appear. Dangerous fixed and shifting rocks lurk beneath the surface. And the rocky, machete finger of a "half mountain" pointing righteously heavenward is a visible reminder of what *they* can do. A few years ago a pre-dawn earthquake sucked the other half into the inlet, created great fissures in surrounding areas, and panicked the population lest the entire island sink into the sea.

Against this striking background, the two logging camps at Aero and Moresby retained so many of the ugly features of nineteenth-century camps that no one went ashore at either place. But young loggers, scrubbed until they shone, in clean shirts and slacks, hair so smooth the marks of combs' teeth showed clearly, swarmed into the ship's lounges. With luxurious sighs, they sank into the deeply upholstered chairs, to lie back, eyes half closed, until sailing time.

Sandspit, port and airport on a levelled headland jutting into Hecate Strait from Moresby's northeast tip, was our last stop in the Queen Charlottes. Beyond it rose green mountains. And beyond them others, the shape and colour of bluebells, rose higher still.

So new it still is in the making, Sandspit may be another finger pointing to things to come! Its pier was the best on the islands; its airport, completely modern. Half a mile away were the equally modern white homes, duplexes, and quadruplexes for the personnel.

From a neighbouring pier, an A-frame of perfectly matched spruce trunks soared more than a hundred feet in the air. In one swoop its steel-hooked crane lifted and lowered tons of 30-foot logs, three and four feet in diameter, from ever-arriving giant trucks into waiting bagbooms below. The logs came from the famous interior stands of Sitka spruce which contributed millions of feet of lumber to the manufacture of fighting planes during the two World Wars.

Thinking these magnificent specimens must be on their way to render some new important service, I was foolish enough to ask. They will be towed to Ocean Falls, Powell River, even to Vancouver, to be ground into newsprint or possibly into pulp for the carton containers of soft drinks the *Coquitlam* left in wholesale quantities at each port!

For a time I could not trace the source of an unfamiliar sensation that irked me as I watched. Suddenly I recognized it —in the metallic throb of engines, ship's and A-frame's, giant trucks' and cars', commercial and private planes' taking off or arriving at the airport. Man-made noise! Like the crows, I wanted to shriek my resentment.

Just when the prophecy, implicit in modern and noisy Sandspit, of development to come for the Queen Charlottes will be realized is as uncertain as the dates for Old Masset's funeral feasts. The islands are believed to be rich in minerals. Coal, gold and oil are known to be there. Graham's plateau offers good farming and grazing lands. Commercial forests cover Moresby and most of the 150 small islands. Some of the finest halibut fishing banks in the world lie off their Pacific seaboard. Other commercial fish and shellfish inhabit their shore waters.

Nevertheless, because those same waters are the most difficult to navigate of the entire British Columbia coast, the islands are handicapped by lack of transportation and no lack at all of high freight rates. Hecate Strait, deep at its southern end, progressively shallower to the north, is the main hazard. Ship's officers swear that its name is short for "Hell-cat."

44

NORTH-CENTRAL
BRITISH COLUMBIA

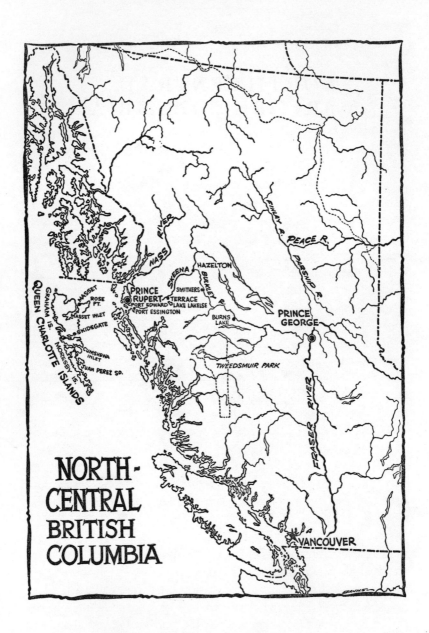

NASS RIVER

PEACE R.

FINLAY R.

PARSNIP R.

HAZELTON

SKEENA

BULKLEY R.

SMITHERS

PRINCE
RUPERT
PORT EDWARD   TERRACE
PORT ESSINGTON   LAKE LAKELSE

BURNS
LAKE

PRINCE
GEORGE

MASSET
ROSE
PT.
MASSET INLET
GRAHAM IS.
SKIDEGATE
QUEEN CHARLOTTE ISLANDS
CUMSHEWA
INLET
MORESBY IS.
JUAN PEREZ SD.

TWEEDSMUIR PARK

FRASER RIVER

NORTH-
CENTRAL
BRITISH
COLUMBIA

VANCOUVER

6

DOORWAY TO EIGHT DIRECTIONS

As though to deny the epithet, Hecate Strait all afternoon was a complacent tabby whose little grey waves tumbled about like kittens on a sunny, horizonless floor. Gradually the dark clouds ahead took shape as mountaintop islands. While they advanced to meet, flank, and circle dimly behind us, Coast Mountains, deeply blue and rounded with snow, piled up range after range on the Mainland. And suddenly and perpendicularly, a short, very wide rainbow hung before them a translucent, seven-panelled tapestry.

The closer we drew to the Mainland, the more futile appeared the ship's stubborn progress toward small, evergreened islands so interlocked that, though buoys bobbed and beckoned, no trace of an entrance showed. But the buoys were right. Soon we were unwinding a twisted skein of narrow channels into a spacious harbour, walled on all sides by more islands. Though not more than twenty-five hundred to three thousand feet high, their summits were scrolled with snow in delicate cloisonné.

There, white also against the green, tall concrete columns of an immense grain elevator framed the doorway through which, next to Vancouver, passes the largest share of all Canadian grain exported via the Pacific. Another turn, and Prince Rupert hung between sky and sea like an over-exposed panoramic photograph.

One glance was all I had of a warehouse-lined wharf more than a mile long, of commercial streets on a levelled ridge above, of homes mounting low green hills, of the massive 1,000-foot ridge that bisects the island on which the city stands. Joe, my resourceful steward, had me and my bags racing off the ship and down that endless dock to "cop" a taxi. Within five minutes I was hanging out a fifth-floor window of the Prince

47

Rupert Hotel for a bird's-eye view of this most northern seaport on the British Columbia coast.

In light so clear I could distinguish the small pink sprigs patterning the skirt of a woman more than a block away, this gateway to north-central British Columbia, to Alaska, to the Queen Charlottes and other islands, and to Kitimat, appeared the frontier town it is geographically. Narrow, one- and two-storey frame buildings of a half century ago, yesterday's brown brick and today's white stone and concrete buildings lined its commercial streets. Only here and there did imaginative home-owners realize all the scenic and architectural possibilities of a site overlooking one of North America's most beautiful natural harbours.

But the city vanished quickly in wonder at the view. Against the high, cloudless, Virgin-Mary-blue sky, mountaintop islands fitted together in a crenellated rampart to imply that island and harbour were all there was to this earth, that all beyond was outer space. The unreality of that impression was so real that I began to feel as though I were poised on the edge of a dream.

That is not a popular word in Prince Rupert. Three times disillusioned by the collapse of high-powered dreams, the citizens now, though with all the rest of the Province mounting the seventh wave of growth and development, proceed with what they call "enlightened optimism."

One such dream founded the town in 1903. Then Charles M. Hayes, president of the Grand Trunk Pacific Railway, while searching for the site of an ocean port to serve as terminal for his transcontinental mainline, came upon Prince Rupert's land-locked harbour.

Not only was it some five hundred miles closer to the Orient than any other Canadian Pacific port. Its ice-free waters were deep enough for ocean-going ships. And Kaien (Mist of the River) Island, at the mouth of salmon-filled Skeena River offered a site for a city that could rival if not surpass Vancouver in beauty and advantages.

By 1908, steamers, stern-wheelers, fishing craft and tugs had

48

brought thousands of super-optimistic people to clear the island's northwest shore of muskeg and forest and to blast down rocky hills in a townsite laid out for fifty thousand! The winner of a national contest had named it Prince Rupert for the "first governor of Hudson's Bay Company." And when the Grand Trunk staged an auction to learn what men would pay for land here, bidding soared to $40,000, to $60,000.

Excitement and effort had reached the boiling point when far away in the Atlantic the S. S. *Titanic* struck an iceberg. Mr. Hayes and his great dream went down with the ship. Fickle thousands left the island. The Canadian National Railways swallowed alive the Grand Trunk Pacific and, "turning left at Jasper," ran its mainline into Vancouver. By 1914, when its secondary line reached Prince Rupert, only four thousand people occupied the wooden homes, buildings, streets and sidewalks balanced on wooden piles above the tree-cleared but boggy muskeg. With World War I their numbers started to climb, but with peace came depression.

Again in 1942, the population ballooned from five thousand to thirty-five thousand as tens of thousands of American troops rushed in and out en route to Alaska and other Pacific bases. Canadian troops were stationed here. Naval ships took over the harbour. Canadian National trains brought in thousands of civilian personnel. But, again, the war ended, troops, civilians, ships and extra trains departed.

Among the five hundred new homes, acres of warehouses, a waterfront lengthened to more than six thousand feet, and other vacated installations, Prince Rupert sagged in inky gloom. Until 1947. Then the Columbia Cellulose Corporation announced its decision to build a $27,000,000 pulp mill on a Kaien Island bay.

The sun rose again as other industries and new businesses came in. German, Italian, British and other European immigrants arrived to swell the city's Canadian mixture of British, Indian, Oriental, Scandinavian, beyond ten thousand. Soon all the vacated buildings had new owners and more were going up. Only the American encampment high above the harbour, now named Roosevelt Park, remains idle though almost every resident keeps one eye on it as the site of a future home. City fathers are holding it until the original townsite is occupied .

With the muskeg long since cleared away to bedrock, commercial and residence streets alike are so clean they look hand scrubbed. The citizens take no credit for that. "Rains," they say. "More than ninety inches a year." And they say it thankfully.

Muskeg, if one may say so, is possibly the earth's meanest substance. If a bog when wet, when dry it is a glacier-ground rock powder that infiltrates lungs, clothing, homes, everything.

From the beginning the port's location endowed it as trade, distribution and transportation centre for a vast timbered, mining and agricultural area. But it was surrounding rivers, coastal and deep-sea waters, alive with fish, from salmon, halibut and tuna to herring and shellfish, that early elevated Prince Rupert to be the fishing capital of British Columbia, "Halibut Capital of the World."

This is a distinction, as a pinch of figures will show. Fishing is number five among the Province's ranking industries. Annually, it contributes about $70 million—sometimes more, sometimes less—to Provincial coffers. In one way or another, fish supply the daily bread for about fifteen thousand British Columbians.

At Port Edward (an industrial suburb), canneries, reduction plants (to transform fish by-products into cattle foods and fertilizers) and allied industries wall Seal Cove. Among them are the largest cold storage plant in the Commonwealth, and the cannery of the internationally known Fishermen's Co-operative.

Alas for the romantic-minded who think to find Seal Cove picturesque with fishing boats, deep laden with silvery hauls. Or to see in the shelter of the breakwater even a few of the hundreds of gillnetters whose owners tie up between fishing seasons along narrow piers in a fishermen's village.

Every gillnetter is at work and so far away that big cannery scows anchor in bays off the fishing grounds to receive their daily catch. While they anchor in bay or cove overnight, to be off to the fishing grounds at dawn, "fish ferries" shuttle between scows and canneries.

Despite the millions of dollars the fishing industries harvest annually, they are not the chief source of the maxim, "There's always money in Prince Rupert." That honour belongs to six thousand Indians, the largest concentration of native peoples in the Americas, who live in the city or in surrounding reservation villages. Largely Tsimshian and largely fishermen or employees of the fishing industries, they consider money as made to be spent and, when spent, to buy only the best and for cash. When they have no money, they do without. Merchants, taxi drivers, and everyone else who has access to this lucrative trade view that philosophy with such favour that white customers run a poor second in their consideration.

Save for their darker skin, there is little difference between the Indian residents and others in appearance, friendliness and courtesy. Many are well dressed, well to do, obviously well educated for a profession. For the most part, these are Indians who have left the reservations to live and work as enfranchised, self-supporting, income-tax-paying Canadian citizens. Any Indian can do so.

Indians from reservation villages, however, give colour and interest to Prince Rupert's Saturdays. Beginning Friday evening, harbour waters are busy with their fishing boats hustling in from a week of netting salmon off some isolated river mouth. Saturday's streets are crowded with family groups, shopping or clotting on corners to chat with friends. Teen-age youths, redolent with bravado, swing along, arm in arm, to appraise the young girls in dirndls and blouses strategically clustered about the doors of sweet shops. Small fry in Davy Crockett or cowboy hats, with well-filled holsters, lap vividly-colored popsicles.

Saturday evenings, hundreds of Indian and white fishermen, loggers, construction workers and miners fill the beer parlors for their one good time of the week. At 11:30, closing time,

51

they pour out again so rapidly that by midnight the streets are deep in Sunday quiet. In British Columbia, that is quiet indeed.

Early one Saturday afternoon, an unusual stir in the lobby of the hotel introduced me to another Indian feature of Prince Rupert life. The family of a neighbouring chief whose eldest son was to be married had assembled to march out to festooned and flowered cars to drive to the church. (In another hotel, on the same schedule, the bridal party gathered.)

With the aplomb of a ruling monarch, the chief, his wife on his arm, headed the march. Behind them, two and two, followed the groom and best man, six groomsmen, and two pretty teen-age daughters. Charging about on his own was a seven-year-old son. The men in sober black, the mother in a tailored grey suit with black accessories, the daughters in pink and lavender, they were as handsome a group as any bride could wish for.

Overlooking Miller Bay seven miles from the city is the hospital for tubercular Indians of the north. With its colourful, ranch-type buildings, sunlit, pink-walled wards and pale-green corridors, it bears little resemblance to a hospital. And the Drs. Harris and Fraser and the entire staff, including two teachers who help children under treatment keep up with their classes, seemed dedicated to the idea of making time spent there both a pleasant and healing experience Unfortunately, I arrived during a rest hour so had only glimpses of dark heads motionless against snowy pillows.

Just as I entered Dr. Harris' office, a radio call from Nass River, where there are no telephones, doctors or nurses, reported that a sick baby was turning blue. Within minutes, he had chartered a plane and assigned a young medic, with respirators and other equipment, to fly north. "Three hours from now," he told me, "that baby will be under hospital care in Prince Rupert."

While he and Dr. Fraser were explaining that the hospital is responsible for any of the nine thousand Indians in northern British Columbia who need treatment, a telephone call came

52

in. "Yes, Mr. Adams," he said. And "Yes," "Yes, certainly," and "See you on Saturday, Mr. Adams." The caller was an Indian fisherman who wanted his wife to enter the hospital immediately. Although he could not pay for her transporation until the fishing season ended, he had given his word that he would.

"He'll be here on Saturday to sign the necessary papers," Dr. Harris said, and went on to tell me that within foreseeable years tuberculosis among British Columbia Indians will be stamped out. Between 1944 and 1954, the death rate in this area dropped from 700 per 100,000 to 45. Best sign of all is the change in the Indians' own attitude toward treatment. Most patients now come voluntarily. If not, their families or villages, aware that one tubercular member is a danger to them all, exert pressure.

East of the Rockies in both Canada and the United States, where immigration was heaviest fifty to a hundred years ago, one is seldom conscious of the variety of nationalities represented on street or bus. In Prince Rupert, the influx of Old World immigrants has been constant since World War II. Many languages are heard, many foreign customs and manners observed. Yet old- and newcomers of all origins accept one another in the easy fashion of eastern communities.

The crowded bus which carried me to Miller Bay and Port Edward was a most cheerful boiling pot. As they exchanged autograph albums for signing, high school boys and girls, readily identifiable as British, Scandinavian, Oriental, Indian, Italian, plainly recognized but one nationality—Canadian. Beside a window, a pretty young English mother and the old Indian who had lifted her son to his lap chatted along like old friends. Behind me a Chinese housewife explained some supermarket procedure to a newly arrived Ukrainian.

My admiration for the French-Canadian bus driver soon outweighed my interest in the passengers. Constantly he made change, gave directions. At almost every stop, he passed out or took in mail, bundles of newspapers, cartons of groceries. A dozen times he had to contend with the aging vehicle's reluctance to climb one more slight incline. Yet when we reached Port Edward at last, he leaned back in his seat with a loud sigh of satisfaction, and exclaimed, "Boy! Does *this* beat driving a dog team up north!"

People rather than scenic beauty or prospering economy give Prince Rupert its quality and atmosphere. Drop in to see the Museum's valuable collection of Indian artifacts. Shortly you may find yourself smoking a cigarette with an income-tax consultant whose Japanese clients have their figures so well in hand that she can complete twelve reports in an hour, but whose Indian taxpayers may take two days to recall, item by item, exactly what they bought and exactly what they paid.

Drop in at the French milliner's and she may tell you of Prince Rupert forty years ago when she and her sister arrived with an elaborate assortment of Parisian feathers, flowers, laces, to find but sixty potential customers among the four thousand residents. Or, at the offices of the Prince Rupert *Daily News* where suspense-ending messages go out by radio to areas which lack all means of quick communication:

To Mary Doe: Safe, but will not be home for two weeks. Joe.
To Scotty Roe: Janie out of danger. Can leave hospital in ten days doctor says. Mother.

In their homes, ultra-modern or Victorian, Prince Rupert citizens are at their hospitable best. Then around tea, cocktail and dinner tables, talk ranges over the arts and the surprising number of local musicians, painters, writers. Over the exploding economic growth of the north and the interior. Over all the world, but particularly over the problems and opportunities nations facing on the Pacific must solve and realize together. Or not at all.

Several times as I listened I was reminded of that proud northerner's boast aboard the *Coquitlam*—"You can't do that with Fraser River oolichan."

7

TOMORROW WILL BE A GREAT DAY

A *Canada goose, if so inclined, could take wing at Prince* Rupert and after flying almost due east for three hundred miles, alight at Prince George. Earthbound Canadian National Railways trains and Highway 16 first must describe a mountain-peak bounce to the northeast, then by a series of diminishing bounces descend to Burns Lake and so continue east for a total of nearly five hundred miles.

That, in reverse, is the "Corridor" the Nechako, Endako, Bulkley and Skeena Rivers have blueprinted from the interior plateau to the Pacific. Between the two Princes, it lies like a sleeping Gulliver as yet undisturbed by Lilliputian efforts to bind and exploit it.

Logging camps and sawmills everywhere make no impression on its forests. Small farms, sheep and cattle ranches, villages, occupy only a fraction of the million and a half arable acres that here provide British Columbia with one of its largest agricultural areas. As yet unharnessed for power, the rivers and lakes, alive with fish, and the forests, inhabited by moose, mule deer, and black bear, supply a local food and sports preserve.

Scenically, the best way to travel the Corridor is from east to west. Then the journey builds to a climax in the Coast Mountains. Through them the Skeena, second longest river in the Province, is outlined by the celebrated "Mist on the River." This snow-white garland of cloud, caught between the canyon's sheer walls, undulates softly above the river's furious twists and falls without ever touching the water. Here are Indian villages, colourful with totem poles. Hazelton and Port Essington, too, are villages now, but in the days when stern-wheelers and prospectors plied the river between them they were boom towns.

55

And here, cradled among mountains at the junction of three fertile valleys, is Terrace, an eccentric among British Columbia towns for its lack of interest in attaining a fifty thousand population. Already it is bursting its seams as airport and food supply center for Prince Rupert and Kitimat. And it sadly foresees the day when lovely Lake La Kelse, its private summer resort, must become a tourist playground.

Because a "washout at Jasper" had delayed until after midnight my early-evening train's departure from Prince Rupert, I woke at Smithers, in the Bulkley Valley. There, behind us, the Coast Mountains' black-rock, snow-slashed crests loomed en masse above a forbidding wall of heavily forested foothills. From some such view primitive man must have got his idea for the first cosmetic—the white clay or ash he rubbed into his dark skin to scare an enemy out of his wits.

East of Smithers, the Corridor rises on a stairway of valleys, defined by foothills, dark with untapped forests, and distant, blue and white mountains. Perpendicularly or diagonally laid logs of farm homes and buildings and split-rail fences do more than identify Bulkley and Endako Valleys as frontier country. They underline the youth of the land itself, land so new it still is in the making.

A frenzy of fishbone rivers drains it. Narrow lakes, a few rods or many miles long, are wild and inviting now with birthday-cake islands and evergreen walls, a lone duck in command of the waters, a lone deer of the shore. But their outlying bays, webbed with silt-gathering water lilies and rushes, are in the process of becoming marshes. Marshes everywhere are in the final stages of becoming land. When all are firm and fertile, this untamed Corridor may reproduce the peaceful plenty of prairie farms.

Not until we left the Endako's brief tumble of rolling lands and foothills for the Nechako's were we in domesticated country. And there, to prove it, were robins and bluebirds. After the ubiquitous gulls, terns, crows and occasional bald-headed eagle of the coast region, they were an exotic sight.

Here fields were lushly green. Among tough grasses and

56

shrubs along the right of way a whole season's wild flowers bloomed in unison. Every clearing shimmered like fresh snow with millions of dandelion seed balls, two and three times normal size.

Perhaps because this was Sunday, our only sight of human life in action was a fast midafternoon glimpse, through interlaced branches, of a baseball game. Or, residents of the Corridor may have been oppressed by the heavy, troubled atmosphere and low, gray skies which neither lifted nor rained. At the infrequent stops, a few villagers stared up at us as dully as we passengers stared down at them. Between stops, everyone slept or drooped in lethargy.

Toward evening, a sudden change of scene roused me to the discovery that we had left the valleys for a plateau of rolling lands, glacier lakes, dense forests. Below us, the Nechako wound between high, wooded walls broken by stunning sandslides. It led at last to miles of sawmills, sugar-loaf wasteburners, and piles of new lumber whose fragrance even penetrated the train.

"Prince George!" the porter called, and had to repeat it before anyone moved.

Neither sea nor mountains give depth and height and colour to this inland city. Spreading over level lands within the sweeping curve the Nechako makes to join the Fraser, it resembles many a small industrial city east of the Rockies. Even on Sunday evening, the air throbbed with cars, trucks, trains. As though paced by a drum, feet marched to a brisk beat along cement sidewalks.

At first glance, the freshly painted or stuccoed, straight-lined commercial buildings appeared as new as the asphalt pavement. But a second glance uncovered behind most of the functional fronts (including the picture window of my hotel) their original pioneer structure.

In the hotel's long lobby, every massive black-leather chair (circa 1900) and modern banquette was filled with men. Most of them wore logging shirts or jackets. All of them were youngish, vigorous and, save for a rumbling murmur here and there, silent. With studied indifference, the clerk watched my approach until I reached the desk, then wandered over to the newsstand to await a young boy's slow choice of a candy bar. In the modern café, all but one seat held other silent men. As I slid into the empty one, the young Chinese manager placed a menu before me by the touch system.

I missed every cue.

That more than a corridor lay between Prince George and Prince Rupert I learned next day. On the streets I heard no voices, much less laughter, saw almost no women. In a coffee bar I asked a young office worker beside me for a direction. She picked up her glass and napkin and moved to another stool. In a department store, while I amused myself and a newcomer-clerk trying to find a billfold with a Canadian design, a mother and teen-age daughter edged steadily closer. When I suggested that the clerk serve them first, the mother protested, "No, no. We were just listening. It's so nice to hear people talking easy like that."

Before twenty-four hours had passed, I felt as though I had stepped into the path of a football star so on fire with team spirit, so tense with determination to win next Saturday's game, that he was oblivious to all else. Though that is the hard way to learn, I did grasp that Prince George was so intent on forgetting its checkered past to realize its glorious tomorrow that it viewed its present merely as an economic springboard.

Checkered is a pale word for its past.

After almost a century as the setting for Hudson's Bay Company's Fort George, the bowl of land rimmed by the Fraser and Nechako became, between 1908 and 1913, the battlefield for three rival townsites. To clarify the confusion of their similar names, I'll call the first two Townsite A (Central Fort George) and Townsite B (South Fort George).

Primed with inside information that the Grand Trunk Pacific Railway on its way to Prince Rupert would establish a division point here, George Hammond rushed in to subdivide acre after acre for Townsite A. His flamboyant advertising of its *eleven* railroads and kindred advantages brought in hundreds of credulous land buyers—via steamer, sleigh and shank's mare.

His success inspired rivals to lay out Townsite B just three miles away. In lieu of advertising, they ran it on such wide-open lines that at one 90-foot bar, whisky drinkers daily rolled $7,000 across it.

To meet that competition, Townsite A built an opulent "house of pleasure." Outwardly Townsite B remained calm, but secretly its leaders used their influence. At the height of its lavish and costly opening, attended by all prominent citizens, the law stepped in. A's house of pleasure closed then and there, to reopen as City Hall.

When Townsites A and B each boasted fifteen hundred citizens, the Grand Trunk belatedly bought up the land between them for its own town of Prince George. Within a year, Prince George had fifteen hundred citizens and its rivals were melting fast.

George Hammond then staged a campaign to force the Grand Trunk to build its depot in or near his town of A. When the railroad refused, he spent a fortune fighting it through the courts. He won, but the Grand Trunk was not defeated. It tossed up a flimsy shed which served Prince George as station until 1922.

By that time, it didn't matter. The Canadian National had absorbed the Grand Trunk Pacific. And, since its incorporation in 1915, Prince George, dazzled periodically by prospects for super-sawmills, super-power plants and other such installations, had expected to absorb A and B at its leisure. Deaths, tragic or violent, depressions, Federal or Provincial political muddling, one by one, killed every hope.

"Prince George," as its leaders chorus today, "stagnated until World War II." Then, as in Prince Rupert, business boomed. The United States built a $5 million airport which, with modern improvements and equipment, now ranks second only to Vancouver's. It also installed an electric plant which helps to solve the city's crying need for power. Thousands of Canadian and American troops stationed here spent money freely.

But now, a thoroughly burned child, Prince George expected to return to stagnation when the war ended. On the contrary! Came the great housing shortage in Canada and the United States, with louder and louder cries for more and more lumber.

"And there we were in the center of the Fort George Forest District. Its 110,000 square miles of commercial timber includes the largest stand of western white spruce in the Province, to say nothing of lodgepole pine, cedar, fir and balsam. Or of the alder, aspen and birch, excellent for plywood manufacture and other building materials."

Prince George's few small mills multiplied like guppies. Today, two hundred sawmills and planer mills operate within the city or within immediate range; between six hundred and seven hundred in the District. Their snarls and screams rang like bells in Prince Georgian ears. Their smoke plumes, black, white, tawny, pale blue, grey and scent of spruce, pine and cedar were sweet to other senses. The forest industries provided year-round employment for thousands of loggers, supplied more than half the city's payroll. Their lumber products totalled some $40 million annually. For a time, joy and pride were unconfined.

But when the forest industries began to represent some 80 per cent of the city's economy, the city fathers recalled an old adage. To have 80 per cent of their eggs in one basket, they decided, was too much. That's why Prince Georgians now build for Tomorrow with a capital T.

Then they will have all the power they need to diversify their industries. They will have better railroad and highway transportation. They can increase their few hundred part-time farmers to enough full-time food producers to free them from their present dependence on outside areas for even butter and eggs.

The cornerstone of their confidence in the phenomenal promise of Tomorrow is Prince George's location just a little south of British Columbia's geographic center. This strategic position at the crossroads of all main routes early made it the market and transportation center for an immense area, east, west and south. Construction of the Alaska Highway in 1943, and of the John Hart Highway in 1952, to link it directly with Prince George, added all northern British Columbia.

Until these highways were available, the rich Peace River Block and the wilderness beyond might have been a desert island as far as the rest of the Province was concerned. Perforce their trade, traffic and loyalties went east, over third-rate railway and highway to Edmonton, Alberta, and so to all parts of Canada and the United States. Now they are turning south, to Prince George.

Keystone of Tomorrow is the power potential in the Fraser and other rivers. The Fraser's harnessing has been delayed because of the tens of millions of dollars it pours into the Provincial pocketbook by way of the salmon which ascend its clay-toned waters as far as Lake Burns to spawn.

How to save the fish and yet provide power has long been a local and Provincial headache. Now with almost every city clamouring for power and rivers from the Yukon to the Columbia involved, the headache has taken on national and international proportions. However, even a layman who doesn't know a watt from an erg can pick the winner! Prince George will get its power and diversified industries.

Meantime, Prince Georgians have not been idle. By a complete face lifting and the addition of shops and services, they have provided a commercial district sufficient for the fifty thousand population they expect to achieve within ten years and a 2,000-acre tract for industries capable of supporting it. They have absorbed Hammond's old townsite and intend to enclose the entire Fraser-Nechako bowl within the city's boundaries. Between 1951 and 1956 they increased their census figures from less than five thousand to more than ten thousand, to head the list of British Columbia's fastest growing cities.

Even newcomers are so confident that Tomorrow is just around the corner that they no longer build inexpensive homes in the hope of moving soon to greener fields. They build $50,000 homes, to stay. An even surer barometer is the fact that five of Canada's leading banks now are housed in substantial new or remodelled buildings. Aiming his pen at a high window through which I could see the roof of an aging frame structure, the manager of one of them told me, "That's where we were until three years ago. We bought this corner, put up this stone building—not for today, but tomorrow."

No matter where I went, with whom I talked, the story was the same. That I wanted to learn about Prince George was introduction enough. Who I was or why I was there had no interest for anyone. While I listened, I sometimes watched men, grey with tension and fatigue, come to life, their eyes sparkle, their faces flush with colour.

Vainly, I asked what part the women of Prince George played today or would play tomorrow. Shrugs answered me. Vainly, I tried to learn about other than economic developments. "Oh, the Board of Trade can give you a list of those," they'd say. Then as one man, frequently using the same words, they'd assure me:

"As soon as we get the power—and we'll have it *soon*—nothing can stop us. Next to Vancouver, we'll be the largest and richest city in British Columbia. What is more, we'll be one of the most important cities in Canada."

More power to them!

Not until the eleventh hour did I glimpse the possibility that Prince George's well-grooved record might have a lighter side. In flight from its grim skies, I dropped in at the hotel's cocktail lounge the evening before I left. There, between two attentive sailors, sat Mabel. One of her escorts must have disparaged her home town, for suddenly into the silence that wrapped everyone else floated her clearly indignant soprano.

"You don't know a thing about Ottawa. It's a prim and prissy town, of course, and I'd like to live a prim and prissy life. But"—dramatic pause while she tossed open her hands in frustration, yet smiled dreamily—"*fortunately* I'm far, far away."

THE NORTH

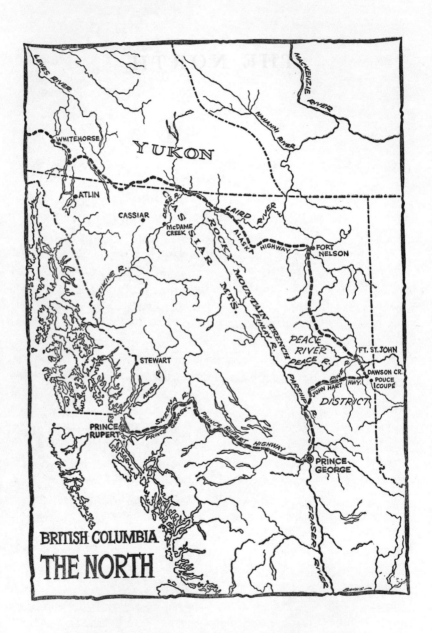

LEWES RIVER

MACKENZIE RIVER

WHITEHORSE

YUKON

NAHANNI RIVER

ATLIN

CASSIAR

DEASE R.

McDAME CREEK

LAIRD RIVER

CASSIAR

ROCKY MOUNTAIN TRENCH

ALASKA HIGHWAY

FORT NELSON

STIKINE R.

MTS.

FINLAY R.

PEACE RIVER

FT. ST. JOHN

STEWART

NASS

PEACE R.

DAWSON CR.

POUCE COUPÉ

PARSNIP R.

JOHN HART HWY.

DISTRICT

SKEENA R.

PRINCE GEORGE R.

PRINCE RUPERT

PRINCE RUPERT HIGHWAY

PRINCE GEORGE

FRASER RIVER

BRITISH COLUMBIA
THE NORTH

BANKS

8

TANDEM KEYS TO TREASURE

Prince George vanished the moment the Northern Stage bus crossed Fraser River to turn north on Mile Zero of the John Hart Highway. True, this 260-mile link between the Alaska Highway and the Cariboo to the south is paved for some miles and along them small suburban homes and broods of tourist cabins rise out of newly cleared land. Others come and go at intervals. Dirt roads lead off to "Sawmill" or "Campsite." But for all the impression they make on the immensities of sky and forests they might be paper cutouts the first breeze will blow away.

As though an enemy had pinpointed our bus for artillery barrage, small stones bombarded it when we left the pavement for hard, grey gravel. But soon even that metallic clatter, like the roar of the engines, was absorbed in the yawn of silence. Though aspens jerked their leaves like persistent hitchhikers' thumbs, not a tree rustled. No bird sang or called. If man or beast was abroad in the early-morning light, our windows did not record it.

In the valley below the rising, dipping, but steadily mounting highway, small lakes glistened. One of them, Summit Lake, marks the divide between waters flowing into the Arctic and those that prefer the Pacific. Everywhere brooks ran down to join a vagrant stream which incessantly disappeared and reappeared, always a little wider and swifter, to attain identity as Crooked River.

Against tall ferns flooring the outskirts of the unkempt spruce and lodgepole pine, tidy cedar and fir, the highway banks were as madly gay as Fifth Avenue's Easter windows with six-foot fronds of prairie rose, blue larkspur and columbine, copper honeysuckle, goldenrod, butter-yellow daisies, and a dozen varieties of white flowers, among them wild strawberries in reckless bloom. With every opening of the door their delicate scents blended with the fresh breath of pine swept through the bus.

After a quick lunch at Crooked River Lodge among nightmare souvenirs conceived in eastern Canadian and American minds for the wild and woolly trade, we entered historic fur country. First seen by three of the old North West Company's "Great Northmen," it still retains its primitive atmosphere.

At Fort McLeod, established in 1805 by Simon Fraser, Indian men, women and small fry, wrapped in shawls or blankets, squatted on the floor of the porch, backs to the wall, while they waited for the agent to pick up the cartons of supplies our bus disgorged, or perhaps just waited. Sekanis of the Athapaskan nation that once roamed all north-central and north-interior British Columbia, they still continue their semi-nomadic life of hunting, trapping, fishing, in the Parsnip, Finlay and Peace River Valleys.

Not far to the west lay Stuart Lake, since 1806 the site of Fort St. James and of the small field of potatoes, turnips and barley with which, in 1811, David Harmon founded the Province's agricultural history. Soon we crossed the Parsnip River, which Alexander Mackenzie ascended in 1793 on the last, near-fatal lap of the expedition which won him the honour of being the first white man to traverse the continent overland to the north Pacific. With every mile my wonder grew for the courage and skill of these explorer-traders, who not only found their way here through trackless forest and hostile tribes, but survived to thrive.

During the next hour we stopped at intervals beside unbroken bush where no house, road or even path showed. Singly or in small groups, Sekanis—short, squat, with an oddly Oriental cast to their broad faces—joined us. Each had his thirty-two cents or other exact fare in hand. Each made his or her silent way to the shadowy rear seats. There they remained in complete withdrawal until at some other undistinguishable point on the highway they'd materialize before the door. When it opened, they'd step down, push aside branches and brush, to vanish, leaving no trace.

For that matter, logger passengers were almost as taciturn. "Here," they'd say at some sawmill sign. But invariably as they left they'd add, "B'seein' you."

A road sign slipping by announced "Peace River Block"— so named in 1883 when the Provincial Legislature granted the Dominion government three million northern acres in exchange for southern land needed for construction of the Canadian Pacific Railway. In 1930, the Dominion returned the Block to British Columbia.

The sign really announced the beginning of Peace River Electoral District of which the Block is a part. But, too interested to remember that the Block lies *east* of the Rockies, I thought this the beginning of British Columbia's breadbasket, producer of 70 per cent of its small grains and most of its forage crops. Myself the product of one of the world's most fertile valleys, I dusted off a professional eye and looked around.

What I saw were hills growing wilder, higher, more rugged, as the highway climbed between walls of solid granite, sometimes grey with blue insets, sometimes cream, with yellow, rust and golden brown. But nary a cultivated acre. For the very good reason, according to the driver, that we were on our way to Pine Pass, the 3,800-foot elevation around Murray Range, one of the northernmost spurs of the Rockies.

Soon the hills grew so high they shut out all but a blue baby ribbon of sky from the windshield view. Not one, not two, but dozens of lacy waterfalls sprayed out of evergreens high on their slopes to cascade from one granite ledge to another before plunging straight down into long, dark-jade green Azouetta Lake. But with whitecaps and eddies foaming about sandbars, the gorgeous minx produced the effect of a racing river.

Hills yielded to granite-crested mountains which yielded to granite-shouldered and -crested peaks, striped like zebras with snow. The Rockies, I thought, until one by one twenty-three authentically snow-crowned and glaciered pinnacles, bumper

67

to bumper in an endless file, swung out of the east and round to the west to bar our way.

Like an answer to prayer, Halfway House appeared, a rough, two-storey lodge overshadowed by spruce and pine. While passengers and driver hurried inside for tea, I remained in clean, crisp pine-scented stillness with ten whole minutes to feast my eyes on that awesome parade. But before it dawned on me that the narrow valley between us which gave them almost full perspective must be part of the fabulous Rocky Mountain Trench, the driver was sounding his horn. Is anything more frustrating than to see something one has longed to see without knowing he is seeing it?

Under way again, I needed several pairs of eyes. To watch that spur of Rocky arrogance curve eastward into misty distance. To glimpse deep in the valley on the west the glitter of West Pine River, which more or less accompanied us north to join the East Pine and so continue until, as the Pine, it poured into the Peace. To keep in sight its erratic twists and turns as it picked up speed to boil in rapids through a gorge of harsh and heavy granite walls. Above all, to follow the highway's lofty course west round that spur of Rockies, east down a "two-mile hill," to cross Murray Pass almost at the feet of a lesser spur.

Up, up, up again, round more jutting shoulders, while on all sides more mountains grey with granite outcroppings and dikes lolled in the sun like lazy, idly curious pachyderms to watch the bug-sized antics of our bus. Ahead we could see another range so black that, though the late June afternoon could not have been more radiantly beautiful, we might have been heading into the Land of Night. And as we left it we could see ahead another and another.

Glimpses of man's presence did nothing to reduce the isolation and dimensions about us. A logger walking the highway from nowhere to nowhere, as alien to the scene as a platypus. A broken fruit crate nailed to a log from which our driver removed the red rag dangling above it, extracted a handful of letters, left a handful in return. A lone helicopter, a speck in space, flying north. Signs warning of "open range cattle" though we hadn't seen so much as a dog since morning. Occupants of two Alaska-bound cars picnicking on the stones of a drying creek bed, the only level spot for miles.

Crossing the Rockies was, all in all, so absorbing an experience that I forgot my interest in Peace River's arable acres until four o'clock. Then we stopped at Pine Valley Lodge, a primitive structure which more aptly could have been named "summit" or "divide." South of its ridge, both conifered mountains and foothills densely wooded with alder and poplar came to an end. Ahead lay rolling, hilly country where the first small distant farms drifted like life rafts on a Pacific Ocean of progressively deteriorating trees.

Shortly we began a long descent, escorted by bluebirds, into East Pine's valley. There the river, as tranquil as West Pine had been turbulent, wandered through fields of plum-brown soil beautifully harrowed or faintly green. Looking at them, the driver suddenly found his voice.

"Funny thing!" he said. "What people think about Hart Highway depends entirely on where they come from. Folks out here, anywhere, who've always been accustomed to dirt roads, think it's fine. And it is. Only once in the two years I've been driving it has the ice been bad enough to make me turn back. But listen to Vancouver drivers, or eastern Canadians and Americans, accustomed to asphalt, and you'd swear it was an old cattle trail. And that's about what it was until 1952. Not now! Just give us time, and they'll be rolling on asphalt right into Fairbanks, Alaska."

Up again, to the valley's eastern rim where East Pine village's neat white homes, lawns and old-fashioned gardens, in contrast to the wild, lone land through which we'd come, wore a long-established air. Miles beyond, in the midst of an alkaline stretch which enclosed no sign of human life, a bow and arrow range fluttered bright flags. Miles more, and we ran again into rolling country where plum-brown fields, others in all shades of green, formed larger and larger islands in the sea of aspens. Spindly things, twitching and shivering, they looked as though

69

a pre-school child could pull them up with one good jerk on their ankles.

I bore with them until they began to throw long grey shadows across the highway while all the rest of the world was a sunlit noon. "Oh, go away!" I told them then and looked at my watch. Seven o'clock. At 7:01, glancing out again, I caught my breath with shock. Not a tree was visible, ahead or on either side! Looking back, I could see them, twitching and shivering, behind a line as straight as though King Canute had drawn it with a ruler.

Apparently glad to be free of them also, the bus rushed on across wide, sunny prairies, patchworked with rich black or greening fields, toward a rounded rise that but for a single, low cluster was treeless, too. An imposing skyline of eight red grain elevators towering above a crisscross of youthful-looking buildings and homes identified it as Dawson Creek.

Halfway down Dawson Creek's main street, Hart Highway comes to an end at a stocky, white-winged pillar which, for the benefit of the tourist, begins Mile Zero of the Alaska Highway. The official beginning is a concrete cairn at the eastern end of Alaska Avenue.

Japanese bombs bursting over Pearl Harbor on December 7, 1941, focussed a white glare on the immediate need for this 1,523-mile thoroughfare through northern British Columbia and Yukon Territory to Alaska. Three months later, United States Army engineers with "coyote instincts" were blazing a route through or over muskeg, mountains, forests, hundreds of rivers and streams. To clear, grade and bridge it, fifteen thousand American troops followed. So did everyone else who could carry a pail, push a wheelbarrow, drive a Bennett buggy, truck or bulldozer.

(When a Model T Ford or a Chevrolet wore out, early settlers stripped it down to the chassis, placed a box upon it, hitched a team of horses or oxen to it, and in ironic tribute to R. B. Bennett, Canadian Prime Minister at the time, named it a Bennett buggy.)

Despite a climate that can range from 70 degrees below

zero to 95 above, the great distances from supplies, and the plagues of insects, with mosquitoes in the starring role, eight months later "a pioneer road" linked Dawson Creek and Fairbanks, Alaska. One year more and the "Alcan" Highway was ready for thousands of trucks to roll over it continuously. Renamed "Alaska" Highway, it came under Canadian jurisdiction in 1946. Two years later it was opened to tourists.

As a military measure it did not justify the $139 million spent on it. But to British Columbia it was worth all that and more. The first artery of communication and transportation through the almost unknown northern half of the Province, it opened the present era of discovery and development. It "built Dawson Creek," started Fort St. John on its way to becoming the second city in the north, established Fort Nelson (an even more remote trading post) as a river port and outlet to the Pacific as well as to the Arctic Ocean. Above all, it joined north and south British Columbia in geographic, economic and political unity.

Rising gradually to a ridge, descending gradually to a shallow valley, up-down, up-down, always attended by the everlasting aspen, the highway runs to the Peace River, thirty-six miles northeast of Dawson Creek. But for the Kiskatinaw River, which inserts its stony bed, steeply aspen-terraced gorge, and unique curved bridge across it, one might be riding a surfboard over ground swells off a cold-water Hawaiian beach.

The high expectancy with which I had embarked on it was deader than the proverbial mackerel, or so I thought until Don Bell stopped the big green book van in which he was driving me to Fort St. John on a high ridge. There, five hundred feet below, was the Great River of the West.

A powerful monster, the colour of a lion's mane and scaled with sinister eddies, it shouldered its way out of the west round bend after bend. Then, swallowing the surging waters of the Pine in a single gulp right before our eyes, reducing wooded islands to the proportion of scatter rugs, it rushed east as though late for a scheduled appointment. Which it had. With the Mackenzie River and Arctic Ocean.

And there was its mighty gorge! Except for the bench just above the water where farm homes faced the river in memory of the street it had been when the original homesteaders arrived by steamboat, the southern façade was invisible to us. But between that spread of tawny water and a half-universe of sun-scoured blue sky, the northern wall rose like a superb mural, wrought in rich browns, tans and deep greens.

The river's master hand may have shaped its benches. But the patient fingers of rains and melting snows rhythmically had carved *their* façades into Chinese half-vases, bracketed between crevasses up which low shrubs, grasses and mosses climbed like vines.

Level as a floor, Taylor Flat (the lower bench) was a geometric mosaic of green and plum-brown fields and far pastures where motionless black and brown horses added to the impression of a painting in the classic tradition. Beyond them, the face of the second bench diminished the few small, weathered farm buildings to touches of neutral color. The only bright note was the fact that the young farmer who occupied them was a grandnephew of the composer, Felix Mendelssohn.

And there, high above the river, classic too in its Ionic simplicity and whiteness, the 2,130-foot Peace River Bridge spanned the canyon from ridge to ridge. Though ranking with Vancouver's Lions Gate and California's Golden Gate, it resembled nothing so much as a bit of cobweb temporarily caught between pipestem pylons. I found it difficult to believe that without that fragile thread the 1,523-mile highway would have been useless.

To replace the ferries that for a century had served fur trade and pioneers was the toughest problem of the highway engineers, already harried by the need for speed and wartime shortage of materials. Even the strongest log underpinning of a wooden bridge would not stand up to ice floes, four feet thick and seven hundred to two thousand feet long, which early April suns release to lunge downstream like so many battering rams.

A permanent steel bridge was indicated. Yet materials and

men could not be assembled until December, 1942. Before
the early April breakup, men and heavy machinery, working on
the ice, must erect two 196-foot towers and other basic sections.

Once started, work never stopped, cold (many times in 20-
below-zero temperatures), hot, rain, sun or snow. On April 9,
just four days before the breakup. the basic structure was completed. On August 2, less than seven months after construction
had begun, the Peace River Bridge was ready for trucks loaded
with tons of war matériel to roll over it as steadily as the great
river rolls beneath it.

Here in neutral territory is a good place to clarify two widely
and vehemently held misunderstandings about highway and
bridge. One is the belief that the Alaska Highway was born in
1941. It is the culmination of almost 150 years of ideas, of
routes projected on maps, of actual work on specific if uncom-
pleted roads.

The succession of overland expeditions to the Pacific between 1793 and 1812—Mackenzie's, Lewis and Clark's, John
Jacob Astor's, David Thompson's—caused British and American statesmen to think about a road through this northern
wilderness to Russia's Alaska, possibly to Russia itself. Scottish fur traders, exploring its rivers and crossing its mountain
passes, recorded similar thoughts in their diaries, but said no
word aloud lest settlers and settlements, their most dreaded
enemy, invade this rich domain.

After 1896, bones and kits of Klondikers so littered the north
that the Dominion government ordered the Mounted Police
to build a road by the shortest, safest route from the Peace to
the Yukon. When the road neared completion, Ottawa
changed its mind. The wilderness had reclaimed it by 1934,
when Charles Eugene Bedaux, either as eccentric multimillionaire indulging a whim or as spy for his friend, Adolph
Hitler, undertook his opéra-bouffe "Sub-Arctic Expedition"
across it.

Three years later, in the belief that air, not land, routes were
the solution to wilderness travel, Ottawa authorized airports at
Fort Nelson and Watson Lake. By 1941, a freight road of sorts

73

had been bulldozed from Dawson Creek to Fort Nelson. This 300-mile conquest of the "impassable" north convinced American army officers, travelling it by jeep in February, 1942, that a highway to Alaska was feasible.

The second misunderstanding maintains that the Tacoma (Washington) Narrows Bridge, which swayed and fell in 1940, was salvaged there for re-erection here as Peace River Bridge. Bewildered by the heat of the arguments, I took refuge in a letter to the John A. Roebling's Sons Corporation, which, as builders of the Brooklyn, Niagara and other world-famous bridges, had been called in to erect this one.

"The Peace River Bridge has no connection with the Tacoma Narrows Bridge or any other bridge," a company official replied. *"All materials used were made specifically for the Peace River Bridge."*

All unaware at the moment of the controversies swirling about that peaceful scene, I reluctantly agreed with Don that the time had come to leave it.

Crossing the bridge, we mounted to a plateau covered with grainfields. Out of them finally rose a collection of low, frame buildings. Too many for a farm, too prosaic for my romantic notions of what British Columbia's most northern city would be, I asked, "What's that?"

"Fort St. John," said Don.

74

9

ALL ABOARD THE CAROUSEL

Before I could voice astonishment at the 75-cent fare for a two-block drive from Dawson Creek's bus station to the Windsor Hotel, the driver said, "It's not right, I know, but the law says, seventy-five cents whether we drive you from boundary to boundary or twenty feet. Trouble is, very few people want to drive from one side of town to the other. The rest feel if they don't drive that far, they aren't getting their money's worth. So they walk."

As I registered, the hotel clerk said, "You had a beautiful day for your trip from Prince George, didn't you?" And a jovial character, reading a newspaper nearby, looked up to inquire, "Prince George, eh? How does it feel to be back in British Columbia?" As the bellhop left me in a large, attractive room, with a spotless tiled bath and shower, he asked, "Want me to tell the dining room you'll be here for dinner? It's almost closing time." In the dining room, my friendly waitress suggested fried chicken as *the* choice of the entrées.

Back in my room I looked for a telephone book to call Mr. D. R. S. Bell, the Voice of Authority on Peace River country, as I had been told in Vancouver. No book. Down to the lobby to consult the hotel copy. No book! "Just ask Central," said the clerk.

Mr. Bell had no home phone, Central informed me, but she'd ring the regional library of which he was the director. The librarian in turn gave me the number of a neighbour across the street. "Someone will run over to call him for you," she said. "No trouble at all."

Mystified and intrigued when the neighbour didn't answer, I called the library again. "Just a moment," the librarian said this time. In a moment, a member of the board, in session that

75

evening, came to the phone. "Glad you're here," said he. "I'll tell Don."

Within half an hour my room phone rang. "Don Bell," said a young voice that had nothing to do with the austere and bearded authority I had expected to meet formally. "How'd you like to drive around town while my wife puts the baby to bed, then go out to our home for a late snack?" Four hours, a gallon of tea, and conversation that ranged from sober fact to hilarious nonsense later, I returned to my hotel with a schedule of people to meet, things to do, places to go for my entire stay. "I'll arrange everything," said Don. "No trouble at all."

That's Dawson Creek!

A town of ten thousand people, it too has doubled its population since 1951. Fortunately it is also a town of young people, bursting with confidence in its present and future and a vitality that even in a quiet room bends the walls outward. Otherwise, the failure of telephones, housing facilities and such essentials to keep pace with its growth and no lack whatever of social, sports, civic and cultural activities would join them all in early union with their ancestors.

Here, as in Prince Rupert, the reason so few can do so much is that no one is at all concerned about "face." The publisher of a weekly newspaper folds copies of the latest issue; owners of large stores sweep their own sidewalks; Don Bell heaves cartons of books for his branch libraries into and out of his huge book van. In no time I found myself aboard the whirling carousel of this exhilarating life which everyone rides as though expecting at any turn to catch the golden ring.

As a matter of fact, that is exactly what everyone does expect. Peace River's history has conditioned them for it. And their present promises it. Try to buy a vacant lot on one of its main streets! Whatever the price—$10,000, $20,000, even more— it is not for sale. Not when another year may double its value! Not because the eight towering elevators make Dawson Creek the leading point of origin for grain shipments in the Commonwealth. And not because, in recent years, its sawmills have begun to ship almost as much lumber as grain.

Alpine meadow, Mt. Revelstoke National Park. (*Photo by Earle Dickey*)

Earlscourt Ranch in the Cariboo-Nicola area, Canada's "Last Great West." (*Photo by Bill Roozebom*)

Anarchist Mountain rising above the Cascade Mountains to dominate the Southern Okanagan Valley near Osoyoos. (*British Columbia Government Photograph*)

Interlocked islands wall Howe Sound. (*Rolly Ford Photos*)

British Columbia's fruit basket, the Okanagan, with its 90-mile-long lake and terraces of white silt patterned with orchards. (*Cleland-Kent Photo*)

"B. C. Ghost," a long-abandoned gold mine in Coast Mountains. (*Photo by Bill Roozebom*)

After raging round the northern spur of the Selkirks in falls and rapids, the Upper Columbia quiets to flow through Revelstoke. (*Photo by Earle Dickey*)

Alaska Highway country in northeast British Columbia. Here at Mile 533 (north from Dawson Creek), it crosses Coal River, one of the hundreds of small streams along the route. (*British Columbia Government Photograph*)

The rugged Thompson River canyon makes life difficult but never dull for the Canadian Pacific Railway and the highway on the right, and the Canadian National on the left. (*Photo by Donovan Clemson*)

British Columbia's Cinderella, the wild, lone Northwest. (*Westcoast Transmission Company, Ltd., Photo*)

Mt. Cathedral, just one of the fantastically eroded Rockies that wall the Yoho Valley (*Canadian Pacific Railway Photo*)

Fraser Canyon's savage walls, as seen from Tunnel Bluff on the Trans-Canada Highway, hundreds of feet above the boiling waters. (*Photo by Donovan Clemson*)

The S.S. *Moyie*, last of the fleet of inland waterways paddle-wheel steamers, entering Selkirk-walled Kootenay Lake. (*From the painting by Alec J. Garner of Proctor, Courtesy Glenbow Foundation, Calgary*)

"Old and New Forest" by Emily Carr captures the centuries of life and death in the rain forest that naps the Coast Mountains. (*Emily Carr Trust Collection, Vancouver Art Gallery*)

In his highly simplified yet grand manner, Dr. Lawren Harris, outstanding Canadian painter, capsules in "Mountain and Lake" the beauty and excitement of the British Columbia scene. (*Courtesy Dr. Lawren Harris*)

Victoria, the capital. (*British Columbia Government Photograph*)

Vancouver, on Burrard Inlet. (*Rolly Ford Photos*)

Chemainus, Vancouver Island. (*British Columbia Government Photograph*)

Powell River, a company town, where 3% of the world's newsprint is manufactured. (*British Columbia Government Photograph*)

South Pender, Gulf Islands. (*Canadian Pacific Railway Photo*)

Trail, on the Columbia; Tadanac in the foreground. (*British Columbia Government Photograph*)

At the foot of Mt. Revelstoke National Park, Revelstoke looks across the Columbia to Mt. Begbie and other peaks of the Monashee Range. (*Photo by Donovan Clemson*)

Nelson, on Kootenay River. (*British Columbia Government Photograph*)

In East Kootenay's Valley of Ten Peaks, Golden lies at the foot of the Selkirks' Dogtooth Range (*British Columbia Government Photograph*)

With northern British Columbia bursting out all over as the source of minerals, oil, natural gas, hydroelectric power, Dawson Creek, now linked with it and all the continent by plane, two railways and three main highways, has become the major transportation, distribution and tourist centre of the northeastern interior.

Casual conversations bristled with startling figures. Of the estimated 250,000-500,000 h.p., to be had by harnessing the Peace. Of the estimated three trillion cubic feet of natural gas to be exploited along the Peace. Driving about the town I saw more than $20 million in new construction, just completed or about to be. The United States and Canadian Armies' Anchor for Mid-Canada's Warning System, for one. The Imperial Oil buildings which represent but a fraction of that company's $90 million investment in the area. New schools, public and office buildings, and street after street of new homes.

Most British Columbia communities trace their birth to the earliest possible date or event. Not Dawson Creek! It grows progressively younger as it discards the year of one significant beginning for another even more so. 1912, when the fertile lands south of the Peace were opened to homesteaders. 1931, when the Northern Alberta Railway arrived from Edmonton to make it Canada's northernmost "end of steel." 1942, when, because of that distinction, it was designated as the southern terminal of the Alaska Highway.

Peace River District is a pie-shaped, 75-mile-long plateau. Rising from the Alberta border, it tapers north and south of the Peace to the spruce- and pineclad uplands and foothills which bring the Great Plains to an end at the Rockies. Small rivers carving their way through rock and glacial drift cut it to pieces with narrow, arid valleys. But the Peace, while deepening its channel from five hundred to eight hundred feet, left bottomlands and terraces deep in black, alluvial soil. These and the silted basins of departed glacial lakes provide the fertile lands.

Long before their fertility was realized, trickles or streams of men flowed in and out of the plateau. Each left behind one or two rugged characters who found Paradise in lone command

77

of lakes teeming with fish, wild ducks and geese and of forests rich in game and berries. Following Mackenzie's and Fraser's expeditions, fur traders and trappers. After 1862, when gold was discovered on the Peace, prospectors. After the Klondike strike in 1896, stranded goldseekers.

In homesteaders from the Prairie Provinces and farm youths from the United States, where free land no longer was available, Edmonton, already fat from its exploitation of the hallucinated Klondikers and Alberta's own landseekers, found a new lode. Nevertheless, with their shoddy equipment and spavined nags, the Peace River pioneers trekked the five hundred miles to Dawson Creek's prairies.

There they cleared their aspen-coated claims, built log cabins, barns and split-rail fences, sowed their raw young fields. After World War I, veterans and European immigrants joined them in the belief that the Northern Alberta Railway would follow on their heels. It did—fourteen years later when each fall saw freight trains hauling sixty thousand bushels of grain a week over the rough, 100-mile trail to Alberta elevators.

Fur traders, goldseekers, homesteaders planted and nourished the belief that Peace River country is an ever-expanding cornucopia of opportunities for health and wealth. Any doubts about it early were laid to rest by "Dal," a Latvian immigrant.

In 1913, after walking and working his way from the Atlantic coast, he arrived with a sugar sack containing a slab of bacon over his shoulder, a hatchet in his hand, and nothing in his pockets. "Where is the land?" was about all the English he knew. Twelve years after he borrowed the $10 filing fee for his claim, he drove into Vancouver behind the wheel of a Model T Ford, a wife, children and the faithful sugar sack beside him. In the sack was enough cash to buy a home, furnish it with "nothing but the best," and still retain more than $60,000 on which to retire.

By 1930, tension gripped the sixty-seven hundred pioneers whose grainfields rippled the prairies, including the rise of ground on which Dawson Creek stands. The Northern Alberta Railway at last was coming in. Seven miles from the rise,

Pouce Coupé (Cut Thumb), the local trading centre tucked into a tree-lined curve of the river from which it took its name, was the logical site for its terminal. Two miles distant, in cabins set haphazardly on grainfields, squatters waited to see "which way the cat would jump." The cat was a Pouce Coupé landowner who had set too high a price on the acres the railroad wanted. Would he or wouldn't he come down?

He wouldn't. The rails ran on west—to the rise. The squatters rolled their cabins over on logs. When the first train pulled into Dawson Creek on January 15, 1931, two hundred residents welcomed it.

But already the shadow of the Great Depression, which had been moving west since 1929, was falling over the prairies. During the next five years 85 per cent of the farmers went on relief. By 1942, Dawson Creek's population had not reached five hundred. Before the year ended, it had passed twenty thousand!

"The Alaska Highway built Dawson Creek," local historians declare and date its birth from the March night when the first American troops arrived in driving snow to set up their pup tents along the railroad track.

What Dawson Creek remembers best of those frenzied years is the hundreds of poor men it enriched. The blacksmith, country storekeeper, and a score of other "small-timers" who became millionaires or multimillionaires on its bounty. "Wherever you see a prosperous business in north or central B.C. today," it is said, "you can bet ten to one the Alaska Highway started it." Locally, the Great Fire of 1943 and an army colonel helped.

One mid-February afternoon, the warehouse in which the Army stored both dynamite and dynamite caps blew up with such force that even farm homes two miles away suffered cracked windows and walls. While soldiers and civilians saved the rest of the town, the Volunteer Fire Department battled until only the chief and one fireman remained uninjured to save the business district. And the surviving two, having refilled their small watertank at the railroad, were returning pell-mell to carry on when the Colonel yelled, "Where do you two think you're going?"

"To wet down those buildings."

"Let them burn! You'll never get a city here till this dump burns to the ground."

> The Frontier Lunch Company,
> And the Alcan Tire Shop next,
> The Blacksmith Shop and Central Garage
> Were all a total wreck . . .

as a Dawson Creek bard sang. Since all records burned, too, many substantial buildings, businesses and citizens today testify to the unchallenged imagination on which owners and merchants drew to recover their losses from the millions of dollars the U.S. Army paid in damages.

A 15-year perspective now gives full play to the sense of humour which enlivens Dawson Creek memories of those days of intolerable chaos and discomfort. The Canadian Ration Board, having allotted supplies since 1939 to a village of 484 people, could not be convinced that between March and December, 1942, it had multiplied its population more than forty times! Estimable housewives quickly learned that a few home-cooked meals offered army cook or lonely soldier could secure a hundred pounds of sugar, flour, hams, canned goods.

The brightest memory of all shines over the "Smart Money Boys." Learning in advance that the highway was to be built, they rushed in to buy up properties around the business district on which to build shackies to rent for exorbitant sums. But the few small mills could only turn out a limited number of green boards a day. These they sold, three or four to a customer. Like everyone else, the Smart Money Boys had to stand in line to obtain their share, tote them to the shackie site, nail them in place, then wait twenty-four hours for more.

Incidentally, Dawson Creek's lack of trees is the only reason why newcomers since 1951 haven't tried to live in them. People have squeezed into basements, attics, lean-tos or sheds until they could buy or build a home, frequently with their own hands. One of the newer streets boasts ten charming modern homes, hand-raised by the "Hillcrest Builders." Seven teachers,

80

a school inspector, librarian and optometrist, they couldn't have known less about home financing and construction. Yet pooling their non-existent experience during every free hour, they couldn't have built better if they had been born with cement mixers in their mouths.

Every day the skies grew higher and bluer, the enclosing fields greener, the light so golden it even gilded the brackish waters of pasture scoop-outs. (These water ponds for cattle are made by enlarging clay-soiled ditches or deepening natural drainage basins to gather and retain water during dry months.)

On the last, most beautiful afternoon of all, three memorable things happened. I saw the first and last of the death-dealing mosquitoes I'd been warned against in Vancouver. Rather, driving with Don Bell in his book van, we overtook the frail little fellow in flight and thereafter viewed his remains on the windshield. I visited one of the sub-branches of the Peace River Branch of the Provincial Library Commission. And I met the *livingest* woman in British Columbia.

At various times I was to encounter the remarkable services the regional libraries give to outlying districts all over the Province. Because of the unpeopled distances involved, the rigors of roads and climate, above all, of the crusading spirit of this young director, however, the work of the Peace River Branch impressed me as unique and colourful.

Its twenty thousand books must be the busiest on the continent. Four or five times a year, from the Dawson Creek headquarters, Don Bell starts different assortments on a round of the sub-branches. Twice a year he takes others in allotments that average four books to each child, to Peace River District's seventy-seven schools. In June he brings them all back for repairs, replacements, additions.

He keeps tiny communities supplied with from fifty to three hundred books. And whenever he hears of someone like the lone trapper deep in the bush six hundred miles north or a farm family in some remote spot, he contrives to supply them also. Unable to bear the thought of anyone, particularly a child, breathing for any length of time without a book at hand, he initiated Summer Reading Clubs to make books available to each school district during the long vacation.

Now we were en route to deliver cartons of summer reading to the Tomslake sub-branch twenty-six miles from Dawson Creek. As the van pounded over iron-dry roads under blazing skies, he told me of other trips in 30- and 40-below-zero weather, over snowbound or iced roads when brakes froze or refused to hold and radiators cracked. Of bouts with Peace River gumbo, which can stop the most powerful trucks dead in their tracks.

In the middle of a sentence he pulled up before a cattle gate. Beyond it a private road ran between manicured forage fields and gardens to a farmyard where cows, pigs and chickens loafed in the shade of an aging strawstack. "I'll just see if the lady is in," he said and was gone.

Shortly he returned with the lady—a short, square woman, her head wrapped in a scarf, her body in a heavy winter coat. Dora, as she apologized gaily, had been doing the family washing and "looked a mess." In her hand was a bouquet of columbines and daisies for me, on her broad, red and brown weathered face, in her sparkling blue eyes, the warmest smile I've ever seen. One of the thousand Sudeten Germans the Canadian Pacific Railway Colonization Board brought to British Columbia in 1939 to grow wheat, now as librarian of the Tomslake Public Library, Dora is a key figure in the community.

Colossal is the only word for her vitality, also her joy at thought of the new books riding behind us. A mile or two farther, when Don ran the car into an open field and stopped before a small white shackie, with "Public Library" over its door, only deeply ingrained courtesy prevented her from delving into the cartons he carried in.

I was looking about the immaculate room, with its few shelves of well-read books, its iron stove, kitchen table and three chairs, when it suddenly filled with striding, bellowing Nazi officers and white-faced, shaken women, their emotions and tensions. In answer to some question of Don's, Dora was describing her years of exile in Czechoslovakia! There she and hundreds of other German wives had thought to live in safety until they could join their Hitler-opposing husbands in France and England. Suddenly they found themselves, without warning, again under Nazi rule.

She did not see her husband until 1939, when in an English port they boarded the *Duchess of York* with 150 other Sudeten Germans bound for Canada. They came, not because her husband, an expert landscape gardener, or she, a one-time office worker, knew anything about growing wheat. Nor because four or five colonies of Sudeten Germans had preceded them. Although Norway, Sweden, Finland, Denmark, France and England had offered them sanctuary, their one idea had been "to get as far away from Hitler as possible."

"Never can I forget those days we come to Canada," she said mistily. "So quiet. So safe. And I had not seen my husband for so long. They were the happiest days of my whole life."

The happiness faded when immediately on debarking in Montreal they were hurried aboard a train that sped for days through rich cities and rolling lands, across fertile prairies, into wild, empty, almost treeless plains. At last it stopped at a point in the emptiness where only a boxlike station, post office, church and a few Canadian farmers and their wives awaited them. Huddling together on the cinders, the 150 exiles promised one another, "Never will we let these Canadians see us cry." And secretly they made a solemn vow, "to stand it here for three years and then we'll all go home again."

For the first year, Dora and her husband lived in a log cabin chinked with clay. An old kitchen stove gave the only heat, but with wood so hard to come by, they had fire only by day except on "40-below nights" when the cold was too terrible to endure. Soon Dora discovered she was pregnant. "Me! An old woman of thirty-one! They—the doctors—said it was the climate. It is so rugged I am now a new woman."

After her daughter was born she got her deepest wish, to live in a "lumber house," though it too had only a kitchen stove. But with her husband working in summer for Canadian farmers and in distant logging camps in winter, by the end of the second year they could begin to buy cattle for the farm they one day hoped to have.

That winter, when her husband again was away, she daily left the baby alone for hours while she cared for the cattle. Then, hitching the horse to a stoneboat loaded with four empty barrels, she drove to a frozen creek where she chopped a hole in the ice and filled them, bucketful by bucketful, with icy water.

"Sometimes when the weather was forty-five, fifty, even more below zero, I was so cold when I got home I couldn't bend. Now—" She stopped to laugh at herself. "Now we have a 240-acre farm and twenty-five healthy cows. Every day I clear stones from the field until sometimes I cannot straighten, and it does not matter."

"But what happened at the end of the three years?" I asked. She looked so puzzled I had to remind her of the vow they all had made to return home.

"Oh, that!" she said airily. "We never thought of it again. The onliest thing—the very *onliest*—in Hitler's favour is that he brought us all to Canada."

10

TALL TOWERS AND TALL PEOPLE

Never shall I forget my first view of Fort St. John!

The short, wide main street was a heavily gravelled mountain range of bone-dry ruts over which Don and I and the heavy van lurched and leaped in different directions. The sloping sides were caked with dried gumbo, puddled with stones the size of dinosaur eggs. Typical frontier buildings faced it at random. A few had smoothed out their false fronts but left unchanged the two high, narrow windows that give such structures a cross and cross-eyed look. Sidewalks—that is, brief stretches of aged boards, each at a different level, alternated with stretches of dusty earth, of disjointed bits of plank, of more stones. Pedestrians who weren't stepping up were stepping down.

Noticing my long face, Don gave me an odd smile, said, "You're going to be surprised." I was. Within minutes after he left me at the Hotel Condil, I was beginning to learn, for reasons as varied as the sidewalks, why the inhabitants were unconcerned about their town's inconveniences.

Pioneers—a pioneer is a resident who pre-dates Fort St. John's incorporation in 1947—ranged from calm certainty to the "sky's the limit" anticipation of the modern city that within five years would replace this frontier outpost. Younger people, reared on similar rosy but unfulfilled assurances, cynically shrugged or twisted their lips to say, "We'll believe it when we see it."

Well, they're seeing it now!

Within a year, one no longer could stop on the high ridge above the Peace to revel in the lonely beauty of its gorge and bridge and the patterned quiet of fields and pastures on Taylor Flat. To the right of Peace River Bridge, an aerial bridge carries the $153,430,000 pipeline of the Westcoast Transmission Company from north bank to south to begin its 650-mile

85

underground journey through southwest British Columbia to the International Boundary. There it joins the 1,488-mile line of the Pacific Northwest Company to supply the entire Pacific seaboard with natural gas.

A refining plant now covers the fields on Taylor Flat. To it, smaller lines from northwest Alberta and Fort St. John's gasfields—one of the largest if not the largest natural gas reserves in Canada—bring the raw gas to be "scrubbed" before entering the main pipeline. The distant pastures now are lined with small, frame homes.

To the left of Peace River Bridge, a second neighbour, the bridge of the Pacific Great Eastern Railway, popularly known as "PGE," is preparing the way for rails and trains to reach Fort St. John. Beyond it, the open country of a year ago houses a small town of construction workers. Motels, tourist cabins, small shops and cafés now rise to the plateau whose grainfields are dotted with "capped" gas wells and tall oil derricks which set the pocket-black nights ablaze with lights and flames.

(Here must be inserted word of another and this time tragic change. No sooner had this manuscript left my hands than in October, 1957, historic Peace River Bridge collapsed—a casualty of intensive industrial traffic and a possible shift in the shale bed of the river.)

No longer does the highway enter a frontier outpost. Fort St. John's three thousand permanent citizens drive down a paved main street, walk on continuous sidewalks. Office buildings, air- and bus-line stations, new shops, banks, another hotel, replace or elbow the doomed false fronts. Housing developments replace the shackies.

Not at all surprised, the pioneers now await fulfillment of the rest of their expectations. All they've been waiting for is transportation. The PGE already whistles at their door. Once arrived, it must go on to open up the north all the way to the Yukon and Alaska. Now the awakened Northern Alberta Railway must come in.

A third possibility is a Rocky Mountain Trench railway. Such a line through one of the most scenic phenomena on the continent, the 1,000-mile depression at the feet of the western slopes of the Rockies, would be a sensational tourist attraction. In case of war, it could carry the heavy modern armaments which the Alaska Highway cannot support. Eventually, and above all, it would realize for the Peace and Omineca Valleys all the prophecies made for their hydroelectric, mineral, forest and other resources.

While we talked, the possibility was on the way to becoming a probability. Shortly, the British Columbia government announced that it had awarded to the Swedish multimillionaire, Alex Wenner-Gren, a priority right to survey forty thousand square miles of the trench for a monorail railroad and the exploitation of its natural resources. If detailed studies fulfill the promise implicit in the area, a billion-dollar project will be undertaken that may do more than develop the northern 40 per cent of the Province. It may revolutionize the Province's entire economic future.

Even with the transportation lines now assured, Fort St. John is confident that the fertile farmlands out of reach of the Alaska Highway will be opened up. That the half billion tons of coking coal, another half billion of semi-anthracite, the manganese, uranium, tin, copper, gold whose locations are known can reach a market. The oil derricks outside the town are merely seedlings, it is said, of the metallic forest that will rise over what may prove to be one of Canada's richest oilfields.

Early, to simplify my confusion, I abandoned all interest in figures under 100 million. But when I heard one man say casually to another, "George tells me that new well on his farm is good for 68 million cubic feet," I thought, *There's a concrete statement I can check right now.* And forthwith did. Said the geologist for one of the investment syndicates, backed by almost unlimited capital, which are exploring the north for base metals and rare elements, "I haven't heard of that well— yet. But I do know of another new one good for at least 71 million cubic feet."

One well I discovered myself by spending part of my evenings in the large, well-equipped motion-picture theatre viewing "A" pictures. Whether I attended the first or second showing, the auditorium heaved and surged with youngsters. A young father of three sons sitting next to me said their numbers were not surprising.

"Peace River Block's had a seventy per cent increase in population since 1951. More than half of all men and women in the Block are under forty. Its birth rate runs around 34.4 per thousand. That's a good bit above the national average of 28." He laughed, then added, "I'm not a statistician, just a father with an inferiority complex. My wife and I have the smallest family on our street."

One well is dry, the historical. If some date the town's origin from 1797, when North West Company erected Fort of the Pines near the junction of the Peace and Pine Rivers, others date it between 1805 and 1925, when five or six trading posts, all named Fort St. John, had brief careers on one bank or the other of the Peace. Still others cite the 1930's, when incoming homesteaders needed a centrally located store, school and church.

"But it was just a scratchin' until 1943," an old-timer assured me. "Then, overnight, you might say, it come alive—with five thousand U.S. soldiers and other folks pilin' in here and seemed like about as many trucks. Highway built, war over—phut! All but a few hundred lit out. Those few hundred built this town."

Whatever its date of origin, the Alaska Highway, World War II, and modern methods of exploration and exploitation have played the heavy roles in giving Fort St. John identity and direction. But the pioneers, by virtue of doing whatever had to be done as a matter of course and character, made up an exceptional supporting cast.

One of them is Mrs. George Murray, better known as "Maggie Murray," the editor and publisher of the *Alaska Highway News*. I had been told again and again on my way north I must meet her. So when I found myself before a low white building, identified as a newspaper plant by the white enamelled twin of the printing press Benjamin Franklin used to such good effect, I went in.

88

"Mrs. Murray," the young man in the office told me, "is somewhere between here and the post office." "If I should meet her," I said, "how shall I recognize her?" "Well, she's wearing a red shortie." As half the women I'd seen wore red coats, I asked, "Is she tall or short, young or old, thin—" "Not young in years maybe, *but*—" He broke off expressively, looked about. "Say, her ten-gallon Stetson is gone. She must be wearing it." Thinking that must be his idea of good, clean fun, I thanked him and departed.

Within half a block I met a woman breezing over the haphazard sidewalks as sure-footedly as an antelope. A red shortie hung from her shoulders. A white, ten-gallon Stetson perched on her reddish-gray hair. "Tell you what," she said, holding my hand firmly while her shrewd blue eyes appraised me, "I'll just make up my payroll—it's Friday night, you know—then meet you at the hotel for a—for a talk."

She did, a bursting "four-bottle portfolio," as she called her brief case, under her arm, bottles of orange crush in her hand. When she had mixed gin and crush to her satisfaction, she said, "Now, we'll talk." And talk she did for almost thirty minutes with such verve and content that my mental watch recorded only two.

Much has been written about the 19-year-old Irish-Catholic girl who, with only three years of formal education and a romantic urge to marry a cowboy, left the small Kansas town where she was born in 1888. About her three-day courtship and marriage to George Murray, publisher of a now defunct Vancouver newspaper. About her political career, both on her own and as the wife of a member of the Dominion Parliament. About her exploits as co-publisher and editor of various regional newspapers and, inadvertently, as "war correspondent." (Marooned on the seventh floor of a Shanghai hotel, she wrote eyewitness cables for Canadian newspapers about the death and destruction Japanese bombs were dropping all around her.)

But how, within a few years of her arrival in 1944 in this rugged land of young people, had she built herself so solidly into their life and times that she became nationally known as the "Salty Sage of the Alaska Highway" and "A Legend in Her Own Time"? Saturday noon, when I picked her up for lunch, I saw and heard the answer

Our progress from her office to the hotel was a continuous series of stops, starts and friendly greetings. "Hi, Bill, got the new baby named yet?". . ."Hello, Mary, your mother coming home today?" . . . "Hi, Joe, get that job?" She asked out of genuine interest, but bong-bong-bong, bells rang in my ears as her mind registered the answers for the next issue's news briefs.

In the hotel café, the sight of four men in the opposite booth lighted blue sparks in her eyes. Though in their wool shirts, khaki trousers, high boots, they looked like every other man in the north, she whispered, "Big shots from the East. Wonder who they are, why they're here." Before we'd finished luncheon, by another series of "hi" and "hello," but not another glance at them, she knew and was off to wire a "hot" story to Edmonton, Vancouver, Chicago and other city newspapers.

Volumes of anecdotes illustrate other facets of her pungent personality. An eyewitness told me of the breathlessly hot day when all the women of a community waited in a stifling hall to welcome and listen to the visiting Lady Tweedsmuir. And waited. And waited. When discomfort and indignation had brought them to the verge of walking out, Mrs. Murray appeared at the front of the hall, to ask, "Would you like me to tell you some stories about what happened to me in the Cariboo?"

As she told tale after tale, gales of laughter blew away all thought of heat and irritation. She had reached an exciting climax when sirens announced the arrival of their distinguished guest. "Ladies," she said, "I'm sorry to leave you out on a limb. You'll just have to get down the best way you can." She faded into the audience on a storm of applause which Lady Tweedsmuir, entering, graciously accepted.

Ten miles from Fort St. John is Charlie Lake, today enclosed by a growing village, permanent and summer homes, and a

$100,000 motel. There Mr. and Mrs. W. J. Powell live in leisured comfort and selfless innocence of the contribution their thirty years of doing what had to be done made to the empty prairies north of the Peace.

Following World War I, when hundreds of Canadians from the Prairie Provinces settled south of the great river, big, quiet, energetic "Red" Powell, a small Alberta town carpenter, took it into his determined head to homestead north of it. His wife, as tall a brunette, was equally energetic if not quite so determined. Having heard that water in those parts was so scarce that "rain had to be caught in stew pans," she refused to take their two small children into such a desert until and unless he first found "good land on plenty of water."

Fortunately, she did not specify good water! In 1919, after searching the country on horseback, he found Charlie Lake, an 11-mile stretch of muddy liquid entirely surrounded by unbroken land. About a sheltered bay on its east shore, he staked his claim.

How fortunate was Mrs. Powell's insistence on plenty of water did not become apparent for a few years. They were facing the fact that Mr. Powell not only was a poor farmer but hated farming when a ramshackle "string and wire," two-passenger plane taxied up to their small dock. From it emerged a daring young man from Edmonton named Grant McConachie. With only a limited knowledge of flying, no business experience whatever, and about the same amount of capital, he was scouting the north for a way to make a living with his plane.

The Powells' sheltered bay was an ideal landing field. Mr. Powell's team and wagon, the very thing to haul passengers and freight between the lake and the steamboat and ferry landing at Fort St. John, then a trading post on the north bank of the Peace. Soon the young pilot was flying between Charlie Lake and Fort Nelson, three hundred miles north. Next he added Edmonton and Whitehorse to his "Independent Airways" route.

About 1934, another independent spirit agreed to fly between Vancouver and the lake to connect with the Independent line. For a time this "expansion" did more for McConachie's reputation than his bank account, but it proved a boon for Mr. Powell. Happily renting his lands to a "real farmer," he devoted himself to hauling gas and oil for the planes over the rough, up-and-down, hairpinning trail from Dawson Creek, sixty miles away.

Those first years were precarious going for them all. Sometimes McConachie was so hard pressed he could not get credit for gas. A contract to carry the mail between Fort St. John and Fort Nelson helped a little. But it was the arrival of four or five trappers, with dogs, supplies and equipment, wanting transport to Fort Nelson that placed the McConachie-Powell combination on firm financial feet.

The plane could carry but one passenger and a little freight. Frequently it had to turn back because of storms ahead. Even so, the trappers reached Fort Nelson long before they could have made the trek overland. Meantime, Mrs. Powell "fed and slept" both men and dogs. That feat transformed the small cabin into an inn. As word of these modern services spread, more and more trappers came.

And now other planes dropped down to Powell's Landing. Some brought big-game hunters and fishermen with their guides and equipment. Many of them were Metropolitan Opera stars and corporation heads from New York. Others brought explorers, already famous or to be.

All but one the Powells have forgotten. That one is Vilhjalmur Stefansson, possibly the hardiest of all arctic explorers. Mrs. Powell delightedly remembers him because of the below-zero morning she carried hot water to his door. He opened it, clad in a spacious nightgown, "*not* nightshirt," complete with yoke and long, flowing sleeves.

With six or eight maintenance men for the planes as permanent guests and an always unknown number of transients, she often had to prepare meals and beds for twenty or more. She could take it and all the laundry for her growing family, but the cabin couldn't. A dormitory addition, with double bunks, was the answer. And when a radio operator arrived to fill one entire room with equipment, static and demands that the children keep out and keep quiet, another addition answered her ultimatum.

Almost from the beginning McConachie had been under increasing pressure by Vancouver, Seattle and other American cities to transfer his air line to Vancouver and fly the coast to Prince Rupert and Alaska. His decision that the inland route offered the greatest opportunity for development proved another turning point for him and the Powells.

His reorganized and expanded "Yukon-Southern Air Transport" line won the interested attention of the Canadian Pacific. Mr. Powell's order for an 18-ton truck with a 40-foot tank, to keep up with the demand for oil and gas, won the equally interested attention of Standard Oil of New Jersey.

Sure that such a mammoth never could negotiate hilly, twisting dirt roads, oil officials wired to ask whether he wanted the tank cut and sealed in two sections or three. "Let her come as is," he wired back. And they replied, "Then name your own price for hauling."

In 1941, the Canadian Pacific decided the airplane had come to stay. McConachie, they said, could sell out to them or compete with the air line they intended to add to their railroad and steamship empire. Unable to compete against their vast capital, he sold out. In 1942 he flew away, to become general manager of the Canadian Pacific Air Lines.

Mr. Powell, "also sitting pretty," now had more time to give to lines of his own. Foreseeing the need for lumber as homesteaders ventured north of the Peace, he had built a sawmill on Charlie Lake. With his own logging crew and small motorboats, he cut and boomed his logs from upland forests directly to his mill. When the need arose for Fort St. John, the town, he turned contractor and built the first store, police barracks, and other buildings.

Mrs. Powell and a neighbour—with a small, justified lie, however—built the school on Charlie Lake, the first school north of the Peace. To secure a teacher, ten children of school age had to be registered with the Department of Education in Victoria. Between them, they had ten children, but only eight who legally qualified.

In 1943, Mr. Powell's ability to foresee and meet the needs of the homesteaders really paid dividends. By that time he had acquired a fleet of twelve trucks. One of them he drove himself, rented out the others. With trucks the priority demand when construction began on the Alaska Highway, he became the Man of the Hour.

The busier he was, the happier, the busier Mrs. Powell was —and during those crowded years she found time to bear and rear nine children—the tireder she became. "I'd lie awake all night, thinking that morning was coming when I'd have it all to do over again."

One 45-below-zero night when Mr. Powell was away, she thus was awake when an overheated stovepipe set the house afire. Somehow she managed to wake the children and get them dressed and out. But the house burned to the ground.

To their new home, President-of-Canadian-Pacific-Air-Lines McConachie returns from time to time to relive with Mr. Powell those strenuous, precarious early years and wish for their return. Not Mrs. Powell! Yet, her dark eyes shining, she loves to tell of the hardest years of all, the years of the Great Depression.

Neighbours were few and distant, the winters unusually bitter. But dances to the music of accordion or fiddle were frequent. "And nobody ever had to dress up, partly because of the cold, but mostly because nobody had anything to dress up in."

11

TWENTIETH-CENTURY CINDERELLA

Northern British Columbia—that is, the section east of the Rockies—is close kin to Peace River Country. The Liard River, with its breath-taking gorge and smaller suspension bridge, dominates it. Small rivers cut it to pieces with their deep, narrow valleys. Aspen and alder mat the lowlands. Spruce, pine and other conifers climb foothills and mountains to timberline. The one real difference is that, while on its way east, like the Peace, to join the Mackenzie, the Liard brings the Canadian Rockies to an end with a fine display of sharp, jagged peaks.

Between Fort St. John and Fort Nelson, the Alaska Highway runs through much the same country as between Dawson Creek and Fort St. John. North of the Liard, it mounts to a rolling plateau of sand, gravel, low hills and deep valleys, to end, as far as this book is concerned, at Yukon Territory's border.

No matter! Wherever one looks, whatever one sees, from valley to mountain, from man trundling the highway in car or truck to man thousands of feet above in plane or helicopter, all that is visible of this earth represents but a thin, faint line drawn across the bottom of a blank sheet of paper. The rest is space and silence.

Against these awesome dimensions, men have carried on a flourishing fur trade for more than a century and a half. Frequently, from the highway, in glimpses of what one day may be handsome marten or fox furs now running around on four legs, one can see it flourishing still.

Each year from this northland more than $1 million in raw pelts, the larger share of the Province's total catch, arrives at Fort St. John, Dawson Creek and Pouce Coupé for shipment to Vancouver and the world's markets. A season's individual catch may be so rich that, as the *Alaska Highway News* puts it, "A trapper can easily afford to buy a hundred-dollar dog, a good farm, or a house and lot in Fort St. John or Dawson Creek, plus a few thousand dollars in government bonds."

But plane and highway rapidly are repainting the old romantic pictures of trapper, trapping and trading post in strong new colours. Every few miles along the highway's curiously winding route, a roadside cabin offers M—Meals; G—Gas; L—Lodgings; or M-G-L—all three. Only Fort Nelson, born in 1946, as the region's only settlement, provides COM—complete services. These reflect the rise of a competitor before whom the fur trade after lo! these many centuries must bow. His Honour, the Tourist!

His demanding shadow stands behind the hotel's private baths and inner-spring mattresses, the café's hot dogs and hamburgers, and the efforts of motel, grocery, gas station, telephone, telegraph and airport operators to produce the service standard anywhere. Where his favour rests, an M may become an L, an M-G-L a Com., and all of them in time the nuclei of other settlements.

Whether the trapper can't or won't read the handwriting on their walls, he takes to the comforts and conveniences of plane and highway with the enthusiasm of a duck long deprived of a pond. He no longer lives the year round in a crude cabin near his trapline, spends weeks trekking in to it by dog or pack train, weeks more trekking his season's catch to some trading post. From home or farm in Peace River country, he now commutes by car and plane to and from his "territory."

Ironic, too, is the fact that to air and highway travellers "Fort Nelson" now signifies the raw young settlement. The historic old fort and trading post which from 1800 to 1946 served as a northern equivalent of an equatorial desert's oasis is demoted to a "sight" the tourist can see across the Nelson River while motoring from settlement to airport. Or he can view it at first hand if he wishes its neighbour, the B. C. McKenzie Navigation Company, to outfit him to explore the Nahanni Valley—

"famous as the location of the 'Headless Valley' and 'Land of Vanishing Men.'"

If these paragraphs appear to dispose summarily of northeast British Columbia, the reason is that, while boning up as I could on the wing about the north, I was astonished to learn that northern British Columbia, west of the Rockies, is a veritable Cinderella. Provincial writers, scientists, and graphs stamp it as "uninhabited" or "insignificant" while they dignify every other section with a title or number. Even geographers callously dismiss it as "what is left of British Columbia." Always on the side of the under-privileged, my interest swung at once to this broken-spouted-pitcher-shaped area.

It is a welter of big, brutal, forbidding mountains bounded by mountains higher still. On the east, the Rockies, snow-white and formidable, rise in a forest of sharp, jagged peaks from that crustal cracking on a planetary scale known as a "trench." On west and north, the International Boundary with Alaska and some of the highest Coast Mountains, notably Mt. Fairweather's 15,300 feet, seal it off from the Pacific.

A primitive land of short summers and long winters, fierce with cold and dense mists, it has known but few exciting moments. A minor gold rush in its Cassiar Range in 1873. A major rush around Atlin in the heart of the gold country of 1898. A flurry of silver, gold, copper, zinc and lead mines opening and closing in the 1920's and 30's. And in 1942 a swirl of high hopes while surveyors seeking air base sites and a route for the Alaska Highway plunged through it. Alas for Cinderella and today's tourists! Already established airports at Fort Nelson and Watson Lake had determined its east-of-the-Rockies route.

It is a land only scantily and recently peopled. A land of few and brief roads, with no railroads except where the White Pass-Yukon Railway scuttles across its broken lip from Alaska's Skagway to the Yukon's Whitehorse. A land of no radio or other quick communication. "Northern Lights play hob with the wireless."

Minerals and hydroelectric power, therefore, are its sole attractions. And those minerals, deeply buried in inaccessible places, have to be as good as gold and as capable of reduction to small compass to engage the eyes of a modern fairy godmother and prince to Cinderella's worth.

No greater tribute to that worth could have been paid than the nature of the two very synthetic and realistic characters who appeared. A godmother born of post-World War II's unleashed billions of foreign and Canadian capital. And a prince of the realm of modern industry where demands for proved metals and for hitherto unmarketable others steadily increase.

Today this long-scorned land is crawling with "discoverers." The traditional prospector, with his pick and pan, slab of bacon, and "hunch" as to where some desired metal can be found. The amateur—truck driver, accountant, schoolteacher, storekeeper, and a motley of other self-mustered recruits. Each is equipped with Geiger counter and list of marketable minerals. Some have a "working knowledge" gleaned from some western university's or Chamber of Commerce's exploration course.

Topping them all are the helicopter expeditions—complete with expert geologists and a battery of high-powered instruments and methods for detecting base metals and rare elements. In a single season, by a systematic dropping of a half dozen two-man teams beside small streams running down from mountains, such an outfit can make a quick reconnaissance of a large area for anything from asbestos to zirconite.

Although a weather-wizened old prospector whistled at me through antennae mustaches, "I sure don't hold with them copter boys and all their gaskets [gadgets]," he was whistling, I fear, to his own courage. The sun is setting on the long day of the pioneer prospector, on the very short one of the amateur. No longer is it possible to make a strike, even a big one, on a shoestring. Not when a processing plant to handle the ore now costs from $150,000 to $1 million. Not when, to justify the investment in equipment and personnel, a deposit of nickel, uranium, copper, whatever, must total a hundred thousand tons or over.

Investment syndicates, with their copter boys and scientific experts, are rapidly taking over the mineral rush of today. And with the cost of the helicopter alone running to $100,000, of a single season's reconnaissance to $250,000, prospecting now has become Big Business.

As Big Business, it has in the past five or six years uncovered in northwest British Columbia some formidable riches, mineral and hydroelectric. But alas again! It also is repainting and restyling this truly wild and woolly scene along functional lines.

Gone are the tumultuous days of the gold rushes from California to Yukon, with their lusty camps or towns, their memorable if obscurely named Deadeye Petes and Gorgeous Georgias. No tinny pianos, orgies of drinking, gambling, brawling, are to be heard in the ordered company towns in what, if closer to civilization, would be de luxe summer resort settings. Miners, with their families, arrive by company plane, to find modern homes, prefabricated in Vancouver, a church, hospital, store, recreation hall, athletic field, waiting to provide them with all, if not more than, the advantages of the communities from which they have come.

"Cassiar," an asbestos mountain near the Yukon border, is a prime example of both the evolution of prospecting and the hazards and costs of production.

No one discovered the mountain. Indians knew of it seventy-five years ago. Some Klondikers saw or heard of it but went their way, looking for the gold they knew had a market. By 1949 when three British Columbia mechanics and a trapper, one of whom had taken an exploration course, started prospecting, its existence was hearsay, its location forgotten.

The foursome never thought of it until, after fruitless weeks, they read in a mining journal of the growing demand for asbestos. Then all they could remember was that its was "somewhere in the Cassiars."

In the Cassiars, after more fruitless searching, they came on a government surveyor. "Know where the asbestos mountain is?" they asked. "Sure," said he, pointing, "right over there."

Right over there, a mountain soared steeply from McDame Creek. Some six thousand feet up, a greenish dike, three thousand feet long, two hundred to six hundred feet wide, and solid with what is estimated to be more than seven million tons of asbestos, stopped them. One to ten feet deep on both sides were 280,000 more tons, split off by frosts and further disintegrated by time, weather and mountain sheep that had bedded down in it. With seven claims the four amateurs staked out the whole mountaintop.

Shortly, the copter boys for an investment syndicate heard of their strike. Within a year the "discoverers" were richer by almost a million dollars and a block of stock. And the syndicate, convinced that dike and talus represented only part of an underlying deposit of equal quality, had staked claims to the rest of the mountain. In 1951, the Cassiar Asbestos Corporation, Ltd., took over their claims and began a production estimated to last for fifty if not a hundred years.

India, North Africa, Quebec and Arizona have asbestos deposits. Cassiar is the only known mine to produce fibres so long, fine and firm they can be spun into durable materials from which fire-fighting suits and other important modern necessities can be made.

To get those fibres the company soon was deep in characteristic difficulties of the region. The shortness of the operating season—June, sometimes mid-July, to October. And the problem of keeping employees and their families comfortable and content. Long winters and lack of radio entertainment add up to a feeling of being shut off from the world. This results at times in an annual labour turnover of 100 per cent.

The asbestos itself contributes one persuasive advantage, however. It yields so easily that miners need use only a short pick. Mine and mill are so clean that a man with a smutty face, hands or clothing would be a curiosity. As a matter of fact, they all are curiosities anyway. Because some substance in the ore acts on the skin like a fine cold cream, their hands are not only clean but soft and smooth!

Lack of transportation is the company's—all northwest British Columbia's—number one headache. Only the best grades of asbestos can travel by truck for three hundred miles to Whitehorse, to be shipped by train to Skagway, to be shipped by steamer to Vancouver. Lesser grades, excellent for the manufacture of other products but not good enough to justify the expense of that long haul, pile up in mountains of slag.

A shorter, cheaper route would cross the Alaska Panhandle to the Pacific, but both Ottawa and Stewart, British Columbia's northernmost port on tidewater, oppose the idea of Canadian products leaving Canadian boundaries to reach Canadian ports. A highway, they agreed, from Cassiar to Stewart would do much more than solve the asbestos company's transportation problem. Running through three hundred miles of untouched country, but known to be incalculably rich in minerals and hydroelectric power, it could prove a "billion-dollar boon" to the Province.

In its 40-odd—and some were *very* odd—years of existence, Stewart has illustrated both the economic hazards of the north and the tenacity of its people. In 1910 it was the scene of a frenzied rush to exploit what was billed as "probably the most extensive discovery of gold in the history of the world." More than seven thousand prospectors rushed in; within two years all but seventeen had rushed out. Its hopes of rivalling Prince Rupert as shipping and railroad centre died one by one. Finally, after producing some $21 million in gold and silver, the great Silbak Premier Mine closed.

During the past few years, however, prospects brightened. The Silback was reconditioned to produce silver, lead and molybdenum. A new mine, the Granduc, with an indicated 25 million tons of copper ore, promised to become one of the biggest operations in the Province. The decision to make this northernmost port the southern terminal of the Cassiar highway came as a crowning assurance that its troubles were over.

A sweeping fire has delayed the Silbak's opening, however. And, though the Granduc perches high on a "mountain of copper," it also perches *above* a 1,200-foot-thick glacier. Planes made daring landings on the ice to deliver men and equipment for preliminary work, but until a way can be devised to get the ore off or out of the mountain to the port, it cannot go into full production. And now, a glacier two hundred feet thick and three thousand feet high, ambling across the proposed route of the highway, may make it necessary to bypass Stewart.

Cassiar, Granduc, and Stewart's problems, possibly also their brilliant prospects, pale before Atlin's. Located in the upper left-hand corner of this northwest British Columbia, it looks over lovely, 90-mile-long Lake Atlin and up to a ring of snow-capped peaks welded together by glaciers. In the heyday of the Klondike rush, it was riotous with ten thousand gold- and pleasure-fevered citizens. It still depends largely on gold production, but unless the price of gold rises substantially, its days are numbered.

The 250 residents, however, have no thought of leaving. For years they have been teetering on the brink of suspense over a plan to combine the waters of Lake Atlin and of a neighbouring chain of lakes with a reversed flow of the Yukon River. Already blueprinted, this plan would create a hydroelectric project "bigger and better than Kitimat."

Although surveying parties still ply in and out and "the place is jumping with prospectors" eager to get in on the ground floor, their suspense may not be quieted for years. With the lakes in British Columbia, the headwaters of the river in Yukon Territory, and the river running across Alaska to empty into Bering Sea, the situation is complicated enough in its own right. But to make confusion complete, the hydroelectric project has become entangled in what the Whitehorse *Star* calls "the big, slow poker game" which Canada and the United States are playing. Its outcome will determine which country can do what on various rivers that gave no thought to a future International Boundary when they carved their courses from headwaters in the north to an ocean exit in the south.

In the face of such physical, economic and political handicaps, it is no cause for wonder that this remote, tightly buttoned northwest wilderness should be among the last of North America's power and mineral reserves to be tapped. The wonder is that within such a short time so many operations of such tremendous scope already have reached the blueprint, if not the production, stage.

Meantime, exploration and discovery go on. Meantime, too, across the Provincial border to the north lies Yukon Territory. With perhaps equal wealth in metals and power still untapped, it waits only for railways and highways to arrive from the south to turn a Yukon of trade and traffic into British Columbian ports and markets.

VANCOUVER ISLAND

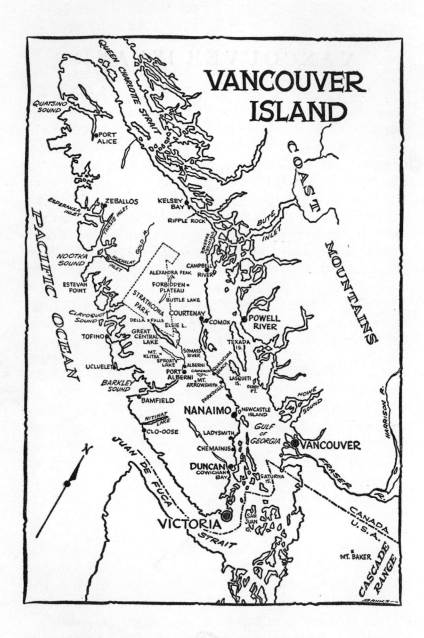

VANCOUVER
ISLAND

QUEEN CHARLOTTE STRAIT

QUATSINO SOUND

PORT ALICE

COAST

BUTE INLET

ESPERANZA INLET

ZEBALLOS

TAHSIS INLET

KELSEY BAY

RIPPLE ROCK

PACIFIC

NOOTKA SOUND

MUCHALAT INLET

GOLD R.

JOHNSTONE STRAIT

MOUNTAINS

ESTEVAN POINT

ALEXANDRA PEAK

CAMPBELL RIVER

FORBIDDEN PLATEAU

BUTTLE LAKE

STRATHCONA PARK

CLAYOQUOT SOUND

DELLA FALLS

COURTENAY

ELSIE L.

COMOX

POWELL RIVER

OCEAN

TOFINO

GREAT CENTRAL LAKE

MT. KLITSA

SPROAT LAKE

SOMASS RIVER

TEXADA IS.

UCLUELET

ALBERNI

MT. CAMERON

NANAIMO BEACH

PORT ALBERNI

MT. ARROWSMITH

LASQUETI IS.

DERBY PT.

BARKLEY SOUND

BAMFIELD

PARKSVILLE

HOWE SOUND

HARRISON R.

NITINAT LAKE

NANAIMO

NEWCASTLE ISLAND

CLO-OOSE

LADYSMITH

GULF OF GEORGIA

VANCOUVER

CHEMAINUS

DUNCAN

COWICHAN BAY

SATURNA IS.

FRASER R.

N

JUAN DE FUCA

VICTORIA

SAN JUAN

CANADA U.S.A.

STRAIT

MT. BAKER

CASCADE RANGE

BANKS

12

POOR MAN'S PARADISE

In rain, fog or sleet, under bleak grey skies, the white steamship that ferries between Vancouver and Victoria is simply a means of transport. But when sunlight twinkles everywhere on navy-blue waters and mountains arch in shimmering heat haze all around, one might be sailing the Milky Way on a night so clear that every star is visible.

Mesmerized by serene blue distances, hundreds of tourists stand motionless and silent along the rails. Even British Columbians cannot long maintain the pretense that such beauty is an old story to them. On such a day I first crossed the Gulf of Georgia from Vancouver to British Columbia's capital.

Soon the islands, sandy-coved, tree-crowned, that make Howe Sound a Vancouver playground appeared on the north. Others, gauzy with haze, to the south, looked more like partly formed thoughts of islands. And a great curve of mainland that seemed to be guiding us to the gulf turned out to be still more islands of all shapes and sizes, tightly interlocked.

In the nick of time a channel opened. We wound slowly through a maze of passages between green slopes interrupted by small homes or the ample roof of some large country place. Here and there on a headland, however, a very white lighthouse warned that, though Burrard Inlet's waters vary in depth from almost 150 to more than a thousand feet, beneath them lie great caverns and cliffs that can send tides boiling in rips and eddies.

Mainland islands behind us, low, flattish, moss-covered rocks, a few grey and white with sunning sea gulls, circled round us and, to judge by the ship's careful speed between buoys and markers, hidden reefs. Here, with no mountaintop islands to shorten the view, bona fide mountains ringed the horizon.

South of the International Boundary, where haze-merged

Cascades formed a low, dark shore, Mt. Baker's 10,750-foot summit, marshmallow white, blue shadowed, set out like some ancient vessel, every sail filled, for the upper skies. Ahead, clearer now, the whole range of Insular Mountains which run like a spine through Vancouver Island lifted a long, snow-glazed wall. Seeing them so, it was not difficult to imagine the rounded icecap almost five thousand feet high that had covered them in Pleistocene times or to recognize some of the places where glaciers had shaped the higher peaks.

Ironically, it is the narrow, rolling benches along both Vancouver Island and Lower Mainland which give the mountains setting and perspective. Had they not risen after the snowcap melted, there would be no eyes in these parts to admire highlands and peaks. On them function the cities, towns and farms which today support at least half of British Columbia's population.

The mountains are more than ornamental. Because of them, the Gulf of Georgia is not exposed, like Hecate Strait, to the fury of the north Pacific's gales. Lined on both sides with these natural skyscrapers, it is a busy commercial thoroughfare approximately 240 miles long and 20 wide, between two of the Province's major divisions. Ships, ferries, even small craft can travel it the year around.

Moving down this highway, we passed between two islands —shinbone-shaped Galiano and Mayne—to turn south at Salt Spring Island. These islands, with perhaps a hundred others lying off the southeast coast of Vancouver Island, make up the group named for the gulf.

The Gulf Islands are Canadian. With the San Juans, a similar American collection to the south, they form an archipelago whose total area is less than four hundred square miles. So small and unimportant did they appear in 1846 that Britain and the United States ignored them when they defined the boundary between their northwest possessions. The line, they agreed, should follow the 49th Parallel to the middle of the gulf, thence run round Vancouver Island to the Strait of Juan de Fuca, and there continue to the Pacific.

In thus failing to mention the islands, they opened the way to three different interpretations of the boundary route. Naturally, when both nations, grown defense conscious, awoke to the islands' strategic position, each claimed the channel best suited to its own purposes. Britain named Rosario Strait; the United States, Haro. Not until 1871 was the issue decided. Then a Joint High Commission, with the Emperor of Germany, no less, in the role of mediator, declared Haro Strait to be the channel most in accord with the 1846 treaty.

With few exceptions, the Gulf Islands lie south of the 49th Parallel. This brings them face to face with the San Juans. But since, to pass back and forth, citizens of both groups would have to cope with the rigmarole of Customs and Immigration, the Pacific might as well lie between them.

Salt Spring, largest of the Gulf Islands, also has the largest population, twenty five hundred. A baker's dozen range from less than thirty to a few hundred residents. A score or two are exclusively owned by wealthy Canadians or by Americans from southern states who make them their summer homes. The rest are unpeopled.

Almost all are heavily wooded. Never is their weather too hot or too cold, too wet or too dry. More birds, more flowers, more sunshine are to be found on them than elsewhere in the Province. In woods, lakes or streams, deer, pheasant, wild duck are to be had in season; from beaches and gulf, clams, oysters, salmon and other fish. Fruits, berries, vegetables grown there come in the large economy size.

The islands offer so many advantages for peaceful, healthful, inexpensive living that non-islanders have dubbed them "Poor Man's Paradise." And retired schoolteachers, civil service employees, small businessmen, clerks and army veterans do form the vast majority of their residents. Only store and resort keepers, a growing number of sheep and cattle raisers, fishermen and loggers, qualify as workers. Millionaires on their privately owned islands perforce come under the head of Birds of Paradise.

Such a life in such a setting naturally attracts or develops ego-ripened characters. Of the peopled islands, almost all can boast of one or more.

Among several such divertissements, Salt Spring has known the hefty Yorkshireman who in devoted memory of his dead sweetheart's conceptions of elegance stepped ashore one day, complete from silk topper to spats as an English gentleman of the Edwardian era. Having made a fortune in the woollen trade, he built an imposing Edwardian mansion where he entertained on a truly Edwardian scale.

So many guests sometimes assembled to dine that dinner had to be served twice. In which case, their punctilious host dined twice. But woe to the gentleman who did not appear formally and correctly dressed. Woe, woe to the woman who failed to include in her toilette the four essentials, all long—corsets, skirts, gloves, earrings. Never did such a one dine twice at that table!

Saturna Island's residents now hold revised memories of a young Norwegian Pan. During the years preceding the advent of the Wurlitzer organ in motion-picture theatres, he did nothing all day long but gather cedar and other boughs. These he shaped into organ pipes, large or small, according to the note of the chromatic scale to which each was attuned.

When he had so many they were stacked like cordwood about his cabin, he left the island without explanation and after several months returned the same way. Not until a ship stopped to take every pipe aboard did someone, adding two and two, reach the conclusion that their island Pan was not as mad as they had thought. But by that time he had departed once more—to live on the fruits of his madness in Norway.

The de Courcy group attained fame or at least notoriety when Edward Arthur Wilson, as "Brother Twelve," founded there a mysterious cult. Whether or not its rituals were as dark as they are painted, their purpose was to attract credulous and wealthy believers. In this they were so successful that within five years Brother Twelve, the lovely young Goddess Isis, and a quarter million dollars were able to decamp on a luxurious yacht, never to be seen or heard of again.

But I didn't need to leave the ship to meet a typical islander. "Madame," said a voice as smooth as the very best butter a moment after the tourist beside me had departed, leaving a newspaper in his chair, "permit me to ask if this seat is taken."

An elderly gentleman with a shiny bald pate and benign face, garbed in a "good black suit" of heavy wool, stood before it, bowing rhythmically. When I said no, he bowed to the newspaper, then to a sign which warned that no one could hold a chair by leaving some possession in it. "Theoretically, that is indeed true," he agreed, "but good manners, you know, require one to be a gentleman."

With a *very* deep bow, he seated himself firmly, added on a sigh, "After three days in that gross cash register known as Vancouver, I am greatly fatigued in body and spirit. I look forward with anticipation to reaching the peace and solace of my island home tonight."

Peace and solace seemed the very words for the islands. Some were solidly green, not even a path showing. On others, small, neat homes, set well back on manicured lawns, with brightly painted garden chairs and hammocks under shade trees, tennis or croquet court at one side, drowsed in the sun as idly as the small motor- or rowboat rocking beside each dock. Sea gulls swirling and screaming about gillnetters anchored here and there in offshore waters were the only proof that day and scene were not something conceived by Anthony Trollope.

The scene at least was not as Trollope-ish as it looked, according to the Victorian on my right. Owners of complete islands want all the islands to remain exactly as they are. But residents whose annuities and pensions are shrinking under the rising cost of living now are as eager as the workers to acquire roads, modern utilities and better ferry service, to realize all the islands' economic possibilities.

"High time," said he. Both Vancouver and Victoria are expanding so fast they soon must look for additional residential suburbs. And Vancouver, the entire Lower Mainland, and the increasing tourist trade require more summer and winter resorts. The quickly accessible Gulf Islands are the answer.

More than 280 miles long, from 50 to 80 miles wide, Vancouver Island is the largest island off North America's Pacific coast. Throughout the voyage it had loomed mistily to starboard. But as we sailed along its southeast shore, the sun burst out and the sea smoothed out. As swiftly as a torn cobweb, the haze disappeared, to reveal the island's green hills, rowed like a typewriter keyboard with homes and buildings.

Soon we were rounding a headland into the Strait of Juan de Fuca, to see only eighteen miles away the shadowy blue wall of the Olympics outlining the northernmost coast of the United States. And there, within the inner curve of the headland was Victoria, a meld of gold and green and blue, flecked with white and brilliant colour.

Sailboats and launches skittered away as we entered what looked like a small harbour, fringed with ships—it is mapped as Victoria Harbour. But by this time I had learned that nothing is what it seems in British Columbia or at least if it is what it seems today, it won't be tomorrow. So I was only slightly bemused to discover that the harbour is the wide mouth of a tortured inlet. As "The Gorge," it corkscrews inland a few miles to end in a bay, bunched like a bucking bronco with all four feet on a dime and called, naturally, Portage Inlet!

But thus bemused, when a great dark dome and small grey towers soared out of massed shade trees, I assumed they topped a cathedral. A snow-white building of classic design I thought was a temple. And as I looked across a blue, rectangular pool, bevelled with formally flowered banks, to ivied walls and acres of well-kept lawns and gardens, I recognized the campus of a college, hoary with age and learning. Very Old World it all looked and a very spacious, gracious entrance it presented to the capital of British Columbia.

When I went ashore, however, the classic temple turned out to be the ferry station. Beyond the balustraded Causeway above the Crystal Pool, campus and ivied walls enclosed the

Empress Hotel. And to the right, across more acres of terraced lawns and gardens, dome and towers crowned the opulent, nineteenth-century Parliament Buildings.

Somewhere Viennese waltzes rippled from radio or amplifier. Flags flew from buildings and standards. Pigeons zoomed or strutted, cooing loudly. From every lamppost swayed twin baskets overflowing with petunias, nasturtiums, geraniums and some blue-flowered vine. Every few feet men and women with footlight smiles passed out circulars advertising antique shops. Beside the curb, gay, red-seated and canopied, horse-drawn tallyhos waited to carry the milling, carefree holiday-makers on sightseeing tours.

Could this be the staid and tradition-bound capital of which I had heard so much? Had quaintly costumed shepherds and shepherdesses been dancing and singing on the green, I wouldn't have turned a hair. If ever there were a place where a tourist could *be* a tourist and welcome, Victoria on a 1,000-carat summer afternoon appeared to be that place.

13

PROVINCIAL CAPITAL, PARISIAN STYLE

If a personality can split into more than two selves, Metropolitan Victoria is a noteworthy example of schizophrenia. There, strangely, considering her 125,000 population and outpost location on the rim of the north Pacific, each resident and visitor finds, as in Paris, the city he seeks.

Her own people split into what a leading citizen describes as "young Turks or rebels and firmly entrenched reactionaries. One group envisions a dream city in one of the most spectacular settings in North America, a progressive city of broad avenues, handsome buildings, thriving industry. The other exists behind what some call 'the crumpet curtain.' Its coat of arms is a monocle and an opera cape rampant on a field of moss; its civic motto, the 'status quo.' "

Modern streets, shops and industries easily are seen. The crumpet curtain set, alumni largely of Queen Victoria's reign, carry on their crystallized social and intellectual lives behind the doors of mid-Victorian homes and clubs or in small, quiet hotels. Their public appearances are limited for the most part to the tea hour and "olde English" functions of the Empress Hotel, which, also schizophrenic, with Old World elegance and New World comfort, manages to remain on good terms with them and the travelling public.

One summer afternoon while I was having tea there, a gentlewoman in fluttering chiffons, shocked by the "unattached" women tourists in backless sports dresses, raised her voice to tell her companion, "I do like people who have got people belonging to them. You feel, in a sort of way, that they'll go on living in their own homes." It sounded like a quote. It was. From Trollope's Mr. Prong!

On a bitter December afternoon, a tired, cold and elderly

woman, in a worn, old-fashioned costume, a paper shopping bag in one ungloved hand, wandered into the tea lounge as I was giving my order. Immediately my waitress and the maître d'hotel rushed to escort her to a table, shower her with attention. Returning, the waitress in an impressive whisper told me the newcomer's name and, to my blank look, translated, "One of the So-and-so's, you know."

So ended my acquaintance with the crumpeteers. But one hears plenty said in a mixture of affection and exasperation about their passionate loyalty to "Old Country" tradition, the leisured life, and disdain for "trade." Though credited with making the capital long known as "The only cemetery in Canada with a business district," they nevertheless have impregnated it with a piquant flavour.

Where else do gardeners sweep leaves from walks with besoms? Where else than in the Empress Hotel's coffee shop would everyone be so well-bred that not a head turned when a masked bandit shouted, "This is a stickup!" To engage their attention, the baffled badman was obliged to fire a shot into the ceiling.

Where else would city fathers furrow their brows for a tactful way to suggest to indomitably genteel ladies that their belief in the right of their pet pussies to multiply into platoons is not necessarily so? To recommend the method widely known to this atomic age would be most indelicate. The alternative—to suggest that each owner of more than three indiscreet tabbies declare herself to be a cat breeder and pay a fee—they well know would be ignored as smacking intolerably of trade.

Primarily, Victoria is a capital—with two centres, political and social. To the stranger within its gates, both are confusing. Though patterned on Britain's Parliament, the Provincial government has but one legislative body. Though, as in England, the Provincial electorate includes Liberal, Conservative and Socialist parties, it also embraces the Social Credit Movement, a comparatively new party in this Province.

The Lieutenant Governor, appointed by the Governor General of Canada, does not govern. As representative of the

Crown, he calls upon the leader of the party which wins the most victories in a Provincial election to act as premier. The Premier names his own ministers, who, with him, are responsible to the Legislature. This combination pleases the traditionalists, who take pride in the booming guns, swords, Speech from the Throne, and other pageantry with which each winter the Crown endows the opening of the Legislature, and leaves the legislators free to formulate policies and laws as they see fit.

From the sweep of muscle-bending steps to the statue of Captain Vancouver atop the copper dome, the Parliament Buildings are truly Victorian in appearance. But the granites that form their outer walls, the cedar, pine, maple and other woods that panel their interiors are as truly British Columbian. The central building, with its dim and muraled corridors, rotunda and marble-walled Legislative Chamber, is the seat of government. A rear wing houses the Provincial Library and Archives; the East Wing, the Provincial Museum. Behind this block-long structure, government departments, from Agriculture to Welfare, function in old, new and interim buildings.

All is not so formal as it looks, however. On summer evenings and for special occasions, Parliament Buildings, outlined with lights, are as gay as the mall of a world's fair. On summer evenings, also, Victorians and tourists gather about the flagstaff on the lawns to witness impressive sunset ceremonies. Though derived from those of the Crusaders many centuries ago, they are executed with the colour and precision of the Changing of the Guard before Buckingham Palace. The sunset ceremonies are presented in turn by one of the armed services stationed in or about Victoria and by cadets from Royal Roads, the national academy which trains young Canadians for commissions in the Army, Navy or Air Force.

Few Canadians, including Victorians, or Americans ever realized that the capital's location at the junction of the Gulf of Georgia and the Strait of Juan de Fuca made it one of the most vitally significant points on the Pacific coast. Because it commands the only two entrances from the Pacific to the densely peopled and industrialized areas of both southwest

British Columbia and northwest Washington State, both Canada and the United States were concerned for its defense.

From 1878, when the first muzzle-loader cannon was set up in Victoria's harbour, until the approach of World War II, fortifications were extended from the capital to Esquimalt, Pacific base of the Canadian Navy. Then, as a result of a Joint High Commission's survey, others were added until, from miles south of the city to miles north, visible and invisible defences ringed the coast. Some of them the most modern in the world, they not only barred access by enemy ships to Victoria, Vancouver and New Westminster, but to Seattle, Tacoma and a half dozen more cities on Puget Sound.

New techniques of warfare developed during and after World War II rendered them and lesser fortifications at Vancouver and Prince Rupert obsolete. In 1956, all were dismantled and "mothballed." Defence of the British Columbia-Washington coast now rests with the Canadian and American Navies and Air Forces.

Physically and psychologically removed from law- and defence-making, Government House, another imposing structure, is made more imposing still by lawns, sculptured shrubbery, formal gardens. Here members of the Royal Family stay while in the capital, and dinners, balls, presentations give the city festive association with the Court. And here, as hosts for the Crown and leaders of the capital's social life, the Lieutenant Governor and his wife reside.

When there is a Government House, that is. Since the first one was erected in 1852, three have been destroyed by fire. The third burned to the ground with all its priceless art and historical collections in April, 1957. On the same day plans for the fourth, on the same site, were begun.

Victoria also boasts two of the most imposing castles built in North America. As a young Scottish emigrant, Robert Dunsmuir brought to the Fort Victoria of the 1850's his young bride. He had promised her that one day she would live in a castle, surrounded by formal gardens and filled with footmen, just like those in Scotland. Thirty years later, when Vancouver

Island coal mines and railroad had made him a multimillion-aire, he built Craigdarroch ("Place of the Oaks on the Rock") Castle. From its rocky knoll, it still dominates the capital's skyline. In 1907, his older son, James, built even more preten-tious Hatley Park on a 700-acre estate in Esquimalt.

Today they are occupied by Metropolitan Victoria's School Board and Royal Roads. But while their original owners lived in them and ever since, the elegant and robustly colourful goings-on among the Dunsmuirs have furnished Victorians with a highly spiced conversation piece. Despite this and the fact that the current generation lacks the wealth of the first, the capital maintains that "Once you've dined at a Dunsmuir table, you've arrived!"

Second in interest if not in importance to Victoria the capital is Victoria the tourist mecca. Ships, planes and ferries from Vancouver and Seattle bring it a major share of the five hundred thousand visitors who annually swarm over Van-couver Island.

The city itself is a prime attraction. Whether the "nearest thing to England" in architecture and atmosphere or as modern as tomorrow, its residential areas are distinguished by beautiful trees, hedges, gardens. So infinite is their variety and sometimes stylized perfection that they give the illusion of tapestries hung against home or garden walls. Buildings and shops are bright with window boxes, lampposts with flowering baskets or, in winter, holly.

My winter months there began with a three-day blizzard and continued through rains, fogs, snow, sleet, low temperatures and high gales. But, as one and all assured me, my experience was "simply too unusual." Looking me straight in the eye, they declared Victoria's normal climate, with an annual average of 50-degree temperatures and two thousand hours of sun, to be so mild that roses bloom the year round.

The very thought brings hundreds of refugees from the snows and cold east of the Rockies to bask with them. For the "winterers" and others who return for the holidays, Victoria stages two weeks of "Old English" festivities, highlighted with traditional "boar's head" Christmas dinners and New Year's Eve balls.

Parks, lookouts, and marine drives from which to enjoy city and setting, fresh- and salt-water fishing and swimming and other sports, and tours to man-made beauties like Butchart Gardens telescope the visitor's days. So do the shops. Modern shops, with woollens, tweeds and porcelains from looms and kilns of the British Isles. Antique shops, with everything from the exquisite to the grotesque.

Many of their owners pine for the halcyon days when only gentry with plenty of money and time to spend could enjoy holidays. One suffered so acutely from the sight of "two-week and weekend tourists" whirling in and out of his doors that he now locks up and goes away during the midsummer madness.

Though many an overweight Victorian structure has been replaced by streamlined stone, steel and glass, some remain in new roles. Behind the carved stone façade and bricks brought round the Horn in British sailing vessels to wall the old railway depot is the City Market. Still in tune with the nostalgic, it offers among today's radishes and eggs, clotted cream, "Old Country" herbs, jams and, in season, sweet Devon violets.

"Young Turks" from time to time add new features. Their masterpiece to date is the challenge to channel swimmers to conquer the eighteen miles of cold-and-tide-harried Strait of Juan de Fuca between Victoria and Port Angeles on the Olympic Peninsula. Each summer, amid global publicity and local hysteria, contestants and spectators overwhelm the city.

For low-pressure visitors, there is lovelorn Cadborosaurus. Centuries ago, as a young Indian brave, "Caddy" defied the gods by carrying off a maiden too beautiful—in their opinion—to know human love. Now, a sea serpent, doomed to haunt inshore waters for a billion years, he occasionally displays his coils to the susceptible.

Still another Victoria is sought by thousands, among them Britishers with decades of service in some Pacific post behind them. On fortunes, savings, pensions, they come, as to Nirvana, to enjoy the late afternoon of life among balmy temperatures, a slow tempo, and a countryside reminiscent of England.

For much the same reasons, numbers of artists and craftsmen call the capital home. Agnes Newton Keith, author of *Land Below the Wind* and *Three Came Back*; Arthur Mayse, a novelist as popular with Americans as with Canadians; Bruce Hutchinson, whose *The Unknown Country* is a Canadian classic, are only a few of the writers here.

Among many artists, Victoria-born Emily Carr is outstanding. Although she and her canvases were almost unknown before her death, today both are prized far beyond Dominion boundaries. The first Provincial painter to see in British Columbia's Indian life and scene an original field, she developed an original palette to portray them.

Perhaps no other Canadian city has so many men and women dedicated to continuing or preserving ancient crafts. An artist illuminates parchment scrolls in the manner of medieval monks. A wood carver specializes in old religious themes. A clock doctor gives new life to timepieces of the ages. Others restore precious porcelains. As a member of both groups, Mungo Martin, aging Indian artist, is the creator of the tallest totem in the world and preserver of others in Victoria's fine collection.

Often overlooked by the visitor is Victoria the manufacturing and trade centre, with the highest per capita purchasing power in Canada. And Victoria the port, whose ice-free harbour, immense dockyard, and the largest drydock in the Dominion, is important as shipping and shipbuilding centre.

Of all the ships that come and go, one of Victoria's own, the deep-sea salvage tugboat *Sudbury*, is most famous. As a corvette, she made no headlines during World War II, but ever since she has been a page-one familiar. Her 30-day, 3,200-nautical-mile tow in the winter of 1955 to bring the Greek freighter *Makedonia* to Vancouver from a point off the Kamchatka Peninsula, did more than break all distance records. Continuously battered by the worst storms the "terrific Pacific" could hurl at her, she won, according to shipping annals, one of the toughest battles ever fought by men and ship against the sea.

Victoria comes naturally by its cosmopolitan population and conflicting schools of thought. It was born of strife and, if one may say so, reared during its formative years by firmly entrenched reactionaries.

Britain and the United States ended their bickering over which owned what in this Northwest in 1843. Three years before, Hudson's Bay Company began to transfer its Pacific headquarters from Fort Vancouver on the Lower Columbia River to Camosack Bay on the southwest corner of Vancouver Island. There, from Fort Victoria, it re-established the status quo—absolute control over a fur domain extending from Rockies to Pacific, from the new boundary to the Arctic. Into that vast domain no settler dared set foot.

By 1849, thousands of Americans, including twenty thousand Mormons under Brigham Young, were voicing interest in Vancouver Island's climate, forests, soils, fisheries. The British government thereupon created the Crown Colony of Vancouver Island. And, on condition that a British colony be established at Fort Victoria within five years, it placed the Island under Hudson's Bay control.

Still viewing the settler as Enemy Number One, the company made its terms so stiff that the one settler who did come had to take up land twenty miles away. And when the first Colonial Governor arrived from London to find no colony, no salary, and above all, no welcome, he soon resigned. The company then appointed its chief factor, James Douglas, as Acting Governor and carried on as before.

Discovery of gold on the Upper Columbia in 1855 and on the Lower Fraser in 1857 shattered the status quo. Prospectors, recognizing no boundaries, swarmed in. Among them were thousands of 49-ers from California's fading mines and eight hundred escaped Negro slaves. Within two or three years, Fort Victoria was embedded in a sea of tents and shacks and a reputation which rivalled that of the Barbary Coast.

By canoe, raft, anything that would float, the miners crossed the gulf to the Mainland. Others walked across the boundary. By 1858 so many were fanning out so rapidly over the Fraser and Thompson Valleys that, to establish control over them,

Britain created the Crown Colony of British Columbia.

This second colony was no more peaceful than the first. Though British Columbians welcomed James Douglas as their governor, they were outraged when he and his staff continued to live in Fort Victoria. To pacify them, the British Colonial Office, in 1864, gave them their own governor—Frederick Seymour.

Inevitably, the infant colonies became rivals. That rivalry became hostility when Vancouver Island Colony's citizens, to rid themselves of a new and unpopular governor, clamored for union with British Columbia. British Columbians would have none of them or it.

To simplify the situation, as it thought, the British Parliament, in 1866, merged the rivals under the name of British Columbia and the governorship of Frederick Seymour. The Governor set off a new uproar. By-passing the "City of Victoria"—so incorporated in 1862—he chose New Westminster, a collection of stumps and shacks on the Fraser, as capital of the enlarged Crown Colony.

To New Westminster, the Mainland choice was eminently wise and logical. But Victoria flamed with such heat that within two years she recovered the capital.

Meantime, another burning issue was in the making. As the Provincial historian, F. W. Howay, puts it, "From the union of the colonies in 1866 . . . there always had been a distinct possibility that British Columbia would . . . join the United States."

The reasons were plainly mapped. Canada was almost three thousand miles away. Even as the crow flies, Britain was six thousand. Neither felt concern or interest in the north Pacific coast or for the maddened goldseekers pushing deeper and deeper into its wilderness. The United States was right next door.

Almost all the Colony's trade and traffic, including its mail, wearing American stamps, came and went through San Francisco, then with sixty thousand people the metropolis of the Pacific. So many San Franciscan shipping and banking services, newspaper publishers and merchants had established permanent businesses and homes in Victoria that the colonial capital was little more than an outpost of the California port.

Because of these geographic and economic ties, mid-Victorian Victoria was so ardently in favour of American annexation that she twice petitioned the U.S. Congress for admittance to the Union. Vancouver Island and Governor Seymour supported her.

The death of the Governor changed the picture. His successor favoured union with Canada. And by 1870 Canada, her interest awakened by rich gold strikes in the Cariboo, was convinced that Vancouver Island was "the key to all British North America on the Pacific." When the Crown threw its weight behind her and Ottawa promised to build a transcontinental railway from Atlantic to Pacific, the long and loud debates over the merits of British versus American citizenship reached a full stop.

On July 20, 1871, British Columbia closed its colonial history, to enter the Dominion of Canada in the full stature of a province.

Elated Victoria invested almost a million dollars—an astronomical sum for that time and place—in an anchor strong enough to fix the Provincial capital forever to the southwest corner of Vancouver Island. The Parliament Buildings.

14

FROM BLACK STONES, A HOT FIRE

Nature required centuries to raise the rolling, 250-foot-high bench that outlines Vancouver Island's rocky, irregular east coast. But the Island's rapidly expanding population and economy are as rapidly smoothing out the rolls to make room for more homes, farms, industries, settlements growing into villages, villages into towns.

So far they have done nothing to change the splendour of the gulf and its islands, backed by the continuous march of Coast Mountains on the Mainland. And coastal steamers, freighters, tugs, stolidly at work, do try to maintain the gulf's original function as commercial highway. More and more sailboats and yachts, sports fishermen in smart white craft, pleasure launches and outboard motors, sunbathers and swimmers, however, are claiming it for a playground.

From Victoria, the new marine highway runs north between long-familiar scenes. Quaint English cottages, bowered in roses, flowering vines, shrubs and trees border the waterfront. Inland, deeply green foothills of the Insular Mountains scallop the cornflower sky. One of them, Malahat, or "Caterpillar"— Indian named for its many humps—is prized for the view its 2,000-foot summit affords of island, gulf and mountains.

But at intervals, our bus lost sight of them between walls of freshly cut granite or evergreens so recently exposed to sun and air that their pale, pipestem trunks and outstretched naked branches appeared as pitiful as crowds of famine refugees. And at Malahat's foot we came on a badly bruised status quo.

The bus stopped suddenly, because—as I thought—fog blinded the highway. But, no, here was a lower lookout from which to enjoy a tremendous panorama. Far below, Saanich Inlet curved in around foothills from the gulf to shape Saanich Peninsula. Across the upper sky, Mt. Baker spread her snowy masses. To the south, a horseshoe of Olympics glistened like real rock-candy mountains. Not fog, but clouds of white dust belching up from a cement factory on the inlet's shore obscured the view almost as effectively as its fumes had destroyed the trees far and wide.

Between gusts we could see that the inlet's hill-and-tree-shadowed waters were clotted with small craft whose sportsmen watched their casts with the concentration of scientists on the verge of discovering the origin of life. They had reason, said the envious driver. Each angler was dedicated to the task of catching a salmon weighty enough to qualify him to compete in the Victoria-Saanich Inlet Association's upcoming Salmon Derby.

In contrast with the suspense-full inlet, the peninsula was a medallion of pastoral peace. Level and green with well-kept orchards, mink, chinchilla and vegetable farms, it claims to have a greater variety of agricultural projects than any comparable area on earth. But round its edges broad roofs of new homes inlaid in heavy green signalled change for this cornucopia too. A few more years and another of Victoria's residential suburbs will cover it as completely as the tall conifers and oaks of only a century ago.

Its first resident was the humiliated young Scot who, in 1855, followed a 12-mile Indian trail north from Fort Victoria. Sight of the oaks wiped from his mind the jeers he had suffered for lack of a seat in his trousers. To his thrifty soul, oaks meant acorns; acorns, pigs. "Here I will settle," Willy Thompson promised himself. And when he had worked out the price of the blanket with which Hudson's Bay Company had ransomed him, a shipwrecked sailor, from slavery among the Indians of the Island's west coast and earned the money to buy nineteen pigs, he did.

On again, into a ferment of contrast and change. Inland, generously dimensioned homes and barns of dairy farms, their hayfields cut and drying, Herefords and Holsteins grazing in Acadian pastures, alternated with stretches of evergreens coming down to make way for more. But also, under the impact of the east coast's ballooning charms as a playground, motels, inns, boxlike tourist cabins, trailer camps and campsites alternated with more trees crashing down. Almost every home on the waterfront offered "Tourist accommodations."

Small wonder! The east coast is scrolled with stunning bays, sheltered between distant black-green ridges and rimmed with beaches that wax or wane from new to half moons depending on the stage of the tides. Each has its own appeal. To each the bus lost passengers.

Cowichan Bay is a year-round fishing and logging village. Cottages and scarlet-poppy gardens ignore gravity to cling to the ridge that here runs steeply to a harbour where log booms ride shoulder to shoulder. Boats for hire along each private dock wait for the sports fishermen and coho salmon soon to swarm in. Chemainus, a flower town though centred about a lumber mill, has the earmarks of an Atlantic fishing village, as popular with artists as with fishermen.

Ladysmith's bay has special distinction as one of the finest man-made oyster areas in the world. Years ago, when heavy demands depleted the natural beds, the Provincial Marine Laboratories here developed the "Pacific" oyster, a Japanese species of the same flavour but faster growth.

Gathering grey skies now gave sea and land a long, quiet look. They brightened sun-faded wild flowers and the dull green of Scotch broom that in May is a golden glory and enhanced the beauty of maples, oaks and arbutus tropical in size and density of foliage. In one tree a huge, horizontal branch overhanging a thread of tree-lined stream supplied a barefoot boy with a perch for long, long thoughts.

His example must have been infectious. The next thing I knew, voices, running motors, honking horns, brought me back to blue skies and sunshine. I had just glimpsed still another vast bay when the bus ran into an asphalt plaza, walled with docks, to stop before the loading platform of a massive transportation centre.

In a city 105 years old, a transportation centre of such proportions and activity ordinarily might not have seemed unusual. But for Nanaimo, a retarded child during ninety-four of those years, it seemed to me phenomenal.

One day in 1849 an old Indian of the Island's Nanaimo tribe, hopeful of having his gun repaired, arrived at Fort Victoria's blacksmith shop. No one paid any attention to him until, pointing to the coal that fired the forge, he remarked that he knew where many more "black stones" just like them were to be found. Since those black stones had had to come from England by way of Cape Horn, Hudson's Bay Company officers pricked up their ears.

Within months they were testing coal seams on shore and islands of a bay seventy miles north. Within three years Vancouver Island's first white settlement, Colvilletown, was operating there as a primitive mining camp.

Renamed Nanaimo—"Big Strong Tribe"—in 1860, it continued until 1946 as a typical mining town. Then, its mines closed, some two thousand miners departed. What was left emerged, fretful and lean as a bear after a long, dark winter's hibernation.

Nanaimo still is fretful, but no longer lean. The residue of citizens, swelled now to almost fifteen thousand, have made it one of British Columbia's most dynamic cities. In a little more than a decade, they have confounded the departing colliery manager's prediction that grass soon would cover its streets.

Only one vestige of the grime and slag era remains. That is a white, hexagonal Bastion, built in 1853 to shelter the miners during Indian attacks. Today it is a museum.

And today a farsighted and most articulate percentage of the population is electric with ambition to realize the many prophecies Provincial and industrial leaders have made for their city. "One of the largest industrial areas in Canada." . . . "Centre of one of the greatest paper and pulp producing areas in the world." . . . "A World Port." "Playground of the Pacific Northwest." . . . "A city of fifty thousand, if not seventy-five thousand," including many Vancouverites who will live here and commute to the Mainland metropolis by helicopter.

But for three things I might have thought myself in Prince

George. Nanaimo's setting and location. The fact that it has no need to seek ways to diversify its industries. And the fact that its "realists," as they call themselves, are balanced by what they call the "sentimentalists." The first would be happy to place all its eggs in an industrial basket. The second are determined to preserve as much as possible of the city's natural beauty.

Like a vast amphitheatre, Nanaimo mounts from the nose of a twisted promontory to spread in tier after tier of streets over the lower slopes of 3,300-foot Mt. Benson. To left and right of the promontory, an enormous, unbroken bay curves between low hills to two islands, Newcastle and Protection, which landlock it from the gulf. So defended on all sides from Pacific and Mainland gales and temperatures, it won from wearied early Spanish navigators the title, "Bay of Rest."

In one sense, its subtitle, "Hub of Vancouver Island," is a misnomer. Nanaimo is less than halfway along the 186-mile east coast highway which must almost double in length to follow the coast to the end of the Island. In another, the term is not a creation of the Board of Trade. It is a fact.

Vancouver is only forty-odd miles distant; Victoria, seventy. About these two centres more than 75 per cent of British Columbia's population is concentrated. North of Nanaimo, another 110,000 people live in fishing and logging villages and sports resorts.

Such a location automatically makes it the distribution and transportation point for most of the commercial traffic to and from the Island. Sightseeing and spectator tourists by the tens of thousands may prefer Victoria. Touring, camping and sportsmen tourists in equal numbers, bound for local streams and mountains or the increasingly sought beaches and fishing grounds of the northern Island, prefer Nanaimo.

Instead of the ubiquitous drugstores characteristic of most cities' commercial districts, Nanaimo's Victoria Crescent is a succession of sports shops. Some of their display windows are Monacan in the luxury of their fishing, hunting, golf and other sports equipment. My first impression, that to be an eligible

resident or visitor one had to be a radio fanatic, collapsed when
I discovered that the antennae rampant fore and aft on almost
every car were fishing rods!

In addition to planes and buses, twenty-one steamship ferries
arrive daily from Vancouver—only a token, it is said, of the
days to come when one will dock every twenty minutes. Small
steamer, launch and barge ferries for passengers and cars ply
back and forth to various Gulf Islands.

Its location also explains why Nanaimo does not need to seek
ways to diversify its industries. Central and north Vancouver
Island still are deep in commercial timber. Giant sawmills
within easy highway reach annually ship hundreds of millions
of feet of lumber in deep-sea ships from Nanaimo's harbour.
Among its factories, presently or soon to be operating, are
secondary industries on which the mills depend.

Its own waters (to say nothing of the gulf's, one of the finest
fishing grounds in North America) make it a market from
which fresh and cured fish and fish products are exported.
Thousands of tons of salmon, ling cod and other fish are
caught here. Shoals of herring are salted to the Orient's taste.
Crab, clam and shrimp are frozen or canned.

A city official with a long view raised the only anxious voice.
Like Prince George, he said, Nanaimo is handicapped by lack
of power. "But even if we harness every river, lake and waterfall
on the Island, we wouldn't have enough to supply all the
industrial demands of the east coast in the foreseeable future.
Our power must come from the Mainland. Eventually it will
—as hydroelectric or atomic. Meantime, I'm afraid we're
destroying some of the very assets that attract permanent residents and tourists to the Island."

Only sterling character forced me away from my windows in
the Hotel Malaspina to learn about Nanaimo's current and
future developments. Those windows overlooked one of the
most beautiful harbours in this land of beautiful harbours.

On the right, it curved round to the wide, deep channel
between Newcastle Island and green hills; on the left, to the
narrow channel between Newcastle and Protection. Through

one or the other, ferries, large and small, freighters and fishing boats in all sizes and colours, sailboats, cruisers, launches came and went. Canoes and rowboats toured from point to point of the harbour. And just when I thought I had seen a sample of everything navigable, a tug no bigger than a wink chugged by as though unaware that at the end of its towline rode one of the float villages characteristic of British Columbia's coast.

A dozen white cottages, every white or flowered curtain drawn, lined its single street. Centred at one side was the general store and post office. A schoolhouse, bell beside the door and gay tulip and daffodil cutouts dancing across its windows, sealed the top or bottom of the raft. No one occupied them at the moment, of course, and everything movable had been put away, but it was obvious that when it arrived at its new location its residents would take up life just where they had left off.

Arched beneath pine, cedar and spruce, whose uppermost treetops stood out like fern fronds against a snow-white crescent of Coast Mountains, Newcastle Island also appeared unaware of its recent escape from a fate worse than death. As the primary issue of a municipal election, it had brought out the "realists" to vote for its transformation into an industrial park. But a larger number of the "sentimentalists" had voted to preserve its beaches, woodland trails, mysterious caves and beauty as places of recreation.

"That's a woman's point of view," one of the losers snorted at me. "Sentimental. Unrealistic. B.C.'s overloaded with parks and playgrounds as it is. Make the country work for you, earn for you, I say."

"To cover Newcastle from end to end with industries would have been ruinous to the city's beauty and all-round progress," one of the winners countered. "And not only for the city. All around us, lakes, streams, and some of the best mountain scenery on the Island provide a playground for our own people. And for hundreds of Mainlanders, too. As Nanaimo goes, so will go the country about it. Balance. We must maintain a balance."

Nanaimo

For a model they might watch their own harbour. By day, it is a spectrum, rippled and banded with every shade; at sunset, a glowing opal, set in green-gold; by night, ebony, stroked with light—of docks, ships, moon, stars. Its waters play with colour as an expert juggler balances bells.

15

FOR A FISH, A RUBY

Overlaid with a sparkling trammel of light, the Gulf of
Georgia was so deep a blue it often appeared purple. Like
the rhythmic whorls of a shell, the Coast Mountains rose in
curve after curve of dazzling white. As though jealous of their
Mainland rivals' display, the Insular Mountains, higher now,
emerged from soft blue haze to stand out so clearly one could
distinguish individual trees on their lower slopes and, in their
rocky upper basins, each little sun-flame dancing on snow.

Fortunately, the highway builds like a Chinese feast of
"eight big, eight little" courses to climaxes, then modulates to
simpler fare. At such times we wound through flowered villages
or cool conifers. Once or twice we stopped at a resort concocted
for the pleasure of the tourist and the profit of the residents
whose own homes, embedded in cabins, traced the mushroom
growth of this new industry.

Qualicum Beach is such a place though its bay commands a
breath-stopping panorama. The gulf rolls lazily toward long,
green islands off the Mainland. Beyond and above them coastal
mountains roll north, south and inland as far as eye can see.
Its pebbled sands were strewn with sunbathers and castle-
building toddlers. Swimmers, dogs, sea gulls, and a coot or two
companionably shared the water. Far out, small boats at anchor
marked the limit of low tide.

My seatmate on the bus came back from a long, wistful look
at one of the islands to say, "Years ago I tore an advertisement
about that island—Lasqueti—from a Victoria paper. I—I still
have it. The people living there then had too few children of
school age to qualify for a teacher. So they offered permanent
residence, rent free, to any couple with at least three youngsters
over five years who would move there. We had three and I

longed to go. I could even have taught the school. But my husband was a city man. He . . ."

Miles of dense woods laced with small streams led unexpectedly into open country. On one side across narrow Union Bay a peninsula, like Nanaimo a one-time seat of Robert Dunsmuir's coal mines, now sheltered an agricultural and fishing village. On the other, grainfields were so aggressively green they should have been behind bars.

"Comox Valley," said my still pensive seatmate. "You'd think it was as old and rich as Prince Edward Island, wouldn't you? Yet it wasn't really settled until after the first World War."

Remembering the woods we had come through, looking at others climbing foothills to the west, I asked what had happened to produce a prairie here.

"It's not a prairie. Every foot was covered with fine timber when the first settlers came in. But they were Australian miners and sailors who reached Victoria too late for the 1862 gold rush, plus a few British farmers. None of them had any idea the trees had value. They burned everything off to get at the soil. With what they grew and with plenty of fish and deer, they didn't starve, of course, but with no market they had to do without almost everything else. My grandfather wore flour-sack socks until after he was married."

While I wondered where the flour sacks came from, we ran into Courtenay, a prosperous, English-looking town of big, comfortable homes, magnificent shade trees, and a startling view. Miles away, in Strathcona Park, two steeply precipiced peaks, gallantly escorting between them a glacier smooth and white as a gull's wing, appeared about to stroll down Courtenay's main street.

My companion introduced them as Mt. Alberni and Mt. Edward, both seven thousand feet, and Victoria, or Comox, Glacier. "They mark the beginning of the Forbidden Plateau which ends with Mt. Alexandra—about sixty-five hundred feet. You'll see them as you go north."

"Why *Forbidden* Plateau?"

"Indians named it. Long before the white man came, they say, the warriors of an island tribe parked their women and children up there while they fought off another from the Mainland. When the battle was over and they sent for their families, not a woman or child could be found. After that, the plateau was forbidden ground."

When she left the bus, the man behind me leaned forward. "The lady is mistaken," said he. "The name, Forbidden, comes from the Indians' fear of the 'red snow' sometimes seen on the plateau. The snow, of course, is red algae, a natural phenomenon. But, unable to explain it, the Indians took it as a warning from the gods to keep out."

Far blue shadows were gathering over the 4,000-foot-high plateau as we followed the highway round its southeast bulge, and over the distant shimmer of Mt. Alexandra. But Oyster Bay, with another all-embracing view of gulf and Coast Mountains, still was luminous with sun. By that time, however, I had reached the point on scenery frequently achieved by a young friend who, after a surfeit of sweets, demands a pickle.

The town of Campbell River was my pickle! A brief row of locked and padlocked pioneer buildings strung along the inland side of the highway, it gave no hint that four thousand people lived in the low hills about it. Or that tourists and sportsmen flocked to its lodges, auto courts and camps. The elderly taxi driver who talked me to Painter's Lodge, four miles away, agreed.

"It's this way," he explained. "Until ten-fifteen years ago, Campbell River was just a small fishing village. Then the government built a breakwater across our harbour and a whale of a dam on Moose Lake. Now, hundreds of fishing boats work out of here every season. And we supply power to Nanaimo, Port Alberni, most of the Island. Besides that, we've got more than a thousand loggers cutting down trees and a big Forest Service nursery growing new ones. And miners—we've got big coal and iron deposits around here—may have a steel mill one day. Right now, we've got a $40 million paper and pulp mill. Add everything up and we've got a year-round payroll that even

Nanaimo wouldn't sniff at. Get the picture?"

"Clearly."

"Well, now, take the tourist. He's seasonal and he wants fancy service and fancy things. But what we want's a town that caters to *us*. And we figure to get it. This time next year we'll have a million-dollar shopping centre, as fine as you'll see in Vancouver. Won't be many years before the highway runs through to the end of the Island and we want to be Johnny on the Spot. It only goes a few miles more to Kelsey Bay now."

It was just as well. The Campbell River he scorned held plenty of interest.

From what I had been told about Painter's Lodge as the favoured haunt of well-to-do sportsmen and from its four-star rating, I had expected a Sun Valley or Camelback Inn. But the main lodge and cabins set back on lawns scooped out of evergreen forest were as simple as the proverbial old shoe.

The only difference was that during the dinner hour the dining room was as still as a chapel. Men in Savile Row and Brooks Brothers wool shirts and tweeds, their faces freshly burned or bronzed, devoted themselves in relaxed content to their food. Their wives, roughing it in cashmere sweaters and single strands of real pearls, wore also an air of withdrawal amusingly reminiscent of the Sekani women on the Hart Highway bus.

With minor variations that scene probably has been standard in most corners of the sportsman's world since or before the days of Jane Austen. But to come on it here after weeks of travel through a Province bursting with economic and social change was the equivalent of waking up in King Arthur's Court.

To reorient myself, I looked out my table window. Lo! instead of another wide and peopled bay, here was the wilderness again. Below a steep, irregular ridge lay Discovery Strait, a branch of the Gulf of Georgia, sliced to little more than arrow-shot width between Vancouver and Quadra Islands.

Shadows were gathering in its canyon. Above Quadra's copper-tinted treetops, the Coast Mountains were a gouache of deep blues and purples. High above them and far away, Mt. Sir Francis Drake's dented white cone glittered like a star in the last rays of the sun.

Less than half a mile south, Campbell River followed a head-land into the strait. A little more than that to the north, the strait pulled itself in to squeeze through Seymour Narrows, a short, tight passage where Quadra pokes a blunt finger at Vancouver Island's chest. There a long-prayed-for change was under way.

"Graveyard of ships," the narrows often are called. The real villain is a submerged mountain, innocuously known as Ripple Rock, right in the middle of them. Over its two rocky peaks, one of them less than nine feet below the surface at low tide, the sea rips and pounds at eight to sixteen knots to create fearful crosscurrents, eddies and whirlpools.

Since 1875, they have sucked down 114 ships, taken more than that number of lives. Rather than make the long detour round Vancouver Island, modern steamships travelling the In-side Passage have learned to cope with them. Small craft and whales wait for intervals of slack water.

All attempts to decapitate the peaks from the surface have failed. Now men are building an undersea tunnel into the mountain's side. There they will blast shafts and pack them with hundreds of tons of nitrone. One day, if "the world's big-gest underwater explosion" is successful, "the greatest single navigational hazard on the north Pacific" will not be even a ripple.

In itself Discovery Strait is a natural fishway where hump-back, coho or blueback, and spring salmon offer sport. Within an hour's drive are at least twenty lakes where good rainbow and cutthroat trout offer more. Elsewhere on the continent such fishing grounds would be polka-dotted with fishermen. Here they are overshadowed by Campbell River. Rather, by its mouth, or pool.

Returning to the rivers of their birth, many salmon still have hundreds of miles to ascend against strong currents, rapids, waterfalls, cougar, bear and other four- and two-legged animals with a taste for fish. Many must make their way through waters polluted by cities and mills, and miles of commercial fishing boats' deep-lurking nets. When at last the survivors approach their spawning grounds they are battered wrecks.

Campbell River salmon are the fatted calves of this piscatorial world. Their river is too fast for fishing; its banks are too densely wooded to attract the insects that attract the fish. Its own non-migrating finned residents feed in the strait, return to their up-river homes for a day or a week as city dwellers visit the country. No commercial fishing is permitted in the strait within a half-mile radius of the river's mouth. And the salmon's spawning grounds lie only a few miles above it.

Depending on when they arrive within tasting distance of their home waters, they know they have weeks or months to travel those miles. So, while they mature, they linger in the strait, to feed so complacently that they "take the line easily." For a sportsman to use anything but light tackle, consequently, is considered very bad form. And the fish put on so much weight that to catch anything less than a tyee is almost as disappointing as to catch none at all.

Technically a tyee, or champion, is a spring salmon, but in Campbell River's sport fishing circles the title applies to a salmon of thirty pounds or over. At Saanich and other Provincial fishing grounds, a salmon of twenty pounds or more is accepted as a tyee.

The Tyee Club of British Columbia, whose lodge overlooks the pool, does not even recognize thirty pounds as prizeworthy. To win just a silver lapel button, its distinguished members must weigh in a 40-pounder. To win a gold pin, 50 pounds; a diamond, 60; and, for a ruby, 70 pounds or over!

With wide and green-eyed wonder I watched the ritual of Campbell River sportsmen. At breakfast, hardly recognizable in dress or manner as the diners of the evening before, they definitely were where they wanted to be, doing what they most wanted to do. But, lest anyone suspect it, they disguised their elation under most inconsequential banter.

Breakfast over, they picked up their lunch boxes and an armful of sweaters and casually departed. But a moment later they'd be striding purposefully down the long pier to the launches waiting at the loading dock. Behind them ambled a guide, with big metal boxes, handfuls of fishing rods and other equipment. One sportsman and guide per launch, they roared away. Two or three minutes later they were dropping anchor for the day at their chosen spots off Campbell River's mouth.

Meantime, the three or four wives who had appeared for breakfast gathered before the picture window in the lounge to watch these departures and arrivals. Though the sky was cloudless, the strait smooth and shining as a silver tray, their eyes were tight with worry, lips compressed. "It's no use saying a word against it," said one. "The more one says the madder they get." No one answered her. Chins up, bravely smiling, they retrieved their parked books from various corners and settled down in *their* chosen corners to read the morning away.

About four o'clock, to the relief of hungrily waiting gulls, the fishermen began to return. A few—easily identified as newcomers—waved wearily to the guides to take over and, empty handed, started cabinward, walking as though each step might be their last. The rest, with days or weeks on the strait behind them, stripped off sweaters to clean every fish as though under the lash of Simon Legree.

Soon, lodge and cabins echoed to the thunder of showers. And despite the custom of serving only wines and beers, a young boy moved mercifully from cabin to cabin to enquire, "Ice, anyone?"

Sitting in sunshine so hot that the Scotch broom's black pods burst to scatter their seeds in a tiny, ticking rain, I had not watched the happily perspiring fish cleaners long when I had to eat my first impression of such sportsmen. They were not and never had been of the past; always of the future.

In this age of increasing leisure and earning power, opportunities for sports that can so absorb and renew surely should be provided as automatically as highways. And here was Vancouver Island's east coast—more than two hundred miles of it—with rivers, lakes, bays, mountains, forests, beauty as yet almost untouched.

If only, before it is too late, too many of its assets (like Campbell River's own Elk Falls) are not destroyed for the waterpower which another generation's atomic or solar energy will render obsolete. If only its "realists" can learn before it is too late what communities east of the Rockies and south of the Boundary are learning at such cost: that beauty and recreation are commodities as necessary as bread and meat; as profitable, if not more so, as steel and chemicals! Then British Columbia could have here a "Continental" playground, a Canadian Riviera.

Shortly after arriving in Vancouver, I asked the guests at a small dinner party if a land as famous as British Columbia for its hunting and fishing had an Izaak Walton. Raising a finger, one said, "All together now!" and all together, they replied, "Haig-Brown!"

Roderick Haig-Brown of Campbell River, they told me, is not only the Province's ranking authority on its major sports; he is one of Canada's foremost and most respected writers. Of his sixteen books to date, six concern fish and fishing.

The slender, reticent man of Campbell River was hardly the robust outdoor type I had pictured. But his home was a writer's dream. On one side, Campbell River raced full tongue over large rounded stones for the strait. Its far shore was a solid, forbidding wall of forest. On all other sides, the big, ivy-clad house and lawns, shaded by fruit and nut trees, bordered by gardens and hedges, further were isolated by acres of his own woods.

For half an hour in his workroom, book-walled except for a log-burning fireplace, we did talk about fish and the history and philosophy of fishing and hunting. But when he early said, "I like to fish off my feet. I wouldn't give you a word of thanks to sit in a boat," I lost interest in fish, grizzlies and moose for interest in the vigour, colour and forthrightness of the man and the writer.

As a schoolboy in England, he had begun to write about fish and birds. At eighteen, some sure instinct impelled him to cross the Atlantic and America to the Pacific coast. During the next eight years in Washington State and British Columbia, as logger, cruiser, trapper, fisherman, he found in the Big Woods and the fish-filled coastal waters, rivers and lakes the creative world he was seeking. Round the edges of work and sport, he wrote about them in articles, short stories, books.

One day in a Seattle bookstore, he met an auburn-haired, brown-eyed creature, all energy, humour and charm, named Ann Elmore. In 1934, they were married and came to scantily settled Campbell River country where they could enjoy the best of fishing and hunting and he could write. Now four children fill house and grounds with activities. And he has achieved a rhythm of almost one book a year, writes also for motion pictures and television.

When he writes is invisible to the naked eye. Because in 1934 the village of Campbell River had no one to serve as magistrate, he took on the office. Soon he was given "extended powers" to hear all cases except those of treason, murder and "combines"; then Domestic Court cases and, with the aid of a probation officer, Juvenile Court.

Not until later did I learn from Victoria newspapers that Haig-Brown, the "noted conservationist," had been engaged for months in a losing battle to prevent the merging of Buttle Lake, one of Strathcona Park's beauty spots, with Upper Campbell Lake, to increase the power the Campbell River system supplies to industry.

From somewhere a fragment of verse floated into my mind—

. . . the saddest task a man could choose;
To fight to win while knowing he must lose.

I don't know why. It certainly doesn't apply to the Haig-Browns of this world. However personally grievous or disappointing an experience may be, a writer always wins—ideas, knowledge, understanding, compassion. A writer whose life and interests are deeply and widely woven into the life of his family, community and country tills an ever-renewed field.

16

DEFINITELY NOT A "PICTURESQUE PORT"

The "Twin Cities" of Port Alberni and Alberni have fifteen thousand people. In the surrounding trade area there are ten thousand more. One and all will forgive me, I hope, if I confess here that I thought my sole purpose in going to the port was to catch the *Princess Alberni*, the Canadian Pacific freight boat which plies up and down Vancouver Island's west coast.

No one on the east coast had so much as mentioned that a west coast existed. Though it was known to European navigators long before either east coast or Mainland, no Vancouver, Victoria or even Nanaimo showed on my map. Only an occasional dot on some Pacific or interior headland indicated a fishing village, a logging or mining camp. And my travel folders described *them* as "Canada's last frontiers" and "picturesque ports."

My contour map of the west coast was the chief culprit. Except for two or three small breaks, it pictured the coastline for about 150 miles north of Victoria as even as a hemline. Above that it was in rags.

No rolling bench outlined it. No Mainland protected it from the Pacific. Rearing out of the sea, the Insular Mountains rushed inland like a swelling comber to solidify at the moment of breaking in a spine of 4,500- to 7,000-foot peaks. And the Pacific rushing after them had riddled the coast with bays, sounds and inlets, gnarled and branched as coral, and stripped down the headlands between them to open roadsteads.

Long since open roadsteads of other lands had destroyed my taste for leaping from bounding rowboat or tender to bounding ship split seconds ahead of yawning seas. Had there been a highway across the northern end of Vancouver Island from

141

Campbell River, I would have hesitated to take it. Yet I didn't want to return to Victoria to meet the *Princess.*

From Parksville, however, a 28-mile highway and bus line crossed the Insular Mountains to the head of a canal so long and almost straight that it penetrated to the centre of the Island. There a dot marked Port Alberni. That seemed safe enough.

Leaving the east coast behind at Parksville, the trans-island highway angled northwest straight into mountains which loomed up fast and high to cool their heads from the blazing sun in snowdrifts of cloud. The farther we went the taller and darker the cedar, pine and other conifers everywhere, the wilder the scene.

All at once, on the left, an immense sprawl of rugged slopes joined to rise toward Mt. Arrowsmith's invisible peak, miles away and more than a mile high. On the right, a long, narrow, black-green lake rippled about slopes so heavily wooded and cragged that the "Stag at Eve" well might have posed there for his portrait.

"Cameron Lake," someone murmured. "Watch! The Cathedral's just ahead."

Cathedral? In a mountain pass?

I did not wonder long. Almost immediately an eerie quiet fell. Even the roar of the bus's engines and their bouncing echoes stilled. For a minute or two we glided along in utter and increasingly awesome silence while more and more mountains folded in and out to form a gorge whose walls enclosed a truly grand cathedral setting and that peculiar peace which great cathedrals know.

As far as eye could see, Douglas firs rose arrow-straight in aisle after aisle of columns whose capitals arched to meet more than a hundred feet above in a deep and deep-green vaulted dome. Dimly visible beyond them, snow-capped peaks shimmered like candles before a distant altar. From overhead, the high sun's rays, pouring through the green, diffused as radiance to fill the aisles and twine the columns with vinelike patterns of light and shadow. Fresh young firs, cedars, pines, clustered in the open, needle-strewn aisles like devout communicants come to worship.

Not a passenger moved or spoke until a little pebbled stream wriggled and gurgled into view. While I looked into massed crowns of more Douglas fir rooted in a gorge far below, the driver told me I had not just imagined the silence that preceded our entrance into Cathedral Grove. Some combination of rocks, forests, mountains and lake creates an atmospheric condition which absorbs all sound. "Gets you, doesn't it?" he said.

That mountain wall behind us, another loomed. We never reached it. We had crossed the mountains into the valley of the Somass ("Something-you-throw-away") River, so named by the Indians who used it as a disposal before the white man came.

After miles of winding through newly blasted rock and dreary logged-off brown foothills, the pretty village of Alberni, all pastel homes and flowers, seemed out of place. It did, that is, until a mile beyond we descended a long hill into Port Alberni. Hardly a frontier! Definitely not picturesque!

From the top of the hill, I looked down on a waterfront curved like a showcase about Alberni Inlet—not a canal, at all! —to display the town's two main industries—manufacture of lumber and lumber by-products and fishing.

The meeting of the Somass River and the inlet shaped a crookedly tapering peninsula, buried beneath tall chimneys, pulp, newsprint, plywood and other mills. Beside a long dock, two ocean-going freighters were loading. Nearby a wide row of log booms waited. Together they formed the most important unit of the MacMillan and Bloedel Company, the foremost fully integrated forest products industry in Canada and one of the largest of its kind in the world.

Beyond the peninsula, chimneys, waste-burners and buildings of the East Asiatic Company's Tahsis Sawmill covered another headland. Warehouses, docks, more mills and anchorages ran for a mile or more. Out in the harbour, gnatlike tugs identified the dark patches creeping behind them as incoming log booms. Scores of white flecks turned out to be gillnetters' and sports fishermen's anchored craft. From the waterfront, the town climbed slow slopes, broken by massed conifers, to the foothills.

Before starting out to see the world, I glanced at the two newspapers. The weekly *Twin Cities Times* featured an article about the significance of MacMillan and Bloedel's new $35 million expansion program. The *West Coast Advocate* head-lined the 60½-pound tyee which an 18-year-old youth had caught while trolling on the inlet. I could have read the first story later, but the second explained everyone's eagerness to "chivvy" as many minutes as possible from shop or office that Friday afternoon for an early start on his weekend fishing.

Two engaging high school boys gave me a play-by-play account of the lucky young fisherman's struggle to boat his tyee. "Know what?" said one. "He'll get a *diamond* pin!" "Know what?" said the other. "His mother *canned* it!"

"Better stay here," they urged when they learned I was waiting for the *Princess Alberni*. "When the weather's perfect like this, that means fog on the coast; rainy here, clear there." And they offered plenty of inducements. The annual late-July Sproat Lake Regatta. The Junior Salmon Derby in September, which closes the tyee season for eight-to-sixteen-year-olds. The Senior Derby about October 1. "The inlet's one of the best places for salmon fishing in the whole world. Why, fifty-pounders are *common*." On condition that I'd visit Sproat Lake, at least, we parted friends.

"Too busy to see you," the publisher of the *Advocate* was telling a group of men as I entered the outer office, but from the gleam in his eye I suspected that he, too, had fishing in mind. He did stand still long enough, however, to build an impressive picture of Port Alberni's forest industries.

British Columbia's 90.5 million acres of forest—conifer and deciduous—are its most valuable asset. The conifer forests not only are the most valuable in the Province; they are the most valuable forests in all the Commonwealth. In commercial timber alone they could supply enough lumber to girdle the equator 147 times with a boardwalk twenty-five feet wide and two inches thick. Each year's cut is more than enough to circle it once.

Of the eleven most important varieties of conifers, the great stands of Douglas fir on the Mainland's south coast and on Vancouver Island today are the most important economically. And the most valuable of all are the stands on Vancouver Island's west coast.

Vancouver, Powell River and Ocean Falls, the publisher said with raised eyebrows on his voice, get their logs from the Queen Charlottes and the Mainland. Every log that enters Port Alberni's mills come from the Island's west coast. And will continue to come for another century at least because of a conservation program to keep them self-sustaining. "Timber," he said in conclusion, "is the past, present and future of Alberni Valley."

His "past" included little more than thirty years, I learned when I caught up with Mrs. Margaret Trebett, editor of the *Twin Cities Times* and authority on the valley's history. "The first man to enter the inlet was the Spanish lieutenant, Francisco Eliza, in 1791. He named both inlet and valley for his captain and sailed away."

Seventy years later an English company set up the first saw-mill, but within five years they also sailed away. Reason? After shipping out millions of feet of dressed lumber and the whole conifers with which the Clyde River shipyards won fame for supplying the world's finest masts, they believed they had logged off "all suitable and accessible timber."

In 1887 came the pioneers—farmers all. To supply them with lumber, one built a small sawmill on a creek. It was the ancestor of dozens of short-lived others until the 1920's when, with the first paper mills, Port Alberni took root. Still unconvinced that the forests had a future, the farmers living in and about their trading centre a mile away refused to move over. Today Alberni remains as a residential suburb for the rapidly growing port.

And today almost everyone in both towns earns his living in the forests and especially in the mills manufacturing pulp, plywood, shingles, processed fuel and other forest products. Not all. Port Alberni is admirably located for both commercial and sports fishing.

As favoured spawning grounds, the many rivers draining into the inlet make it and the coastal waters a gathering place for salmon. Pilchard and herring also are plentiful, and halibut in the deep seas. Gillnetters, seiners and trollers or trawlers by the score work out of the port.

Remembering my promise, I consulted my map for Sproat Lake. In outline, with its long, narrow head and body, two wing-shaped fin bays, and Taylor River as a thin, rattish tail, it resembled some fearsome prehistoric monster. But it was only five miles away and I had an hour before dinner. A hungry taxi driver drove me out a conifer-banked highway into a scenic and sportsman's delight.

Low mountains enclosed the 14-mile-long lake. Their slopes —the whole landscape—were deep in virgin stands of Douglas fir and red cedar. Down the slopes, waterfalls and white-water streams tumbled toward the lake. Above them, to the south, loomed Arrowsmith's massive, snow-capped 5,976-foot peak and Mt. Klitsa's 5,388; to the north were the white tips of a bevy of Strathcona Park's striking summits.

Half hidden among firs were lodges, public parks and picnic grounds. On beaches tourists sunned or swam in clear, placid waters. Here and there, in sole command of a whole bay, a fisherman stood like a totem in a rowboat casting into mountain reflections for steelhead, cutthroat and rainbow trout. Ah, me!

This seemed enough for one community. But in the evening the Trebetts, while driving me out to see the Fish Ladder at Sproat Falls and sunset on Great Central Lake, told me of other lakes and fishing streams.

A few miles from the city, about a hundred feet of tumbled rock interrupts the Somass as it carries the waters of the Sproat, Stamp and other rivers between palisaded and forested banks to the inlet. Boiling up in great white curls or slithering in thick, sea-green glassy folds over flat surfaces, it crashes down terrace after terrace to the smooth bed below.

In years of high water, like this one, Mr. Trebett said, the salmon easily could ascend the river to their spawning grounds.

146

But until the ladder was built in 1950, in dry years men had to sandbag what water there was into a narrow channel to save them. I peered and peered through the grated roof of the long, concrete tunnel at waters hurtling down broad steps and scanned the open river, but not a salmon appeared. "Keep watching," he urged. "Miracles do happen here."

One day while the ladder was under construction, the crew worked most reluctantly. Queen Elizabeth—then Princess Elizabeth—was to dedicate something on the east coast that afternoon, but with the river low and the salmon due any time, the need to complete it was so urgent they could not take time out. All at once cars poured down the road and people down the bank. And there was the Princess right beside them!

"And did the salmon put on a show! Out of nowhere they swarmed, to leap, not by ones or twos, but by dozens at a time. And not, as they usually did, just high enough to clear the falls! None of us who had watched them year after year ever had seen anything like it. We stood rooted, just like the Princess, our eyes falling out."

No miracle occurring for me, we sped through miles of Douglas fir and cedar forests to a scene as savage as Sproat Lake (just five miles south) had been peaceful. Held prisoner in solitary confinement by Insular Mountains, Great Central Lake turns and twists for twenty miles through peaks and valleys known, if at all, only to loggers. From its surface, unbroken forests climb to summits one to three thousand feet above; below the surface, the slopes may descend as many more. No one has plumbed its depths. Nowhere on the lake we saw could a man step ashore from a boat.

Although we arrived in clear daylight, the sunset which inflames sky and waters and throws a double glow of direct and reflected light over the forests, had faded. We looked up a narrow canyon, floored with polished ebony and, except at one high point, walled with concentrated night. There the last of the afterglow, falling through a mountain gap, touched a slope, to suggest that a hidden army waited, with bayonets bared.

Hidden from all but sturdy hikers and climbers who can

147

follow an old, ten-mile trail through snow- and icefields bordered by wild flowers, is Canada's highest waterfall. Dropping 1,443 feet into Drinkwater Creek, Della Falls compares in height if not in volume with Venezuela's Angel Falls and California's Yosemite.

As we drove back to Port Alberni through the cool, starlit night, the Albernis seemed the most fortunately situated of all the communities I had visited. They had every means of livelihood and recreation at hand, yet were free of the pressure elsewhere for power and more power.

"By the way," said Mrs. Trebett, "has anyone told you of the British Columbia Power Commission's plan to harness the Somass River watershed? With a network of dams and power-houses on Elsie, Great Central and Sproat Lakes, they can develop a hydroelectric project that . . ."

17

"NONE OF THAT TOURIST STUFF HERE"

Though Alberni Inlet is twenty-two miles long, more than a thousand feet deep, and that rare thing, a British Columbia fjord less than a mile wide, mountaintop islands divide it into a series of gentle lakes. From the moment the *Princess Alberni* turned her bow into it until, four hours later, we entered Barkley Sound, I knew the delight Noah must have felt while his ark approached Ararat over an emerging world.

On either side, low, smooth-lined mountains accompanied us. Their blue-green or yellow-green forests, dripping with moisture from night mists, glistened in the early-morning light. Above them, others rose to summits frequently dappled or swatched with snow. Every few miles from one shore or the other a small stream joined us. Dominating us all was Arrowsmith, miles of Arrowsmith. A whole range of green slopes supported its enormous broken crown, snow-white and dazzling against the soft-blue eastern sky.

From time to time an overgrown road or, high on a mountain shoulder, a rounded scar, ugly as an old-fashioned vaccination mark, told of loggers who had come and gone. Otherwise, we moved through sunlit blue and green silence. Not a bird, beast or man was to be seen. The only sound, felt rather than heard, was the low beat of the ship's engines.

Suddenly Arrowsmith vanished behind pygmy foothills. One gull, then another and another appeared, to flutter, pygmy too, as moths over the forests. High above, an eagle drifted, apparently trying to see how long he could remain aloft without batting a wing. Sawmills and logging roads broke the green. The quiet blue waters began to roll in lazy swells and to widen rapidly as we sailed out into Barkley Sound.

From its shape and size, the sound once must have been

three inlets whose land boundaries the Pacific has eaten away to rows of small islands, rocks and reefs. Against them, mounting combers broke in crystal sheaves. The farther we nosed into it, the higher Strathcona Park's peaks, topped by snow-striped Rooster's Comb (7,219 feet) towered over the shore mountains, but the *Princess* turned her back on them to head straight for Asia.

As the one ship on which west coast villages and camps must depend for all supplies, the *Princess* herself was not lacking in interest. So much cargo had been waiting for her at Victoria that some had been sent overland by truck to replace what she discharged before reaching Port Alberni. Even so, much had had to be left on the dock. With no road running north from that port, only "priority" freight had a chance.

Her hatches were stuffed to the exploding point with fresh fruits, vegetables, meats, milk, beer, soft drinks, cigarettes and "other foods." The freight deck was man-high with lumber, machinery, spools of heavy wire, coils of rope and crated furniture. Atop everything balanced a shining new "fridge," a washing machine, a rowboat, and a slatted crate from which two handsome goats regarded the heavy Bermuda-green seas with aplomb.

Priority for space in the four tiny cabins on the bridge deck also was given to island residents. Though I had one, it was with the proviso that, if need arose, I would share it. One paid a flat fee for passage and could bring his own food, eat and sleep in the small lounge off the galley or engage cabin space by the day, night, or both. Meals also were "optional." After my first one, I had a calorie-count reason to be grateful for that. Though the chef looked like the dean of Oxford's Graduate School, he probably was Escoffier's reincarnation.

"Poor things!" One of the five cabin passengers, an attractive, middle-aged woman, joined me to admire the goats. "They're the third or fourth pair a neighbour of ours has ordered. Cougars always get them."

She and her husband were returning to Estevan Point, site

of a lighthouse, radio station, British Columbia Electric Company plant, twenty-five people and, as one of the west coast's boldest projections, a most hazardous open roadstead. Ships must anchor far out and shorebound passengers leap for a rowboat as it rises deckward on a wave.

Understandably nervous, she said, "If the sea's too rough for me to jump, I'll have to go on to the next port and wait two weeks for the ship to bring me back. But, thank Heaven, once home, I won't have to leave again for fourteen months."

"Fourteen months?"

"That's not time enough for all we want to do. My husband's the radio operator. Besides that, he has a complete workshop where he makes all sorts of things. He's also a camera fiend and develops his own film, both in black and white and color. I have our home to manage, and I garden like mad—everybody does—and paint. But I like most of all to clear more land for more garden and to clean and polish pieces of beautiful wood the tides bring in. I have some lovely things, one as exquisite as a Grecian vase. The only fly in my ointment is our oil stove. The only thing it will bake properly is scones, and the one thing I love to bake is johnnycake."

"Wouldn't cougars come under the head of flies?"

"Well, they are bad," she admitted. "Especially now that the east coast is settling up so fast and all the cougars there are crowding over to our side. No one goes twenty feet at night without a gun. But at night we can tell where they are. They whistle or mew like a cat. By day, one *never* knows."

She told of small children's narrow escapes from death, of a nine-year-old Indian boy a cougar did drag into the forest. "We have a most useful neighbour, however. She has only one good arm, but in the past few years she's shot seventy-nine of them. She gets a twenty-dollar bounty on each one and makes their pelts into rugs."

Cougars she could take, but fish—! "We get more fresh salmon, halibut, cod and crab given us than we can eat, though sometimes we have to. In stormy weather the ship can't come in, so we keep supplies on hand for a month ahead. If the ship misses us twice—well, with cupboards bare, we eat fish."

She talked cheerfully, but from her I got my first inkling that Vancouver Island's east and west coasts are not sisters under the skin. While we talked, another came into view.

First, Ucluelet ("Yewklet"), a herring-fishing village, spread small, simple cottages over a narrow headland; then, across a splinter of water, West Ucluelet appeared. Between them they share five hundred people, but not a soul was visible. Not a dog or a cat, either.

When the ship tied up beside West Ucluelet's silent cannery, we walked ashore to look up its one short, wide, almost perpendicular street. From the crest, a dry torrent of loose, glacier-rounded stones poured down between faded frame buildings. With bare and stony ground everywhere else, it appeared as stark and gray as the mud-walled villages on the desert north of China's Great Wall. No, there, human voices, dogs', goats', gongs', and bells' fringed the stillness.

Picking precarious courses upward past the general store, we came on a town hall alive with Brownie and Boy Scout posters. A library no larger than a grand piano box, its corners balanced on piles of flimsy bits of rock and two-by-fours, but its steps well worn. A gift shop whose one window displayed everything from cups and saucers to dacron blouses to potted plants. And at the top of the hill, an austere Church of St. Aaron's. Set back from the street between them, cottages faced minute lawns and gardens, window boxes, tubs, riotous with golden glow, dahlias, nasturtiums, geraniums, mango-toned begonias.

While I gazed with awe, thinking of the effort expended to gather and enrich the soil to support them, my companion said, "Life is very real and earnest on this coast. But it has its compensations. A good garden is one of them. Oh, not the garden itself, I suppose, or a library or anything else tangible. One's satisfaction comes in knowing he can do the hard way what others—in Vancouver or Victoria—do with everything provided."

Smaller than the Ucluelets but otherwise a carbon copy, Tofino, twenty miles north, climbed a small headland jutting into Clayquot Sound, which one day will be as large as Barkley. Already the Pacific has chewed the peninsulas between three or four inlets into islands that provide the fishing village with a landlocked harbour. One day also, a highway will link it with Port Alberni. Meantime, the ship's crew unloaded an astonishing amount of freight, including week-old Vancouver newspapers, for distribution to surrounding logging camps and to Kakawis, an Indian reservation on an island across the bay.

While I watched from the deck, a man, in appearance and dress very unlike the lean, hard-bitten handful of elderly observers gathering on the dock, emerged from the captain's bridge. Stopping nearby at the rail, he looked the village up and down with a strange and sombre concentration.

All at once he burst out: "Nobody here is interested in television. Because their radios pick up all the ships' reports and all the chitchat between fishboats and R.C.A.F. planes, they can't get any kind of reception until after eleven p.m. And then, just as they're enjoying a good program, bing!—some fishboat in distress calls the Life Saving Station and the air is full of crackles, calls and instructions. So they think television will be even worse."

He spoke to no one in particular but, with that off his mind, he seemed approachable, so I asked if Tofino held a Salmon Derby. "Oh, no!" he exclaimed, shocked. "None of that tourist stuff here. All commercial fishing. Even on Sundays the boats go out, work day and night. For salmon and halibut chiefly. Some crab." Nodding toward stacked cartons waiting on the dock to be loaded, he added, "We have a small crab cannery here."

To redeem my frivolity, I spoke of the beautiful harbour. "People here aren't conscious of it," he said. Infected by his cynicism, I remarked as he turned to leave, "They probably pull down the shades so the beauty won't bother them."

Whirling round, he stood stock-still to stare at me. Then, his eyes sparkling, his whole face alight, he walked toward me. Pointing to a small island, he said in a roguish, what-is-the-world-coming-to voice, "Two women bought it a few years ago.

153

Built a hotel on it, by Jove! Practically with their own hands. And now, *they run it themselves.*"

As again he turned away, I said, "The modern theory is that anything men can do women can do better." Back he came, all smiles. "What," he asked, "is the greatest laboursaving device ever invented? A wife."

He did leave then, but on the dock he stopped, half turned, hesitated, then with a reluctant wave, went his way, visibly chortling. But, watching him go, I felt inadequate. He'd asked for cake and I'd given him very dry crusts.

While the last of a brilliant sunset still glazed the harbour with colour, I watched low-riding gillnetters return from an 18-hour fishing day. Angling heavily, wearily, through the narrow channel between two small islands into the bay, they anchored some distance from an old, unpainted fish-buying station. From there, one by one, they moved in to sell their catch to the buyer, who came out to the edge of the short pier twenty feet above.

When his catch had been sold by shouts and gestures, the fisherman tied his boat to a log piling. The buyer untied a rope to let a wooden crib slide down between two poles. Bending and lifting, the fisherman tossed his catch into it, one at a time. Crib full, the buyer hauled it up, emptied it, one fish at a time, into a large bin. Over, over, and over they repeated this routine until every fish had changed hands.

Boat and fisherman then sprinted for home. The fisherman, sitting erect now, flexed his arms, stamped his feet in a little jig. The boat, a small bone in its teeth, skipped gaily, lightly, from wave to wave.

As we left Tofino, one of the officers showed me the small, dim island of Disappointment. Time was, he said, in the heyday of the British remittance man, when life in Tofino held plenty of interest. Of the four rich exiles there, one had bought the island, built a castlelike home and a race track where he bicycled round and round every morning.

One calm day he rowed far out to sea to fish. The wind rising, he could not row back. Discarding boat and clothing, he set out to swim to the nearest shore. But when at last he reached it, to rise naked from the surf and collapse, he did so at the feet of two righteous Tofino ladies. Horrified, they departed posthaste. He died of exposure where they left him. When his will was read, he had left his island and everything on it to two Tofino ladies.

Because of their historical importance if nothing else, two points on the coast I especially wanted to see. The first was Estevan Point; rather, its lighthouse, which in the darkness of June 20, 1942, had been the target for the shells of a Japanese submarine. No one was hurt and little damage done, but those guns, the first to be trained on the Dominion of Canada by a foreign enemy, reduced to rubble the belief that Atlantic and Pacific were impregnable Canadian defences. The second was Nootka Sound.

When Spain ordered Juan Perez in 1744 to take formal possession of the Pacific coast right up to the doorsteps of Russia's Alaskan posts, he got no farther than the northern shore of Graham Island. But, while returning to Mexico, he sighted the entrance to Nootka Sound. Gales prevented entrance, but he anchored outside to trade with the Indians. Spain's prolonged secrecy about where he went also prevented his landing in history as British Columbia's discoverer.

Thirty-two years later, the British Admiralty amended its 25-year-old offer of twenty thousand pounds to the merchant vessel that, from the Atlantic, found a Northwest Passage to the Pacific. Naval vessels now could compete and discovery might be made from either east or west. So rich a plum brought Captain Cook out of the land berth to which he had retired after his two strenuous three-year voyages in New World seas.

Sailing up the Pacific in 1778, he entered Nootka Sound to exchange trinkets for sea-otter pelts with the Indians while his crews repaired his ships. Though the Indians wore tiny copper, brass and iron horseshoes in their noses, and even gave him two silver spoons of Spanish design, he never suspected that a Juan Perez had been there before him.

Cook failed to find the passage and lost his life while exploring the Hawaiian Islands. Nevertheless, his sea-otter pelts set off the massacre of the mammals from the mouth of the Columbia to Alaska that opened a trade route between the north Pacific and the Orient. In 1780, his crews, sailing for home via Canton, broadcast the glad tidings that the Chinese would pay $120 for a single pelt.

Among the English traders to engage in the lucrative slaughter was John Meares. In Nootka Sound's Friendly Cove, he threw up a makeshift "shipyard" from which he launched the *North West America*—the first keel laid on the Pacific north of Mexico. He also sent one of his own ships to China with a cargo of spars cut from Vancouver Island forests. Nootka Sound thus became the birthplace of three of the Province's modern industries—shipbuilding, forest products, foreign trade.

As an opportunist with a genius for building a molehill into a mountain, he did even more. His extravagant charges against Spanish seizure of his shipyard and ships resulted in 1790 in the "Nootka Convention" treaty, by which crumbling Spain agreed to permit British ships to enter her closed seas. That treaty notified the world that the whole northwest coast of North America was open to any nation that cared to occupy it.

None did, but two years later Captain Vancouver and the Spanish Quadra met in Nootka Sound to decide what to do about Meares's claims. With the Spaniard denying all claims and the Englishman supporting them, they got nowhere diplomatically. But personally they became such good friends that they named the Island in their joint honour, Quadra and Vancouver.

Unhappily for my nervous fellow passenger and me, the *Princess Alberni* reached Estevan Point through rough seas and fog about two o'clock in the morning. After much effort, the small launch which met the ship steadied enough for her to jump safely. But the inshore tide was too far out for a truck to back into the sea to pick up passengers. She reached shore piggyback! And before the sun rose again, we had left Nootka Sound, to ascend its right arm, Muchalat Inlet.

18

FJORDS "YUST LIKE NORVAY'S"

Like a twisted wet sock, Muchalat Inlet runs inland for about twenty miles, then turns south for a few more. At its heel, just where Gold River comes in like a ravelling, lies a logging camp of the Tahsis Company. That's as restrained as I can be about it.

Behind it rose a mountain so grandiosely apt as a backdrop for *Die Walküre* that I named it Grand Opera. Naked of trees except where narrow ledge or crevice permitted a little silt to gather, it bulges with rough rock faces, golden with lichen, green-gold with moss. At either side, more rock mountains, abrupt and rugged, lift out of the sea. A sea, deep, clear and emerald green; white or gold where sunlight blazes upon it; coal black in mountain shadow.

On levelled, gravelled land, beneath tall Douglas firs, stood the logging camp; an ordered village of white, brown or gray cottages roofed in red, green or brown, lined brief, regular streets. Between it and the harbour ran the road to the working camp fifteen miles away. Trucks rolling on sixteen powerful tires to dump tons of 20- to 30-foot logs into bag booms pounded its gravel to powder.

The air, clear, too, and cedar scented, sparkled as though filled with diamond dust. But silence really filled it. Even the thunder of the trucks and the voices of men working on the long pier directly below us were absorbed. So were the screams of gulls fighting for breakfast morsels at a low dock where fishermen cleaned their catch.

Shades of Campbell River! In battered rowboats powered by outboard motors, and with ordinary fishing rods, two men and a boy had caught half a dozen salmon, each weighing about twenty pounds. Another, who went out and returned within the half hour I waited for the gangplank to be lowered, after

157

beheading and cleaning his single catch, casually dropped it on the warehouse scales. Thirty-nine pounds! And the tyee season here more than two months away!

To reach shore, I skirted the household goods of a ranger and a logger who were transferring to other camps. Among them were the electric refrigerators, washing machines, and complete sets of pale-blue or pink baby furniture that thereafter left or came aboard at every stop.

The young Catholic priest I met on the pier did not—*would* not live at Gold River. Unlike the Rockies, he said, these mountains were not born of a violent upheaval. They had risen, still were rising, at the rate of three inches a year. As they "grow," they develop new faults or weaken old ones. And he showed me several in Grand Opera and another on a neighbouring slope which had sheared an entire shoulder into the sea.

Watching the numerous crows and gulls flying about, I spoke of the lack of birds everywhere. "Lack!" He stepped back in amazement. "Why, we have all kinds of birds. Ravens—not crows!—and gulls, *many* eagles, some osprey, and occasionally a kingfisher."

He had arrived from Nootka the night before to say Mass that morning at the Indian reservation a mile away, was going on to other camps to conduct a funeral, a wedding, and a "batch" of christenings. When I asked directions to the reservation, he shook his head. "No time. The *Princess* sails in an hour. I'm going aboard now. No, I'll just have time to see—" He hurried away, and that was the last of him. No matter, said the captain; any boat going his way would be glad to take him.

Past clean streets named Cedar, Pine, Fir Way, I met a time-keeper's wife who stopped to chat. "I've been in the business eighteen years," she said. She'd had six children in almost as many camps but had lived in only four houses. "When a camp closes, us wives just take down our figurines, place bars across cupboards and closet doors. Then the water and electric hook-ups are disconnected and the houses rolled on skids onto a float in the harbour. A tug tows them to the new camp where streets, water, everything's ready. And soon as my last figurine's in place, so am I—to go on with the baking or knitting or whatever I've been doing."

Logging companies were slow to catch on, she told me, but when they did they "caught on good." Now they prefer married men, with families, provide all-modern homes, schools, stores, everything possible to hold them year after year. "No brawls. No drinking, that way." And except for loggers who fell trees with power saws or drive trucks, "they" also want college graduates. "Degrees, degrees. Everything is degrees!"

Almost everywhere I'd been in British Columbia I had thought the scenery of the moment the best of all, but now, as we sailed round Grand Opera into Muchalat Inlet again, I felt sure I would remember longest this northwest coast of Vancouver Island. The young Norwegian we carried to the working camp thought highly of it, too. "Yust like Norvay's fjords!" he exclaimed repeatedly. "Yust like Norvay's."

Between massive mountains, rock based, rich in fir, cedar, fragrance, space and silence, we retraced our course down the inlet's rippling green. Against a cloudless pale-blue sky, mountains ahead were a clear electric blue; beside us, black, brown and green. But once behind, they veiled themselves in grey mists and clouds as though they tired more quickly of looking at us than we at them. Periodically a mountaintop island barred our way, offering a choice of channels and a new direction.

At noon, while the captain showed me the devious route we would follow across Nootka Sound's lobster-shaped head into Tahsis Inlet, a radio-phone call came in. To its crackles and squeals, he said briskly, "I'll be there at four o'clock."

Exactly at four, the *Princess* stopped in empty Nootka Sound to send a peremptory whistle echoing round the mountains. From between two islands a squeak replied, and a fishboat hurtled toward us as though about to take to the air. Immaculately blue and white, it slid alongside, a woman at the wheel. The ship's derrick swung a net rounded with food supplies and cartons of "10,000 cigarettes" into its empty well. Not more than a minute and not a spoken word later, the fishboat was hurtling homeward and the ship was under way. "That woman runs a logging camp like a good clock," the captain commented.

"Stopping a ship's a pretty expensive service to give a customer, isn't it?" a passenger wanted to know. And the captain answered, "The *Princess Alberni* is more than a ship. She's a good neighbour." A neighbour whose services will end one not-too-distant day, he told me later, when all the fragments of logging roads are joined in a highway that will run from end to end of the west coast.

About twenty miles up Tahsis Inlet, Tahsis curves about a bay dominated by a sawmill and almost floored with log booms. We tied up at a dock among cosmopolitan company. The Greek *Leonidas Nicholas,* one of three 10,000-ton freighters which call here every week to load lumber for East Asia and South America. The king-sized, spit-and-polish yacht of an American lumberman. And a flagless mission boat, en route to a summer camp with sixty-five children.

The sawmill to which the logs had come from Tahsis Company camps up and down Muchalat and Tahsis Inlets was interesting. So was the parting comment of the superintendent who showed me about. "Plenty of cougar around here. Used to be they'd step aside when they met a man. But the logger who met one last night had to do the stepping." Most interesting of all were two of the men who worked the log booms until darkness fell.

No Sadler's Wells ballet dancer ever was more expert and graceful than the man working the boom farthest out in the bay. Never did he break some inner rhythm. Long pike-pole balanced in one hand, he ran on tiptoe across dozens of bobbing logs, or jumped feet into the air to cross open water and light on tiptoe on another. He poised on one toe to prod a log half a boom of water away or, prancing the boom's full length, leaped across water to the back of a recalcitrant log to dance it into place.

The other man herded logs as a cowboy herds cattle, his cowpony a snub-nosed, low-riding craft whose lower, weighted two-thirds was underwater. Astride its saddlelike seat, he dashed from boom to boom, to shoulder a single log or a loose bunch into a corner. He turned on a dime to gallop round a boom and head off escaping logs. Graceful as a cowboy is graceful, he leaped from saddle to boom log to clip a hooked rope into a metal loop and leap back before the log had time to sink enough to wet his feet.

Our first stop the next morning was Esperanza, a health resort at the head of Esperanza Inlet. About the foot of a tall, forested mountain, a large white English inn, a large white hospital and a handful of white cottages snuggled in cedar and pine. A half dozen men, one obviously a doctor, another, with sallow skin and sunken eyes, as obviously a patient, and a lively grey Maltese kitten welcomed the supplies, mail and shiny new garbage can we brought them.

On the bridge a half hour after we'd left that peaceful spot, the first mate yelled, "Good Lord! I put that brat ashore twice with my own hands." In the centre of the deck sat the Maltese kitten. Plainly a much-loved pet, she appraised with practised eye the captain, two officers, the helmsman and me. Leaping then to the chart desk, she wooed the captain as though she had been seeking him alone throughout her nine lives. Before her shameless wiles, he melted like picnic ice. Thereafter, smooth and shining as Brancusi's *Bird*, "Stowaway," sunning herself on the charts, narrowed my nautical research to empty stretches of the Pacific.

Grey skies fitting neatly about the mountaintops, whose upper conifers pulled shredded scarves of mist about them, satisfied all doubts as to whether these inlets could be equally beautiful in sunshine and shadow. They can! Against that subdued light the wild tangle of mountains walling Tahsis and Zeballos Inlets through which we twisted to the village of Zeballos appeared wilder still.

Once Zeballos was a lively supply centre for four gold mines behind the peaks at whose base sprawls its one stony street. Today it is one of the few places in the Province whose population has melted away in the past five years. At first glance, with most of its old frontier buildings closed and no mining, logging or fishing industries of its own, even the "up-island" headquarters of the Tahsis Company did not seem sufficient to support the 154 people remaining.

Yet no ghost-town air hung over its large, modern supermarket, pharmacy and cottages deep in roses, hydrangeas and kitchen gardens. The *Princess* lingered for hours to unload, among other supplies, almost a hundred cases for its licensed liquor store. Perhaps the secret lies in the fact that Zeballos is the metropolis for a number of outlying logging camps.

By way of Esperanza Inlet we returned to the Pacific, to round the coast to a point even maps call Rugged and ascend Kyuquot Sound to Chamiss Bay, its northernmost tip. Entering it in the shallowing light of early evening, I caught my breath, charmed by the tiny white village clinging to the levelled foot of a mighty black-green mountain and ringed with others. Then I caught it again. The village rode an immense float, about three hundred feet long and half as wide. Another logging camp.

To the right of a central square, a commissary, a first-aid station with its Red Cross placard recording "Accident Free Days—89," and the superintendent's home, complete with porch and frilled white curtains at every window, lined the waterfront street; to the left were the general offices and warehouses. Behind them, across another narrow street, bunkhouses stood eave to eave. Every building was two-storeyed. At many windows and running the full length of the superintendent's home, flower boxes flamed with geraniums.

For a moment it appeared that we had reached mezzanine seats just as the curtain lifted on the second act of a musical comedy. Towering mountains, clean, flower-decked buildings merely set the scene. Unconsciously (I *think*) but effectively, silent, slender young men, very country-clubbish and well scrubbed in their slacks and wool shirts, grouped, chorus-wise, about the square. When a large-chested man strode out of the general offices to take a wide stance at the central edge of the float, look up and open his mouth wide, I expected the usual baritone solo to pour out.

"Hi!" said he to the captain. "Hi!" said the captain in return.

And the crew proceeded in their efficient way to put off ten tons of freight, including crates of fresh fruit, lettuce, milk, more mail than we'd left at any other port, and several small metal trunks that from their wooden bands and rounded tops first must have seen the light in Europe a century ago.

These were catching up with Danish, Swedish and German newcomers, the captain said, but they were airplane luggage in comparison with the carryalls from various corners of the world which the *Princess* had delivered to one camp or another. So long as their owners are stable, hard-working men, who cares? The latch no longer is out for the one-time powerful, tireless, but rough and illiterate logger who used to drift restlessly from camp to camp.

No longer are the men forced to tote their own blankets into camp, sleep in bunkhouses tiered with wooden shelves, race through their meals without speaking, eat what is placed before them, work from sunup to sundown. Wherever possible, "dormitories" now house two men to a room; every four men have their own shower. Meals are served in a cafeteria so that they can choose what they wish to eat and eat it at small tables with friends. The eight-hour day is standard.

To my disappointment, the *Princess* carried no freight for Port Alice, almost at the end of Quatsino Sound's long right arm and the west coast's northernmost port. I didn't need to go half a knot farther to be convinced that this northwest region contains more than 50 per cent of the remaining virgin timber stands on Vancouver Island, at least half of the commercial timber in the Province. But I did want to see another island industry—whaling.

Long before the white man came, its Indians had harpooned the great mammals from dugout canoes. But British Columbia's industry dates from the advent of the steam whale catcher and explosive harpoon gun in 1905. For a time, as an Islander quaintly put it, the industry was so well "served" by "transients" of all species of large commercial whales that four processing stations were necessary.

Today's fleet, manned by about sixty men, almost all seasoned Norwegians, work the waters off this northwest coast from April 1 to October 1. In good years they may deliver six hundred or more whales to the remaining station at Quatsino Sound's Coal Harbor. There they are processed for whale oil, whale meal and fertilizer. The fresh meat is frozen as food for the four hundred or more mink and other "fur farms" on the Island's southern tip.

In compensation, the Insular Mountains soared out of cloud-topped foothills, under moonlight and sunlight, all the way back to West Ucluelet. There, the *Princess*, cutting across Barkley Sound to sail down the southwest coast to Victoria, plunged into fog so thick we had only half-mile visibility.

Its ephemeral folds cheated me out of two views. On the sound's southern shore, Bamfield, northern terminus of the 7,830-mile trans-Pacific cable—longest underwater communication system in the world—which, since 1902, has linked Canada, Australia and New Zealand. And the southwest coast. Nothing could be done about Bamfield, but the captain showed me the coast by way of a vivid description of the sea bed a hundred fathoms below. "Their mountains and valleys are the same in appearance and quality."

Clo-oose, an open roadstead, was our first stop. An Indian fishing village of a dozen small houses pinched together on a clearing axed out of crowding forest, it lay between a short headland and bold, black, jagged rocks. Behind it, sea-fed Lake Nitinat ran inland, either as an inlet the Pacific has sealed off or as a lake whose western shore it is eating away to add another inlet to the coast.

Between shore and ship, insistent swells, shiny as tin, appear gentle, but really are treacherous. Said the mate, "They never change except for the worse. A southwester here is terrible." Nevertheless, out of the murk came two young boys in a dug-out canoe, its asthmatic motor coughing and choking, and an old Indian in a light canoe, propelled rowboat fashion, with two flimsy, unsocketed paddles. As they stood in their crazily rolling craft to heave aboard six cases of empty soft drink bottles and a mailbag so thin it looked empty, a crewman grumbled, "Look at them! Risking their lives for the hell of it."

On our way again, only the Island, a low dark blur to port, and the hatch deck below the bridge varied the smothering white. Suddenly, the officer glued to the radar reported a flock of seiners ahead. Everyone stiffened to listen and peer out of lowered windows. "Those little jokers are the mischief in these fogs," someone said. "They can move so fast you never know where they'll be next."

"One is just point one, point two (one mile, two cable lengths) off our course, Captain," the officer said a minute later. The captain pulled the whistle cord. Throaty growls ripped through the fog and tension through the bridge.

"One right ahead, sir! Nine and a half cables." The *Princess* slowed to a stop. For minutes we waited, while the fog closed about us. Then, less than two cables to port, a shadowy tangle of spars and ropes lunged by.

"All clear ahead now, sir." The ship picked up speed. The captain yawned. Everyone drew a deep breath and relaxed.

By early afternoon, when the sun spread a tentative diffusion through the fog, all the passengers and most of the crew were asleep in their berths, and on the bridge only the captain at the radar and the helmsman were wide awake. All at once bells rang, whistles blew, orders crackled. The ship shot out of the white world into a clear, warm, brilliantly sunlit green one. The harbour of Port Renfrew, a fishing village just inside the entrance to the Strait of Juan de Fuca.

About its calm green sea, a crescent of interlocked hills were so thickly and evenly forested that they looked like sleeping, green-coated beavers. Inshore, almost a hundred fogbound gill-netters were snug in their berths along both sides of short, low docks. "The Lord provides for His own," said the captain softly.

Two small Indian girls and a toddling boy momentarily interrupted their efforts to spit into a gillnetter as we neared a pier that led up to the silent, tree-hidden village. Two young boys, asleep in the shade, roused to catch the ropes and warp the ship in, then ambled off. The crew swung some freight ashore, swung aboard more cases of the soft drink bottles that had awaited us at every port. We turned our backs on the warm, green world to plunge once more into fog that cut the visibility to less than a hundred feet and an icy wind that howled through the rigging. The whistle sounded continuously; the ship moved at half speed.

After more suspenseful stops when something showed darkly in the "clutter" on the radar screen, the captain called Victoria to ask about fog conditions at "the corner." A surprised Victoria replied, "Clear as day."

Within minutes, just off the bridge, a low, radiant, creamy glow arched like a baby rainbow at the base of the fog. As a cheer went up, the captain told me, "Whenever you see a fog-eater, the fog is going to lift."

Five minutes later the white gloom thinned. Within twenty minutes green sea and a sky blue as delphiniums cleared about us, though great billows of the stuff boiled away behind and coils clung to the strait's surface ahead. And there, to port, was Vancouver Island, a welcome line of green-blue hills patched with dull-gold heather. To starboard, the Olympic Mountains, an immense blue curve, rose higher and higher to reveal beyond their coastal ranks the crests of the great range, deep in snow the year round.

Steadily the *Princess* moved down the narrowing gap between Island and Peninsula while the sea's sparkling green waves tossed lacy whitecaps before her as Nootka Sound Indians used to strew feathers of welcome about the bows of early explorers' sailing vessels. As, far ahead, a white spot above black signalled the lighthouse on Race Rock, where we would turn "the corner" to Victoria, the waters widened. The Olympics paled to delft blue. The sea became a glitter of gold. Beyond the Island's sun-bronzed tip, first the great white summit of Mt. Baker loomed and then, below it, the white crests of the Coast-Cascade Mountains.

From bridge deck and bow, officers, crew, passengers, motionless and silent, watched that incredible panorama of colour, dimension and space open from horizon to horizon. Of tremendous implication, too, this meeting of two nations in such peace and beauty.

THE CARIBOO

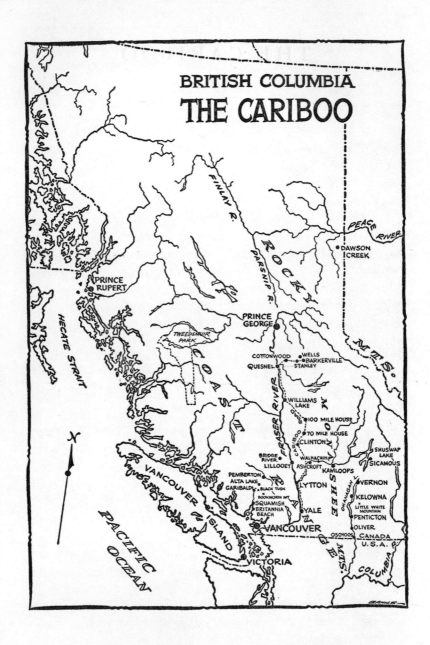

BRITISH COLUMBIA
THE CARIBOO

19

SWITZERLAND WITH INDIANS; GOLD WITH GHOSTS

"Can you swim?" a tourist beside me asked his companion as the overloaded and undermanned little steamer left Burrard Inlet to round Bowen Island into Howe Sound. "No," said his companion. "I'm holding my breath. One good sea in here and it's all over."

To the east, North Shore Mountains rose bluer and bluer to peak or cone; snowfields glistened in their high basins. To the west, mountaintop islands, with bits of cloud clinging like jeweller's cotton to their shoulders, folded together in a solid blue wall, finally to merge as mainland. East and west their forms and folds suggested prognathous-jawed Neanderthal men sprawled on their backs to watch the morning sun climb blue, blue sky. About us, blue sea rippled here and there in the wakes of Vancouver-bound tugs pulling long barges double-lined with tank, freight and flat cars piled with lumber.

At noon we nosed among anchored barges heaped with sulphur to Britannia Beach, where an eight-tiered structure of shining aluminum climbed a steep mountain to concentrate copper ore from one of southwest British Columbia's few notable mineral deposits. Shortly we crossed the inlet to Woodfibre, another village centred about a pulp and plywood mill. Anywhere else, both industries might have appeared impressive. Here, massive granite mountains reduced them to scale models.

An hour later, Howe Sound came to an end in a Yang and Yin of desolation and grandeur. Shallowing waters, miles of muddy tidal flats, both strewn with decaying piers and logs, wound inland round low, rocky hills. Behind them, smooth snow- and cloud-thatched mountains held at bay a whole range of white-spired peaks.

Between two small rivers, a mile inland, smoke tufts and aisled treetops marked the village of Squamish, or "Big Wind." From it a railroad pier picked its way across the flats far into the bay to fork like the open jaws of a hungry crocodile. Into them slid the steamer, to stop below the iron wheels of the Pacific Great Eastern Railway's waiting wooden train.

Except for its small diesel engine, it retained most of the features that for more than forty years had made it a "collector's item" which tourists delighted and Canadians endured to travel. Its original 347-mile route from Squamish to Quesnel corkscrewed over an old trail through the heart of the Coast Mountains. To British Columbians, it ran from "nowhere to nowhere." Tourists knew it as "Switzerland with Indians."

Open iron steps led into threadbare pioneer Pullmans. Though on cold days the diesel heated the cars, in each a potbellied iron stove still shoved its tin pipe through the ceiling, to end in a mushroomlike growth on the roof. The original lanterns, electrified now, supplied a dim light. Between engine and coaches rode a Toonerville caboose. Bringing up the rear was the "observation parlour"—the lower half of a wooden coach fitted with slatted seats and open to the sky.

Alas for tourist lovers of the exotic! At that very moment the PGE was completing a 42-mile rail extension between Vancouver and Squamish. Three weeks later, a stainless-steel, air-conditioned train replaced both decrepit steamer and collector's item. But Quesnel no longer is its final destination. Nor is Prince George, its current terminal. As I write, PGE rails are pushing north—to Dawson Creek, Fort St. John, one day perhaps to the Yukon and Alaska.

Hardly had this modern train settled into its daily schedule than other sweeping changes were begun in order to integrate this long-ignored region into the Provincial economy and culture. First to feel the broom is nondescript Squamish.

In anticipation of the "tremendous trade which ultimately must develop between British Columbia and the billion people across the Pacific," the PGE, and the Provincial and Domin-

170

ion governments are co-operating on a multimillion-dollar face and purpose lifting. When completed, Squamish will be a city of twenty-five to fifty thousand people; its 30-mile valley, an industrial park; the unsightly tidal flats, a vast freight yard; the harbour, a major seaport.

Just thirty miles north, we outran the Big Wind to Garibaldi Park, scene of a third transformation. Although Deception Peak is almost a hundred feet higher, Garibaldi's 8,787-foot, blinding-white summit gives its name to one of British Columbia's thirty-four main parks. Six of the park's twenty-odd glaciers creep down its snow- and conifer-deep slopes. High upon them a glacial lake of turquoise waters mirrors its own and surrounding minarets, pillars, domes.

Other peaks crowd the 600,000-acre park's skyline: Mamquam (8,475), Bookworm (7,910), Sphinx (7,886), Corrie (7,423). A few, including Garibaldi, are the only volcanic mountains in any Canadian park. Black Tusk (7,350) is the solidified basalt throat of an eroded crater.

Since the park was established in 1927, hardy climbers, skiers, and campers have enjoyed its mountains, lakes, trout streams and alpine meadows where more than forty varieties of wild flowers bloom unseen. Now a network of highways, chalets, sports facilities will provide a Provincial playground.

Long after we left the park behind, its peaks appeared above rank after rank of mountains to challenge comparison with other monarchs. Mt. Murchison's Fujiyama-shaped white cone rose above evergreen crests, to multiply the depth of the narrow granite gorge through which Cheakamus River boils, cascades, plummets to Howe Sound. At Alta Lake, Wedge Mountain's (9,484) snowfields and glaciers towered over a corps of rocky black crests. But I soon abandoned all effort to keep track of which mountain, river, lake or waterfall was which.

With breath-taking frequency the train not only wove in and out between sheer cliff and sheer precipice. It climbed up and down a series of heights of land that rose or fell from a few hundred to three thousand feet. One minute a mountain torrent poured south; the next, another raced north. Lakes sparkled everywhere; waterfalls shimmered.

To add to the confusion, rushing water and rushing wind sounded exactly alike. Forests, rivers, lakes appropriated one another's colours. Rocks, shining like patent leather, matched their rust, brown or green lichens and mosses with fading tints in the underbrush. Midsummer's white daisies and blue columbines stood petal to petal with autumn's asters and fireweed. Over everything hung the mingled scents of water, cedar, fir, flowers and baking earth.

Late in the afternoon we entered Pemberton Reservation, largest Indian reserve in the Province. Impassive as the ponderous, almost naked mountains behind them, fathers, mothers and small fry of each little village lined up in ragged rows to watch one of the last appearances of this long-familiar train. The Pontiacs and Mercurys standing about carry their owners north to earn money in the potato fields and south to spend it in beer parlours and movies.

"How they love Westerns!" a Squamish passenger said. "Every time a Jimmy Stewart or Alan Ladd hero shouts, 'Forward, men!—until every redskin bites the dust!' and every time a redskin does, they roar with laughter and stamp their feet."

Ever since Garibaldi Park I'd been fascinated by the march of 80- to 125-foot power towers and cables from one inaccessible, knifelike ridge to another. That they must be going to Vancouver, I knew. Everything does! But where in this isolated wilderness had they come from? How had they been erected? No one could explain *how*, but the PGE led straight to their lair on Seton Lake.

There a simple white powerhouse characteristically understated the dimensions of another of the grand-scale projects British Columbia's engineers have completed since World War II. This time Bridge River, descending from high slopes to the west to join the Fraser, became their sacrificial lamb. With a dam larger than the Great Pyramid of Gizeh, a 13,200-foot tunnel through Mission Mountain, and a 1,200-foot plunge, they diverted enough of its waters to Seton Lake to generate 248,000 h.p. for distant Vancouver and Powell River industries. Now a larger, duplicate construction is under way to raise the river's power potential to almost 700,000 h.p.

One mile north, Lillooet spreads over the high west bank of the Fraser as the entrance to the Cariboo. Aging frontier buildings along its commercial street still retain something of the robust years when the village was one of the main centres of the 1860's gold rush. On the hill above the PGE station still stand the gnarled pine tree, a frayed rope dangling from it, and graves of badmen who met justice-in-the-rough upon it.

But its thousand-odd population represents a 127 per cent increase in the past five years. Cowboys rolling cigarettes with one hand, Ukrainian potato growers from the wide bottom lands, Indian potato pickers, and miners from Bridge River gold mines represent a new and varied economy: modern homes, school, shops, a new way of life.

Here I heard what seemed the most logical of the many versions of how and why Cariboo became the title of the wide and rolling land we were entering. The winter of 1859 was more rugged than anticipated by three goldseekers who stayed to live off the country until spring. The caribou they killed one day furnished so providential a meal that they named—and phonetically spelled—the entire region in its honour.

Born in the Rockies, the Fraser River found the going so easy once it reached the great central plateau's clays and sands that by the time it passes Prince George it has cut a gorge almost a half mile wide. This it deepens on its way south until, as it approaches Lillooet, granite foothills rise hump to hump like embattled buffalo to force it to run the gantlet between them. Pinched and twisted, it bites, hisses or, where boulders also challenge its progress, caldrons into rapids and cataracts.

At that point our train swung east into night over the Cariboo, a night that quickly became so deep and thick with stars that the sky often appeared gold, spangled with jet. Watching it wheel overhead, I understood why, after all the perils of the Lower Fraser, the vanguard of goldseekers believed it a most auspicious omen.

When, twenty-five thousand strong, they poured into that

lower valley in 1858, high water covered most of the gold-bearing bars. "Humbug!" many cried and departed. Those who remained until the waters fell found gold at almost every bend. Their appetites whetted for the mother lodes, the majority pressed on up the Fraser's terrifying canyons.

They found gold, but under such dangerous conditions that they left the great river for the little Harrison. It led them to the lakes we had been passing for hours. The lakes led them to Lillooet. There on the threshold of the Cariboo, they made more strikes.

Sure now that vast mother lodes waited up-river, about four thousand pushed on. Up the Fraser to Quesnel River. To Quesnel Lake. To Cariboo Lake. To streams running in all directions. Again and again they struck gold, sometimes in nuggets. With "Dutch Bill" Dietz's big strike on Williams Creek in 1861, the Cariboo Gold Rush roared into life.

Estimates of its gold production range from $40 million upward. Williams Creek alone yielded $20 million.

In Williams Creek's narrow valley, ten thousand miners and adventurers built Barkerville into the capital of the Cariboo. Quesnel, at the junction of Fraser and Quesnel, boomed as its transportation and supply centre.

But only a few miners struck it rich on Williams Creek. The unlucky either worked for them or rushed away as new strikes were reported on the Big Bend of the Columbia or elsewhere. Primitive mining methods soon exhausted accessible deposits. Fire racing through Barkerville's shacks and tents in 1868 wrote "The End" to the Cariboo's "epic of British Columbia."

From Quesnel the next morning, under an "ardent" sun, as Ralph, the taxi driver, called it, I drove to the Barkerville rebuilt after the Great Fire. As the last lap of the Cariboo Trail which earliest miners broke while pushing north from the Lower Fraser, the 60-mile route once had wriggled round every rock and tree. After the big strike, it had been widened and straightened in spots as the Cariboo Road. A highway now, with many curves cut off and more in the process of amputation, it still curls like a wet spaniel.

The farther we went into hills folding in and out of hills, the higher we climbed toward 4,200-foot Beaver Pass, the more magnificent the fresh, untouched greens of spruce and fir forests that covered everything but the highway itself. A disgruntled grouse zoomed away at our approach. A few sparrows chittered annoyance. Otherwise, for miles at a time, our eyes might have been the first to see this wilderness; our ears the first to hear its singing silence.

Mementoes of the gold rush were not lacking, however. Ten miles from Quesnel, a crumbling log cabin was all that remained of "Ten-Mile House." At twenty miles, "Cottonwood House" was the home of a French-Canadian farmer. At thirty, Stanley was a ghost town of half a dozen weather-beaten cabins, the largest labelled "Hotel."

Miles upon miles of bleached grey flumes and sluice gates, all of heavy whipsawed lumber, fixed high on rugged slopes to last a hundred years, were doing just that. Occasionally a stream, dammed and dammed again to provide "power" for the sluice boxes, ran beside us.

A dozen times, at one creek or another, we sighted bent figures digging and washing for placer gold. "A summer pastime," said Ralph. "Always a new lot trying their luck. The gold's here all right, but the price is too low for those fellows, working on a shoestring, to get it." On one creek a San Francisco gold mining company's rigs worked a "really big operation."

Inevitably the old Trail had had its Lover's Leap, though to title it no beautiful Indian maiden plunged down the 2,000-foot drop to join her lost lover in the spirit world. Instead, on its brink a miner asked a stuffy young thing to marry him. "Marry you?" she cried. "I'd sooner die!" Flinging an arm about her waist, *he* cried, "If that's the way you want it—" and took off.

Beyond Beaver Pass, a hill-walled valley held several surprises. Hardly a tree broke the distance. In its centre rippled long Jack-o'-Clubs Lake. We ran between two operating gold quartz mines to see colourful cottages hung like a Grandma Moses painting on a green hillside,—homes of the mine officials.

At the lake's head stood Wells, a typical mining town. Dating from the 1930's, it is twice scorned by old-timers as a Johnny-come-lately and because its one street boasts nary tree nor flower. As this was Closing Day, not a soul was to be seen. But from the "Ladies'" empty beer parlour in the hotel I looked into an even larger "Gents'" parlour, where most of the male population circled tables covered with beer mugs and tall glasses of livid red.

Beer in these parts is served four mugs at a time. When a consumer is well along on the third, the bar, not to keep him waiting, draws four more. At appropriate intervals a long drink of tomato juice enables him to go round again.

Five miles beyond Wells we left the highway for a dirt road lined with log or frame cabins and weathered-grey, two-storey buildings which followed the curves of a high hill. Not a bird or even a scrap of paper fluttered upon it. Neither footstep nor voice broke the hot quiet.

"Like to live here?" Ralph asked. "Just pick your house and move in. No questions asked. Owners never will be back."

Barkerville—British Columbia's most famous ghost town!

It didn't look the part. Living hands had repaired, sometimes painted, log or frame structure. Limp and faded half-curtains were drawn across almost every window. Hardy perennials bloomed here and there. But the old fire hall still sheltered beneath its high bell tower the wooden-wheeled, hand-drawn fire apparatus. And the street ended with the Chinese section, where hundreds of Oriental miners had centred their life about a Masonic temple which still guards the lodge equipment behind boarded windows and doors.

Yet before the Great Fire this slim and somnolent valley had pulsed and roared with the flamboyant camp of ten thousand men and women. Then every cabin, tent, bar and hotel had poised tipsily on stilts to escape the wet gravel pouring down from sluice boxes on the hill. Then the Jack-o'-Clubs Hotel, with its gaily silked and satined German and Chilean "girls," had been known round the world. Then young, gently bred brides in high, buttoned shoes and swaying crinolines had climbed that 60-mile trail with their husbands, to make homes in tents, wear with grace their elaborate trousseaus, bear and rear children.

Only the Anglican Church of St. Saviour's, built in 1869, and the cemetery on the nearby hillside spoke clearly of the past. With serene dignity, the narrow, little frame church, with its varied windows, the work of dedicated, if unskilled miners, dominates the street. On a summer afternoon the cemetery is peaceful, too. But the tilted or fallen wooden headstones, their roughly burned inscriptions hardly legible, are almost lost among tangled trees, wild flowers and grasses.

Legends and tales—true, embellished or rootless, but all possible to the Barkerville of the gold rush—keep memories of the Cariboo miners green. One stars Cariboo Cameron, the husband who promised his wife that if she died in Barkerville, he would bury her near her girlhood home in Glengarry County, Ontario.

When she died in Barkerville in 1862, he first bought two caskets, one of wood, the other of tin; then filled the double coffin with whisky and sealed it. By horse-drawn toboggan he transported his precious, 450-pound burden over the snows to Quesnel. From there, by pack train, he accompanied it down the tortuous Cariboo Trail to Yale. At Yale he boarded a steamer for Victoria. In Victoria he took passage on an ocean-going vessel that, after sailing round South America, docked at last in New York.

New York customs officials could not be convinced that a coffin, even a double coffin, containing a woman's body, could weigh 450 pounds. Specifically, they could not be convinced that a coffin from the world-famous goldfields of British Columbia was a coffin. Fraud! they charged, and gold smuggling!

Cariboo Cameron had not almost circumnavigated the Western Hemisphere to be stopped now. Calling for a drill, he bored a hole through both caskets. Out streamed the whisky!

Inside, perfectly preserved, lay the proof of his claim. Hastily, the customs officials authorized clearance.

And one day in 1866, in the small cemetery of Glengarry County, Ontario, Cariboo Cameron stood beside a grave; the promise he had made in Barkerville, four years and thousands of miles away, fulfilled.

20

"THE LAST GREAT WEST"

At elevations varying from three thousand to six thousand feet, the Cariboo rolls down from the north through mountains that rise to nine thousand feet and over. It rolls on through hills whose slopes and vales provide most of the Province's two million acres of open and fifteen million acres of timber range lands. Rolls on through dry belt and canyons, to taper to an end about 350 miles later where the high-powered Thompson River joins the high-powered Fraser at Lytton.

Running through it, the Fraser gathers the waters of major tributaries—Chilcotin from the west, Thompson from the east —and minor contributions of hundreds of lesser rivers, creeks and lakes.

From Prince George to Williams Lake, the Cariboo Highway follows the Fraser, there leaves it to caterpillar east on a course that brings it into Lytton also. At either side, lie three of the Cariboo's four different areas of range land which together account for 80 per cent of British Columbia's beef cattle and of the cattle industry's annual $814 million value.

Along this paved and motorized thoroughfare practically all commercial development is concentrated. But alas for "The Last Great West," as the Cariboo long has been known. In an intensive wave of construction, the log cabins and whip-sawed pioneer frame inns, shops, homes, of crossroad centres and villages are being replaced by stucco, "store lumber" and glass in functional designs. Chrome, neon lights, jukeboxes are bright and loud in the land.

Beyond highway and ranches, however, remains a solitude of hills, rocks, forests, lakes, pools, creeks. Moose, deer, bear and numerous small "fur-bearing animals" claim these fast-nesses as their own. So do various game birds that raise their families in forest thickets. So do ducks and geese that rise in

179

clouds from lakes and pools. Fish grow to thirty, even forty pounds in lakes and streams. Many never have heard the crack of a hunter's gun; never been tempted by a fisherman's lure.

The few capsules of information I brought to these wide-open spaces were as useless as my umbrella. Quesnel, trade centre of the northern Cariboo, was a "pretty, tree-lined, drowsy village." Williams Lake, in the southern Cariboo, "a rootin', tootin' cowtown." The main function of the Cariboo Highway was to link booming northern British Columbia with the Lower Mainland. On ranch and range, the free and easy, romantic and lusty way of life portrayed by song, film and story as "western" was here forever preserved. But—

At the junction of the Fraser and Quesnel Rivers, Quesnel is a town of nearly five thousand people. Since 1950, it has overflowed its original townsite and spread over both banks of both rivers. Chiefly responsible for its 200 per cent increase in population and economic growth are forests sufficient to supply plywood, pulp, and veneer mills for another century or two. More than 150 sawmills now operate within a 30-mile radius. Western Plywood, Ltd.'s expanding plywood mills cover acres of nearby Fraser waterfront.

More than five hundred small farms and cattle ranches make it their supply and shipping centre. And a new industry, arriving like a wind-blown sunflower seed, has grown and blossomed almost overnight. Quesnel on the Cariboo Highway and Dawson Creek on the Alaska are about 350 miles apart. As that is just a good day's travel for north- and southbound motorists, motels to serve them line its highway approaches.

Since goldhunters founded the town in 1860 in an old bed of the Quesnel River, its life has been such a series of ups and downs that Quesnelites now speak with crossed fingers. "Prince George is booming," they say. "Dawson Creek is booming. Quesnel's doing all right. But one day—"

When a solution can be worked out with the fishing industry to save both the salmon swarming up Fraser and Quesnel to spawn in tributary streams and lakes *and* the half million horsepower in hydroelectric energy their waters now carry to the sea— When the price of gold rises enough to interest modern mining companies to extract from the hills as much as or more gold than the miners of the sixties ever found— When known deposits of copper, silver, low-grade asbestos, and diatomite in what are said to be the largest, purest beds in the Commonwealth are put to work—

About seventy miles south, Williams Lake, a town of two thousand people, lies in a shallow valley among low hills. During the sixties it was a supply and administrative centre for the gold country. Today, as trading centre for the five to six hundred ranches and farms of the southern Cariboo, it has acquired the title of "Cattle Capital of B.C." and a gaudy reputation for rootin' and tootin'.

Neither title nor reputation applied on the sunny weekday morning I arrived. Two or three drooping cowboys astride drooping ponies led strings of others out of town. Stockpens along the PGE were empty. Behind locked doors, store windows displayed saddles and kindred leather goods. Not a Stetson nor a high-heeled boot was to be seen; not a hitching post or rail, much less a cowpony. In Williams Lake, it appeared to be a rainy Sunday after a large Saturday night.

The race course, paddocks and grandstand on the outskirts, however, wore a depleted, dishevelled look. For half a mile on both sides of the long main street, cars were parked wheel to wheel. Every open spot held more. "What goes on?" I asked a lean, bronzed type wearily jackknifing himself into one of them. Ripping his eyes open, he stared as though I were just in from Mars. "Stampede," he groaned. "Over."

Williams Lake's Saturday nights are rather large but, according to observers, its annual Stampede is more than a year of Saturday nights in one. It is the best amateur rodeo in British Columbia, if not in Canada! Performed by the Cariboo's own working cowboys, it not only includes bulldogging, bronc busting, all the usual attractions, but an original, heart-stopping race when men (and sometimes a woman) risk their necks to ride straight down a steep mountain.

Matching the Stampede in excitement and importance is the

annual fall Cattle Sale. Then in two days of dizzy bidding and nights of bedlam, some thirty-five hundred steers, cows, heifers and calves are auctioned off to the tune of several hundred thousand dollars.

To house the thousands of spectators, ranchers, cattle buyers, dealers, reporters, who crowd in for both events is no trouble at all. Who sleeps?

As headquarters of the Cariboo Historical Society, Quesnel is rich in relics of gold-rush days. On a main street, a Cornish Pump which kept water out of the mines is just one of the many curious items collected for its Museum and Archives. Its residents are as rich in lore. There, while I marvelled at the pump's huge, primitive wooden wheel, one of them stopped "to pass the time of day" and tell me the story of the Cariboo Road.

Built in 1864, this oldest and most historic of all Provincial thoroughfares followed the Fraser south from Quesnel for four hundred miles to Yale, head of steamboat navigation on the lower river. Yet, whether it followed a ledge at water level or at dizzy heights, over gigantic rock-fills or cribwork, few miners fell victim to river, robber or Indian. An army of men, including the pair who pushed their worldly goods before them in a wheelbarrow and the homebound miner with a horse and cart and $500,000 in gold dust at his feet, travelled it safely.

Cumbersome stagecoaches lurched and swayed over it. Freight wagons. Long pack trains. Camels imported from California. Last, but ranking next to the gold in consideration, the "ladies of the evening." Its real hazards were the rough-and-ready resthouses stationed every ten to fifteen miles and, depending on their distance from Lillooet, known as "83-Mile House" or "100-Mile."

All are gone or going now. Even mountains and canyons have had their faces changed. But thinking to see something of the Cariboo of both yesterday and today, I left Quesnel one morning by bus. For thirty miles or more, I saw it under almost 1864 conditions.

Because recent cloudbursts had closed the highway for repairs, we snaked down steep, narrow country roads, along unguarded rims of gulches in whose depths swollen mountain torrents raced for the Fraser. Inches above those clay-heavy waters, the bus rattled across planks to turn at acute angles and climb another steep, narrow road.

During rare, level intervals we wound through a green and fertile world. Of grainfields bordered with yellow daisies. Pastures where dairy cattle grazed. Farmyards where children played as intently before picture windows newly inserted in old, unpainted log cabins as before glass walls of modern ranch-type homes.

Returning to the highway, we ran along the rim of the increasingly wider and deeper canyon the Fraser's drab waters currently are shaping, to see others they had shaped during millenniums. Between ridges so high and distant they were veiled in haze, the great central plateau had been carved into a melee of gorges, lesser ridges and plateaus, topped with forests or fields.

Absorbed in the river's own engineering feats and those of the PGE, whose rails, tunnels and arcades clung to ledges hewn out of the canyon walls, I didn't know we had left the green world until a familiar fragrance drifted in the bus windows. Sagebrush. New hay. Pine. Baking earth and stone. Cattle country!

Hills of sand and clay ran beside us and ahead. On their summits sun- and wind-frazzled yellow pines stood in puddles of their own shadow. On the slopes, toasted grass, tufted with the soft, grey-green of sagebrush, dark greens of cactus, and pocked with sand-scoured stones, ran down to lazy streams not more than two or three feet wide. On lower slopes of the vales between them, massed birch and aspen were startlingly light and white. Cattle country it was.

In a fishtailed area between the Fraser and Chilcotin Rivers and continuing down the Fraser, the southern Cariboo claims a major share of the region's open and timber ranges. More than two-thirds of them are privately owned; the rest leased from the government. Owned and leased lands often are enlarged by obtaining "control" of large or small areas of Crown grazing lands.

Many ranches here are small, but about Williams Lake, the "Big Five"—Alkali, Chilco, Gang, Koster's, and Circle S— thus own, lease and control an average of 450,000 to 500,000 acres.

Water—rather, the lack of water—accounts frequently for the fantastic shapes and sizes of some Cariboo ranches. To acquire "water rights," a rancher may lease land in which a creek wriggles through miles of rockbound, forested wilderness. Lease secured, he seldom, if ever, views that wilderness again. His cattle never see it. One such ranch runs for sixty miles, is said to "control" a million acres. Another "controls" 850,000.

Whatever the size of the ranch, here or elsewhere in the Province, Herefords predominate. Some ranches raise Shorthorns and Angus, but none exclusively. Though to ask a rancher how many cattle he runs is a "shootin' question," it is safe to say that the Gang Ranch herds about seven thousand; others herd an average of two to three thousand.

One ranch, the 100-Mile, though much smaller in acreage and herds, is widely known through its owner. While president of the British Columbia Cattlemen's Association, Lord Martin Cecil substantially improved the Province's marketing methods, prices, freight rates, and the ranchers' perennial problem of feed supplies.

But, though the sun blazed down from an intense blue sky and the air was so light, clear and dry that the grain of fenceposts showed clearly, I could not see a Hereford on any slope. "Of course not," a PGE official told me later. "They're all down on our tracks, being killed." Actually, they long since had retreated for the summer to the high timber ranges back in the hills.

Leaving the Fraser at Williams Lake, the highway followed the old Cariboo Road route for more than a hundred miles through scorched hills and a sampling of the lakes. A few,

184

like Williams and La Hache, miles long and narrow, twisted through lower hills or ridges. Signs and an occasional dirt road indicated that working and dude ranches, fishing and hunting camps were all about. But only here and there a fisherman, drowsing in a rowboat, broke the reflections of blue sky and foaming white clouds mirrored in unruffled surfaces.

As we approached 83-Mile House a stunning electric-blue wall, looming ahead, sealed us in among heat and hills. But when reached it broke into more hills, huge, black with pine and cloud shadows, patched with light-grey rock. At a cross-roads store, I looked out my window to meet the gaze of an enormous pair of limpid brown eyes beneath a battered black sombrero. An Italian cowboy, I thought, until he turned on crooked heels and, from his profile and walk, I saw that he was Indian.

At 70-Mile House, we crossed a 3,568-foot divide to descend to Clinton, "a cowtown" at the head of the Cariboo's third cattle-raising area. Cowtown? All grey, white and yellow cottages, green lawns, climbing roses, it nestled like a baby chick among those black-eagle hills.

Hardly had we left it than the picture-book grandmother who became my seatmate there, dug out pen and pad to write, "I am very deaf. What valley is this?"

Valley of the Moon, I wanted to answer as I looked at the narrowing walls of rock and clay. Bald except for a thin fringe of black and brittle trees, they formed the gorge of the Bonaparte River. Steadily it wriggled deeper into hills of rock, sand and white clay, naked as Chihuahuas.

In searing heat we paused while a wise and patient black dog herded two hundred sheep round a curve of the highway and across a low white bridge. Sunshine filtering through dust haze to highlight their curly grey backs, the wisp of water glinting through tattered alder and chokecherry, and harsh hills linked them all in a pastoral theme for the brush of Constable or Crome.

The native of the Cariboo behind me didn't see it that way. "Except in godforsaken country like this," he told his neighbour, "everything's stacked against sheep raising in B.C. Most of the range land's more profitable for cattle. And British Columbians are beef eaters—don't go for lamb and mutton. But bears and wolves do, and that costs money and trouble. Besides, the price of wool's too low to bother with."

He underestimated this "godforsaken country." As we went on through more hills toward another high, blue wall, more and more wooden flumes wound down the slopes to irrigate miles of level benches where tomatoes and potatoes ripened for the Canadian market and hay for the Cariboo. And a sudden whiff of cedar and fir, of fresh lumber, announced, of all things, a sawmill!

Ashcroft, once a gold-rush camp, now nationally known as the source of Cariboo tomatoes and potatoes, appeared. In this dehydrated tropical afternoon only two things moved there. Heat waves. And the tongues of two small Indians frantically lapping melting ice cream cones.

There we joined the Thompson for the last fifty miles of its descent from Kamloops, one of the most exciting fifty miles in the Province. Pressed between sheer rock walls of Black Canyon, it progressed from deep olive-green eddies to rapids. As the walls narrowed and heightened to a hundred feet, it became a roaring boil of white water. To that roar the wind added another as our bus sped in and out between the ledge hewn out of hills and rock for the CPR tracks and the curling lip of the canyon.

All at once a bridge, a mere silkworm's thread, spanned the waters far ahead. Descending almost eight hundred feet to cross it, we arrived before the "General Merchant" store of Spence's Bridge. And there parked between truck and car, singular as a white robin, was a Bennett Buggy—Model T Ford chassis, rubber-tired wheels, sorry brown nags, and all!

Now wilder and wilder hills squeezed the Thompson into a strait jacket and from all sides tossed little falls and streams into it. Piling higher, higher, and louder, the mad waters plunged into the all too aptly named "Jaws of Death." Eroded rock and clay slopes broke out in bruised shades of yellows, red, purples. Against them dwarf jack and bull pine and sage were black as drifted soot. Sheer cutbanks of white sand, graceful as a waterfall or veined like a leaf with rain runnels, folded about their feet.

Only our debonair driver seemed confident of our ultimate arrival somewhere. Whenever the canyon became too much for her, the picture-book grandmother wrapped one hand tightly into the back of my jacket. Above the Jaws of Death, horrified fascination lifted her to her feet, and me with her, to peer down. Abruptly covering her eyes with her free hand, she seated us both to write, "I'm seventy-eight years old. I don't think I care to make this trip again."

Suddenly the Thompson discovered that the Fraser it was racing to meet was sauntering along just beyond a narrow band of hills. As it slowed to a dignified, clear green pace, the gorge flattened out. We ran into Lytton, a village high on a ridge, to witness their unique meeting.

Here was no question of an 850-mile river gulping down a 100-mile tributary. Recognizing an equal in the quality of the Thompson, the drab and dirty Fraser moved over. Side by side, each maintaining its own colour and character, they set out for the Pacific.

I only had time to see them on their way. Within minutes, aboard the CPR, I was ascending the Thompson to Ashcroft, there to turn right for Kamloops, on the eastern border of the Cariboo.

WOMEN ARE SMART AND MEN
ARE LONG ON MAKING DOLLARS

Smooth as a lake, the Thompson, also turning right at Ashcroft, was a changed river. For about twenty miles of its upper course, it is, in fact, a lake—Kamloops Lake. In the mellowing, late-afternoon light, the blistered hills relaxed like weary elephants, so old their wrinkled hides hung in folds.

Along the highway, hoods and doors wide open, cars cooled while their occupants picnicked on some shaded spot. From the "Bird-Cage," a roofed but otherwise open, breeze-swept observation car, I watched dust devils form and spin while a lean and lanky individual who "ranched for the hell and health of it" offered a running comment on the passing scene.

"Northerners!" he exclaimed, apropos of the overheated motorists. "From Peace River or the Yukon, I'll be bound. Strange—up there, when a blizzard comes along, they know enough to stay indoors and keep warm. Well, this is a heat blizzard in the Dry Belt. Down here, we stay indoors, keeping cool; come out in the early morning and after sundown. Going to *be* in a country, you've got to learn to *live* in it—like the plants and animals." Waving a hand at the upper slopes, black with yellow pine and shadows, he asked, "Don't see them growing down here, do you? Not when we get less than eight inches of rain and most of it falls up there."

As Wallachin flickered by, he translated, "Wallasheen— 'Land of Plenty.' And once it was on its way to that. Years before the first World War, the Earl of Anglesey and some friends, most of them titled, came in here. Brought servants, masons, carpenters. Carpets, grand pianos, paintings—everything. And all kinds of seeds and seedlings. Planned to make this country a bit of England and live in it in the same style they'd had at home—

"Well, sir, they built fine stone houses. And they planted gardens and orchards. And they rigged up their own irrigation system. By 1914, they had apples ripening. But they never saw them ripe. Soon's the war broke out, every last one of them went back to England, leaving everything just as it was. Thought the fighting wouldn't last long and they'd all be back. But not a man of them lived to come back! All they'd had and done here went to wrack and ruin. Tragedy for this country. By now they'd have had it blooming like a rose."

To my regret, he left shortly to drop off at one of the cross-road centres for ranchers and farmers back in the hills. We went on through alternate twilight and daylight as the sun winked off and on behind hilltops and gaps.

Occasional fields, no larger than a city lot, green with grain or beige with stubble, topped clay or sand benches whose slopes were palisaded with rose-red rock or white with stones, thick as barnacles. Gradually the benches divided rhythmically into mesas, erosion-shaped and fluted as though moulded on a potter's wheel and glazed in a kiln until, even when the light was dim, they shone.

When the sun left the deepening sky, the hills and levels broke out colours of their own choosing—subtle blues, lilacs, purples, sharply accented with black. And the Thompson, now Kamloops Lake, captured their reflections so exactly that to look at one was to see them both.

As they faded to shadows, the train ran through a beadwork of tunnels to emerge in an ebony world. From the chair car, I looked across the lake's black sheen to clustered lights that transformed a large white building with tall chimneys into a wedding cake with white candles and flowers. ("Tranquille," said the steward. "British Columbia's tubercular sanatorium.") Then to a more brilliant display where acres of tall, lacy white towers and arches were a carnival of lights. ("Kamloops Oil Refinery and Pumping Station—on the Trans-Mountain Pipeline which carries crude oil from Alberta to Vancouver.")

The field of lights ahead where the hills came together I could identify for myself. Kamloops.

189

From my hotel windows the next morning it was not difficult to understand why the Indians had named this spot *Cumloops,* "Meeting of the Waters." Round St. Paul and St. Peter, two bold if junior mountains of thirty-five hundred to four thousand feet, curved the North and South Thompson Rivers, to merge and run down the centre of an oval bowl of hills in a bright-blue, half-mile-wide band as the Thompson.

Nor was it difficult to understand why North West Company's Simon Fraser, after discovering and naming the Fraser in 1805, waited a year to title this one for David Thompson. Clear, clean, strong, travelling alone through this virile desolation, it must have reminded him of the most admirable of all the "Great Northmen" of the fur trade and the nineteenth century's foremost geographer and mapmaker.

As though focussed by a magnifying glass, the sun burned through the clear, light air on rooftops of business and industrial districts filling the narrow valley on both sides of the river. Directly below me Victoria, the main street, with awnings or drawn shades prepared for another day in the high nineties.

Little effort had been made to rebuild or streamline the pioneer frame and brick buildings because (and, characteristically, as one of the city fathers was to tell me) its citizens refuse to go into debt for the sake of appearances. "We may be short on beauty and culture, but we sure are long on making dollars."

Though not the oldest city in British Columbia, Kamloops has had a longer association with what is called the "white man's civilization" than any other point in the interior. Beginning in 1812 as a trading post, it ran through the history of the fur trade in less than ten years.

Traders from John Jacob Astor's Pacific Fur Company pushed up here from Astoria on the Lower Columbia to build the first post. Within a year, North West Company took it over. With the merger of that company and Hudson's Bay in 1821, it became the important northern terminal of the Fur Brigade Trail. The log cabin built at that time to store pelts now stands in the new Public Library-Museum as "the oldest building in the Province."

Twenty years later, two black-robed Oblates of Mary Immaculate erected here the first mission for the Indians. During the next twenty years more missionaries, Catholic and Protestant, came. But it was the discovery of gold on the Thompson in 1857 that started Kamloops and its neighbour, North Kamloops, on their way to a population of fifteen thousand and a community of diversified interests.

In the early spring of 1862, 150 gullible English, Canadian and American goldseekers arrived in St. Paul, Minnesota, to be transported to the gold strike in stagecoaches of the British-American Overland Transport Company. No such company or stageline existed! Many of the defrauded turned back. After six months of indescribable hardship, largely afoot, some reached Kamloops—only to learn that the gold rush had swept north to Williams Creek. Starving, almost naked, penniless, the "Overlanders" settled down on small farms and millsites to found Kamloops' sawmilling, agricultural and other industries.

Primarily, as headquarters for a forest district that embraces more than fifty-five thousand square miles, Kamloops' interest today is in logging, milling and forest products. Every winter thousands of North American homes celebrate Christmas around trees from its "Christmas market."

As division point for both Canadian Pacific and Canadian National transcontinental lines, as crossroads for highways and airways, it is a transportation centre. Like Prince Rupert and Prince George, it is an administration centre for Federal and Provincial departments. Industrial centre, for canneries, packing plants, factories. Health and medical centre. Tourist and sportsman's taking-off point.

North and east of the city, lakes and streams of all sizes, sparkling in increasingly forested mountain land, explain its popularity with tourists. The North Thompson's valley is Cloud Seven for sports fishermen and hunters. Game birds, elk, caribou, moose, bear, mountain goat, are plentiful; deer and cougar too much so. Trappers set their lines for mink, marten, fox, muskrat. And from spring to fall, nature lovers revel in tree-climbing clematis, starlike yellow arnica, lavender sego lily and other wild flowers.

Just ninety miles north is Wells Gray Park. A million-acre wilderness of mountains and lakes, as yet accessible only by foot or plane, it contains some of the finest scenery in the Province. With a roar and spray that can be heard and seen for miles, Helmcken Falls drops 450 feet out of massed evergreens into a natural rock-walled bowl to spill into Myrtle River. Others, if elsewhere, would be magnets for sightseers. Scores of lakes offer superlative fishing.

But the Cariboo is celebrated as cattle country, and here on its eastern border cattle trails crisscrossed on the enclosing hills identify Kamloops as a cattle town. The first words I heard, via my hotel maid, were "You've come too late for our Rodeo and too soon for the Fat Cattle Show—the best things in town."

During breakfast, a rancher from the South Thompson Valley, who looked more like a businessman than the men of Kamloops in their open-throated shirts and slacks, told me that the city is "the capital of one of the three largest cattle-raising areas in Canada." And, because of its dry climate, excellent bunch-grass ranges and water impregnated with lime and iodine, one of the best. "Up here," he said, "ranches are small —about three to four thousand acres of owned and leased land, run a few hundred cattle and horses. But down south in the Nicola Area, both ranches and herds run big."

Strictly speaking, another rancher with a pronounced professorial air, informed me that the Nicola Area is not Cariboo, but Lower Fraser country. Be that as it may, it was the cradle of the cattle-raising industry while British Columbia still was a Crown Colony. Its grassland ranges are rated as the best in the Province. Year after year, its entries win the blue ribbons at the cattle shows.

There, the largest ranch in all Canada, the Douglas Lake Cattle Company, or "Douglas Lake Ranch," runs ten to twelve thousand cattle on five hundred thousand acres of owned, leased and Crown range land. Others, notably the Guichon Family Holdings and the Nicola Lake Stock Farm until recently covered larger spreads than the Williams Lake "Big Five." Now they have split their holdings or sold several places to cut down outlying operations.

Many ranches breed Arabian and Palomino horses as well as standard strains from riding to heavy draft horses, stock to polo ponies. And the North Thompson's valley produces sheep whose wool commands prices well above the going market rates. Here, the Hayward Ranch, largest sheep ranch in the Dominion, runs about 3,600 ewes. With a yearly increase of at least 125 per cent of lambs, it thus obtains a total of 8,100 head.

Just outside Kamloops is the Provincial Range Experiment Station. On almost a hundred twenty thousand acres, representing every type of soil from arable bottom lands to upper mountain-forest ranges, it is engaged in improving the quality of every phase of cattle raising from forage crops to ranch management.

Assisted by the growth of the Cariboo's population and forest industry, the Station supplies one more reason why the traditional rancher and cowboy, like Wyoming's, are heading for the last roundup with the equally traditional trapper, prospector, and lumberjack. Cattle raising today is not a way of life. It is a business. Or a hobby, Or a dude ranch.

This is not to say that the Cariboo's robust characters and ways have gone. Not with a thousand different cattle and almost six hundred fifty horse brands registered on Cariboo-Nicola ranges!

But sad, oh, sad to say, under the impact of modern education, higher standards of living, two World Wars, the movie, TV, automobile, plane, the human monadnocks are levelling off to a plateau. One still meets or hears about range-ripened characters, men or women, but the tales they tell and the tales told about them are best when flavoured with the past.

Cowboys may slope along on crooked heels, ride the range on cowponies, even into town on Saturday night. But they are more likely to arrive on wheels, hatless, bandanna-less, spurless, their shirts white or rodeo style, their tan or black slacks concealing all but the toes and heels of their boots. Their home on the range no longer is a bunkhouse atumble with blankets, boots and saddles, redolent of leather, cattle, sweat and kerosene. It is a modern home with bedrooms, showers, lounges equipped with radios, card tables, reading lamps, even pictures ordered from a New York art gallery. They may sing nostalgic plaints of the wide open spaces where the deer and (in the Cariboo)the cougar roam, but where they long to be is within easy reach of a town where lights are bright and music gay.

Ranchers drive to town in their own cars—or one of them; they fly their own planes. The "home ranch" may combine the baronial with the last word in kitchen units. But it rapidly is becoming a figure of speech as homes or apartments of convenience are established in cattle-shipping centres; for winter, in Vancouver, Victoria, or some warmer clime from Hawaii to the Caribbean. The modern "character" is the rancher who appears briefly in dusty jeans and Stetson at roundup or cattle show; at home hastily discards his "working clothes" for tweeds or slacks.

Arriving in Vancouver, I had been considerably startled to see beside the entrances of many hotels two smaller ones, labelled "Men" or "Gents"; "Women" or "Ladies." The first, I soon learned, indicated a beer parlour solely for men; the second, for women alone or accompanied by escorts, never for men alone. This is an old British Columbia custom, I discovered as I travelled about but, until Kamloops, I had no opportunity to enjoy it.

Then, although every table in the immense room was filled with young women or young women and young men, both décor and behaviour were subdued. Nothing distinguished ranchers and their wives, cowboys and their dates, from the townspeople.

Speaking of women, those of Kamloops wherever met or seen were smarter in dress, grooming, posture than elsewhere.

This at a time when summer wardrobes have a tendency to wilt like Saturday lettuce in a supermarket. And, curiously enough, in whatever direction a conversation turned, a Kamloops woman starred in it somewhere.

History? The proud granddaughter of Simon Fraser, 86-year-old Mrs. Annie Crum, never refers to the Fraser River by any other title than "My Grandfather's River." Education? When Martha Watanabe, a Japanese teen-ager, graduated from high school recently, three of Canada's foremost universities—British Columbia, McGill and Queen's—offered her scholarships. The unusually interesting Library-Museum? A woman presented the city with the downtown property on which they stand. Women are as active as men in initiating and supporting all manner of social welfare and, despite the "short on culture" disclaimer, cultural activities.

At a dinner party a husband asked me, "How did you like Mexico? I must take my wife somewhere or she'll have a bad attack of arthritis." As I visibly tried to sort that out, he explained, "When she's up to the ears in good works, she never suffers from it. But when a big job ends she's sure to—unless something else is coming up quick. She's just finished helping to raise $110,000 for a housing project for Kamloops' senior citizens."

All at once I knew that a quick departure was indicated for me also. Kamloops' climate is so invigorating, everyone so vigorous, that the unwarned visitor, infected, soars on an illusion of inexhaustible vitality—only to fall! Although the first train pulled out at 5:30 in the morning, I was aboard, destination unknown.

For almost an hour we ascended the milky blue South Thompson between hills smouldering under a smoky blue haze. Then the river widened into Little Shuswap Lake, buried in trees save where summer cottages broke its shoreline. Lower, longer, smoother hills, green with cedar, spruce, pine, led the way into a land of ripening grainfields, pastures knee-deep in forage, comfortable farmhouses. Everything had the *look* of moisture.

We had entered the valley of Lake Shuswap, a most extraordinary body of water. Twenty-nine miles long, in places twenty-five miles wide and a thousand feet deep, it breaks into seven arms that describe among the rolling hills the outline of a terrified jack rabbit, long ears pricked, in leaping flight east.

What a boon if it could have leaped right over the Rockies! There thousands of North Americans would find release from the heat and beat of summer on this lovely lake's blue water, white beaches, green hills. Here, at least along the miles and miles I saw, hundreds of Canada geese and scores of dairy cattle were almost the only living creatures to enjoy it.

I was studying my map for a destination upon it when somewhere in the car someone said, "Nothing ever happens at Sicamous." And there was Sicamous, tucked into the cup of the rabbit's right foreleg. I looked no farther.

Ah, Sicamous! May it live forever!

THE OKANAGAN

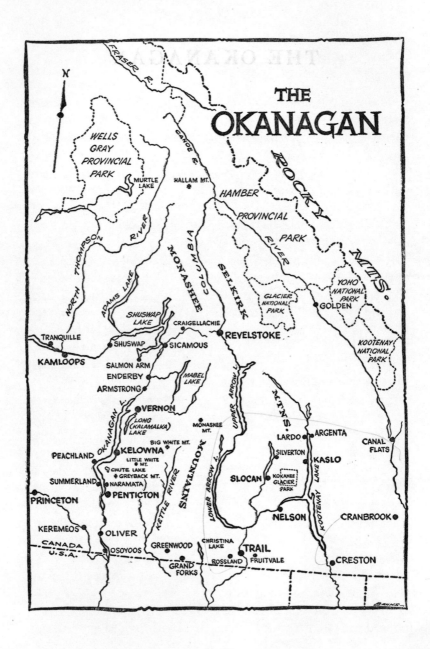

22

ALL THIS AND OGOPOGO, TOO

The ancient observation car dangled like an old-fashioned watch charm from a chain of four freight and three baggage cars. Its mahogany walls and plate-glass windows were dim; its green velvet velours draperies, limp; its upholstered chairs, threadbare. "Brigham Young's private car is somewhere in this part of the world now," said a passenger. "Shouldn't wonder if this is it."

Through its wide-open door I watched Sicamous and the last of Lake Shuswap's seven blue arms disappear. Massed cottonwoods and evergreens and rocky hills rose on both sides of a level green valley and Shuswap River's weaving course. Sagebrush and bunch grass patched the slopes with grey fuzz. On the lowlands, wheat, forage, vegetable and dairy farms slid by. Every village circled a sawmill, lumberyard, or both.

Could this be the Okanagan Valley, British Columbia's prized 130-mile-long fruit basket? Where were the orchards? Where was equally prized Okanagan Lake?

At Larkin, orchards began to roll up lower slopes like dark-green surf looking for a beach to break on. But the lake that rippled into view, aswarm with ducks, coots and hell-divers, was named Swan!

From it, a creek runs through a cup of low, faded hills, enclosed by others, high and blue. Salish Indians named it "Jumping-Over Place," because here they jumped their horses over the stream. When cattle raising was the valley's only industry, incoming settlers renamed the cup Vernon for the owner of nearby Coldstream Ranch. Today a flower-bright, tree-shaded town of about nine thousand people, it is the ancestor of the Okanagan's fruit-growing industry.

In 1892, Lord Aberdeen, then Governor General of Canada, bought the Coldstream. Planting an apple orchard on it, irrigating it with canals leading down from lakes high in the hills, he demonstrated that under the magic of water the black soil was incredibly fertile.

That same year a group of rich and titled Belgians arrived, plus servants, heirlooms, carriages and all the the rest, to plant hundreds of acres to orchards and re-create here a bit of Belgium. Instead, they repeated almost word for word the sad tale of Wallachin's English colony. The only difference was that some of the Belgians survived to return after World War I. Penniless, they sold their treasured heirlooms.

As the centre of the northern valley's fruit-growing industry, Vernon boasts a million-box (bushel) packing plant, one of the largest single orchards in the Commonwealth, and the largest single irrigation district in the Province. It also fills many other baskets.

It is the distribution, packing and processing centre for the grain, forage and vegetable seed-growing farms of the northern valley. For a district in which six thousand cattle produce ice cream and cheese as well as milk and butter; sheep produce wool; and poultry, eggs. For a forest industry that turns out lumber, poles, piles, railroad ties and box shooks for which British Columbia has an insatiable appetite.

In summer, tourists and trout fishermen come to its forty surrounding lakes and streams. In the fall, pheasant, native grouse, Hungarian partridge, ducks and geese bring hunters. Deer are so plentiful that two bucks (double the usual bag) or one buck and one doe (usually forbidden) are permitted, provided the doe is shot "between November 26 and December 4."

The psalmist who sang of

Mountains, and all hills; fruitful trees, and all cedars:
Beasts, and all cattle; creeping things, and flying fowl . . .

must have known and loved a valley like the northern Okanagan. Except for vines, I saw no creeping things, but everything else was there—in abundance. Including thirty or forty churches!

Basically, the people of the Okanagan are English, Scotch, Irish; among them, numerous mid-Victorian ladies and gentlemen akin to Victoria's crumpet set. Newcomers from Greece, Italy, the Ukraine, Netherlands and other Old World countries also find its hills and soils reminiscent of their homelands. With their hopes they brought their religions.

For southbound travellers on the Shuswap and Okanagan Railway's watch-charm train, Vernon keeps its brightest memory for the last. Just outside the town is Kalamalka ("Waters of Changing Colours") Lake. For thirteen miles it twists between hills that range through greens and blues to purple and lilac as they fold into distance. Rocks blasted out of their feet to provide a ledge for the railroad deepen from cream to rose to carmine.

The waters, clear as the air, riffling over a cobbled bed, outdo them all. Now jade, tourmaline, or mint green, now turquoise, pinkish silver, amethyst, rose, gold or all colours at once, they are as beautiful and astonishing as a peacock's tail. Woods Lake, almost as long and separated from Kalamalka by a hair, though a smoothly shining silver, appears a self-righteous drab.

But where was Okanagan Lake? Running along beside us, said my map, and had been ever since we first sighted Swan Lake. The low, continuous ridge to the west which I had been ignoring hid it.

Against the grey-fawn landscape, orchards now cross-stitched lower slopes and lowlands with a dark-green petit point. Villages were a succession of fruit warehouses embedded in orchards.

All apple and all McIntosh, each tree was the same height, the same distance apart, and almost identically shaped. Each apple was the same size as all others, its soft green precisely tinted the same soft rose in precisely the same spot.

Seen individually, each tree might have been a jewelled basket from Cellini's workshop. En masse, they reduced the fields of onions, beets and other vegetables, of grain in shock, of hay cut and drying, of goldenrod and aster, to autumn leaves floating on a deep-green sea. Tractor-drawn hayracks and grazing Holsteins in hay or stubble field to waterbugs. Stands of red pine and yellow, groves of alder and poplar, to reeds and grasses.

One fruit tree in blossom is a feast for the eyes. One orchard, a continuous delight. An Okanagan spring is a festival of beauty that thousands of Canadians and Americans return year after year to share. Then, when hills are green, skies and lakes a forget-me-not blue, almost two million trees foam into white and pink bloom.

As the hills, rising to three thousand and sometimes four thousand feet, took on mountainous outlines, I marvelled that they could be so similar in size and shape, yet so different in effect from those about Kamloops, only a geological hop, skip and jump away. Kamloops hills were virile, red under the sun, and hot. These were softly curved, a cool grey-fawn, faced with dead-white terraces on which more orchards flourished.

"Know why?" asked the one-time World War I officer beside me. "Kamloops hills are composed of volcanic lava and alluvial soils. These are granite, limestone and volcanic rock, buried under white-silt soils, fine as your face powder. Those terraces are almost solid silt."

Way back in Eocene times, a great plain forty-five hundred feet high, with monadnocks rising to two thousand feet, ran through here. In it was a dent twenty-five hundred feet deep. Glaciers eroded the monadnocks and levelled the plain; their ice, melting in silt-laden streams, ran down into the dent.

Silt deposited, another uplift followed, another round of erosion began. This time a river—the Okanagan—brought down more white silt and, flowing in a more or less straight line except for one "wide U turn," shaped the valley and eroded the earlier silt deposits into the 900-foot-high terraces. Finally, in Pleistocene or "recent" times, tributaries pushed the silt into fan-shaped wedges which blocked and divided the river into the Okanagan and smaller lakes that now floor most of the valley.

As he paused on an "Is that clear, men?" note, the conductor called, "Kelowna!"

A pear-shaped taximan drove me to the Royal Anne Hotel, named for a cherry. En route, we wound round immense fruit trucks decorated with man-sized red apples, between block-long warehouses where mountains of crated peaches and vegetables were melting into freight cars beside their loading platforms. Blended scents spiced the dry air.

Office buildings filled with fruit brokers, orchard supply companies, various fruit-growing services faced commercial streets. And when we turned into Bernard Avenue, the main shopping street, display windows were still-life arrangements of grapes, plums, cantaloupes, fat red tomatoes and golden peaches.

This was not surprising. Kelowna is the headquarters of British Columbia Tree Fruits, Ltd., the organization which annually markets, to the tune of $20 million to $25 million, all fruits grown in the Province. Of British Columbia Vegetable Marketing, Ltd., which handles $3 million to $4 million a year as the sole agency for the infinite variety of vegetables British Columbia growers produce. And trading centre for the largest apple-growing district in Canada.

Here are refrigerated storage warehouses with million-box capacities. British Columbia Fruit Processors and other fruit- and vegetable-processing plants, canneries, frozen food and juicing plants, the second largest winery in the Dominion. And, though lumbering is the second industry, it is an accessory largely to the fruit. In box shooks alone, its sawmills turn out enough lumber each year to build five thousand homes.

What is surprising is that all this has come about in fifty years. The Okanagan still was arid cattle country in 1905 when big land companies, inspired by the success of the first small orchards, moved in. Buying up great tracts, they installed irrigation by gravity from high hill lakes and sold sub-tracts to fruitgrowers.

Today, some eighty thousand acres are under orchard. Almost as many more could be if water were available. Their value has risen from $200 per acre in 1909 to $750 or, depending on the extent of planting and irrigation, to $3,000 and up.

Like farmers, fruitgrowers are independent characters. The Okanagan vintage formed and abandoned several mutual help organizations before World War II, dislocating markets and prices, made a single central marketing agency imperative. From this resulted, in 1942, the co-operative popularly known as "B.C. Fruits." Completely owned by some thirty-eight hundred growers, it now markets all fruits grown in the thirty- to forty-thousand square-mile fruit belt that extends from Kamloops through the Okanagan into East Kootenay.

Word of its success in developing national and international markets and protecting both growers and consumers from exploitation spread rapidly. Representatives from fruitgrowing areas all over the world now come to the geranium-gay, white-stucco headquarters in Kelowna to study its organization and methods.

Vegetable growing, however, still is largely a family affair. Chinese and Japanese, with everyone from toddlers to grandparents helping, are the leading growers. Immigrants grow vegetables on five or ten acres until they are able to buy farms and machinery. On the 700-acre veterans' project, young couples grow vegetables while they wait for their fruit orchards to mature. Still others lease lands on the Indian reservations at Vernon, Kelowna, and Penticton.

Vegetable growers do not own B. C. Vegetable Marketing, Ltd. It is their sole selling and distribution agency.

Because vegetables lack the glamour, prestige and magnitude of the fruitgrowing industry, their growers lack the influence to remove the thorns that sorely plague them. Most painful is the fact that every time the B. C. Vegetable Marketing Board tries to obtain protection for them, three older and more powerful industries cry, "Why endanger lumbering, fishing and mining for a few potato farmers?"

And the vegetable growers need protection from an American thorn. California, Oregon and Washington vegetables ripen ten days earlier than British Columbia's. In tremendous surpluses they flood Provincial markets before the home-grown are ready.

Kitseukla, Tsimshian village, on the Skeena River. (*From a painting by Emily Carr, Permanent Canadian Collection, Vancouver Art Gallery*)

From the vast fields of Peace River country . . . (*British Columbia Government Photograph*)

from mountain pockets, like this one in the Coast Mountains near Lytton . . . (*Photo by Jack V. Long*)

the grain of British Columbia farmers . . .
(*Photo by Donovan Clemson*)

. . . is shipped to Pacific and Atlantic ports from Vancouver's elevators.
(*Photo by Harry Cantlon*)

A float village on the west coast of Vancouver Island. (*Photo by Jack Cash*)

Tugs escorting log booms to sawmill or paper mill are a familiar sight on coastal waters, rivers and lakes. This one happens to be on Shuswap Lake. (*Photo by Donovan Clemson*)

By Saturday evening the cannery docks at Prince Rupert's Port Edward are thick with seiners and gillnetters returned from a week at distant fishing grounds. (*British Columbia Government Photograph*)

Gillnetter fishermen mending their nets, Queen Charlotte Islands. (*British Columbia Government Photograph*)

Halibut boats gathering for the opening of the fishing season.
(*Photo by Parry Films*)

From Deadman Valley in the Cariboo, beef cattle go to market.
(*Photo by Donovan Clemson*)

Tomato growing near Lillooet. (*Photo by Jack V. Long*)

Zucca melon "patch" at Osoyoos, Southern Okanagan. (*British Columbia Government Photograph*)

The Lower Mainland's vanishing "Garden of Eden" (*British Columbia Government Photograph*)

Almost anywhere, at almost any level, skiing. This is Grouse Mountain, eight miles from the business centre of Vancouver. (*British Columbia Government Photograph*)

On summer evenings in the primeval forest setting of Stanley Park, Theatre Under the Stars (British Columbia's only professional theatre) presents a series of musical comedies. (*Rolly Ford Photos*)

Day or night, rain or shine, more than 20,000 fans watch professional football games. Here, the Vancouver Lions vs. the Saskatchewan Rough Riders. (*Rolly Ford Photos*)

Ten winners out of 25,000 competitors in Vancouver's annual Salmon Derby. (*Photo by Brian Kent*)

"Merry Christmas" from the Parliament Buildings, Victoria.
(*Canadian Pacific Railway Photo*)

At Bamfield, corner of the Pacific Ocean and Barkley Sound, a private swimming pool. (*British Columbia Government Travel Bureau Photograph*)

Year-round sport in Victoria: antique hunting. (*Canadian Pacific Railway Photo*)

Victoria golf course on the Strait of Juan de Fuca, with the Olympic Mountains in the background. (*Canadian Pacific Railway Photo*)

Cariboo working-cowboy star of Williams Lake Rodeo. (*Evergreen Press Photo*)

University of British Columbia campus from the air, Howe Sound in the background. (*Department of Extension, University of British Columbia*)

In another of Kelowna's interesting combinations of modern design, stucco and colour, B. C. Fruit Processors, Ltd., has made banking and fruit-processing history ever since it was organized in 1946. Then, on a few antiquated buildings and machines, they borrowed more than $250,000. With that and three-quarters of a million more advanced by the growers, they invested in plant and equipment. In 1954, when they were producing a million cases of apple juice, they returned $1 million to the growers.

Some years ago, apricot growers feared they could not market all their harvest. B. C. Processors devised an Apricot Nectar that saved the crop and established a permanent market. For that good deed they recently were rewarded—by accident.

Thirsty delegates to an annual meeting of B. C. Fruits tapped the Apricot Nectar dispenser so steadily that the thick juice clogged the works. To clear them, some helpful soul emptied a half dozen cans of apple juice into the machine. Dispenser restored, Apricot Nectar was served again. To loud complaints that it wasn't as good as it had been!

B. C. Processors' delegates said not a word, but after the meeting they rushed to their laboratories to mix apple juice and Nectar until they arrived at a completely new fruit juice. In itself, "Applecot" is more refreshing than either of its forebears; mixed with gin, a *succès fou.*

The hot afternoon I visited the plant was applesauce day. McIntosh fragrance, delicate as a good perfume, veined the cool, airy workrooms, Skipping along tiny overhead trolleys, little cans tinkle-tinkled like Chinese wind bells. Bright apples tumbled into an involved apparatus to be washed and, twenty operations and as many minutes later, to emerge as sauce, tinned and wrapped in shining red, black and white labels. On their appointed days, peaches, plums and apricots make that same cheerful journey into sauces, fillers, juices.

Most interesting feature of all these young industries was the youngish executives' and technicians' boundless enthusiasm for the "Big Business" possibilities of their enterprises. "It's a game I could play forty-eight hours a day," one told me. "Of course, it's fine to own my home and car, to know I can send my children to college, travel—all that. But that has nothing to do with it, really. And that's rather a joke on me— on a lot of us, I imagine. I remember in college how cynical we used to be, looking across the border, about 'American materialism.' Now, here we are, on the road to the same thing and calling it 'Canadian progress'! Whatever it is, I'm for it. I never had so much fun in my life."

This was the height of the peach season. I listened to "fruit talk," saw, smelled, touched, tasted a variety of processed and cooked fruits. The one thing I could not do was to get a fresh peach. Hotels and restaurants did not serve them! Hostesses considered them too "common" to offer a guest! And, thanks to Kelownians' friendliness and generosity in driving me from appointment to engagement until long after all shops were closed, my every hope of buying them was foiled.

Kelowna lies in a cup of hills, just where Lake Okanagan tightens its belt before making that sweeping U turn. In population, it is a little larger than Vernon; in years, little more than fifty. Yet its modern appearance, facilities and established atmosphere compare with those of cities two and three times its age and ten to twenty times its size.

As one of the first cities in the Province to be zoned, its residential, commercial and industrial districts are separate and defined. No street is a mixture. With a seven-mile-wide control zone ringing its boundaries, no hodgepodge of cheap, temporary structures clutters the outskirts.

The City Centre is typical of its advanced thinking. In long, low stucco buildings, City Hall, post office, Arena, Public Library, all city services, are framed in landscaped lawns and gardens. A municipal parking lot does away with street parking and parking meters. Of its eight parks, five overlook Okanagan Lake. Residential streets are parklike, too, with arched trees and continuous gardens.

Who did the thinking? "Those old jokers," as the city founders are remembered affectionately. Largely British, they did not come here merely to make a living. They came to live a good, well-rounded life. When incorporated in 1905, Kelowna had but six hundred people. Yet, to make sure that Okanagan Lake waterfront did not become an eyesore of sawmills, docks, railroad tracks and warehouses, they bought and transformed a large and beautiful section into even more beautiful City Park. Ever since, city fathers have walked in their footsteps.

Kelowna's origin, however, dates back to 1859, when Father Pandosy and five other Oblates of Mary Immaculate followed the lake to a sandy cove four miles distant. Impressed with the immense "tillable lands" about it, they founded a mission for the Salish Indians. The next year a landseeker, staking a claim about it, elevated the cove to the valley's first permanent settlement.

The city's name derives from *Nor-kwa-stin*, Salish for a hard black rock used to sharpen flints. Or so says the Okanagan Historical Society. Popular local belief holds that it descends from a colourful Frenchman who joined the settlement in 1862. Because of his rampant red hair and beard, the Indians called him "Brown Bear." Because of his prowess as a hunter, the settlers changed that to *Kelowna*, "Grizzly Bear." The name followed him to the claim he staked in what is now the colourful city's townsite.

"If we had an auditorium large enough to seat two to four thousand people," a backer of the Artists Series said, "we could bring the greatest singers and symphonies, the best plays, to Kelowna. We have the audience—particularly among our 'Olde England' set! They seldom appear in public, but for anything 'cultural' they come out in force, feather boas, lorgnettes, opera capes, monocles and all."

Tourists are a million-dollar industry. They come in spring to the "Valley of the Blossoms." They come from spring to fall to the sixty lakes within a 25-mile radius. They come in fall when millions of red-ripe apples glisten like festive tinsel balls in the orchards and, Heaven alone knows why, in this land of milk and honey Kelowna stages a Stampede.

Especially they come in early August for the now internationally famous four-day Regatta. Then against that background of lake and hills and sun- or starlit skies, a crowded program presents world and Olympic swimming and diving champions and Canadian water-ski champions, war canoe and other races, water carnivals with their rhythmic water ballets, and above all, the lovely Lady of the Lake Pageant.

Whenever and whyever they come, they keep one eye open for controversial Ogopogo. The name dates back to a London song hit of the 1920's which lauded a creature whose mother was an earwig, whose father was a whale. But long before any white man entered the valley, the Salish worshipped N'ha-a-itk, a monster living in a cave beneath the waters of Okanagan Lake's U turn. To paddle safely past its lair, they early learned to toss a dog or other animal into the lake as a "sacrifice."

The first white man to claim sight of it may have been the lumber camp cook who went out one morning in 1896 to fish, returned, whey-faced, to babble about a sea serpent looping about the water. Since then hundreds, many with 20-20 physical and mental vision, have testified to its existence.

The creature is described as twenty feet long, with a heavy snake's body and the well-bearded head of goat or horse. Real or mythical, its goings-on titillate Kelownians and visitors alike. As one leaves the city, southbound, the last sight his eyes record is a life-sized conception of Ogopogo in hurried flight from the Museum to the cool depths of City Park.

23

WHERE THE WAYS MEET

On a late August afternoon, Okanagan Lake's final thirty-nine miles are an adventure in beauty. The higher the bus climbed the ridge road above the northern arm of its U turn the wider, smoother, bluer the waters. And, after a near-cloudburst the midnight before, the greener the ponderosa pine and sagebrush matting hills that lifted straight from the far shore.

From the apex of the U, we looked down to see the widespread arms of the lake clasped about miles of interlocked hills. To the east beyond the southern arm, Little White and Greyback Mountains, two 7,000-foot outriders of the Monashee Range, also basked in radiant light. Not a boat moved on the serene blue waters, not a cloud in the serene blue sky. Not a sign of human existence appeared anywhere.

Though only fifty minutes from either Kelowna or Penticton, the entire panorama was a wild, lone land of greens, blues, purples, and dark, rain-washed rocks, sometimes curiously featured with heavy brows, noses, jaws. On just such a day the first Coastal Salish to penetrate the valley must have paused before just such a view and, awed by those eroded rocks, named the lake *Okanagan*, "Big Heads."

Every moment we detoured inland seemed so long that when we returned I was not surprised to see that the hills had grown into young mountains of sheer rock and white silt.

Inland, apple orchards continued to ripen. But more and more cherry, apricot and peach orchards, their labours over for the year, were pulling together their picker-mauled branches. Once the driver paused significantly beside a peach tree bowed beneath rosy, tree-ripened fruit. Woe to the peach-surfeited young man who commented, "Left for the birds, and they can have them!" While the rest of us remained speechless— and peachless, the driver shrugged, drove on.

Midway of the southern arm of the lake, Summerland was a beauty spot with a beauty spot in the Dominion Experimental Station. Its laboratories work to improve old fruit strains and develop new ones, like the Jubilee and Spartan apples. Raying out from this centre, the slopes and benches of small valleys wore orchards and gardens reminiscent of the impossibly perfect illustrations with which seed catalogues seduce the layman.

Too soon a chatter of white notes rising from a green keyboard ahead marked the end of Okanagan Lake and the beginning of Lake Skaha. At one side a white note expanded into an old paddle-wheeled steamer fixed on shore—the S.S. *Sicamous*, last of the stern-wheelers that once plied the lake. Rescued from ignoble decay by the service clubs of Penticton, it now is a delightful place to dine and dance and enjoy a superb view of the lake and king-sized foothills of the Monashees.

The bus coasted down a gentle incline to turn at right angles onto the land bridge between the two lakes. The white notes reshaped themselves as tree-embedded homes and buildings. Penticton!

Its odd name has two possible translations, both applicable today. The Salish, who once had had to migrate seasonally to live on fish and berries in summer, game in winter, here found them all. In addition, Okanagan Lake on one side and Skaha on the other tempered summer's heat; foothills warded off winter's bitterest blasts. *Pen-hic-ton*, they named the land bridge, "Place-to-stay-the-year-round."

To identify this spot "Where-(water)ways-meet" for early fur traders, their descendants said in greeting, *"Pen-hic-ton."* Today, with air lines, rail and highways coming and going in all directions, Penticton is the southern entrance to the valley and one of the most accessible cities in the Province.

For a time, in fact, its diverse interests and points of view appeared to ride off in so many directions that I wondered what held it together as a community. Three towns more unlike than agricultural Vernon, the-good-life Kelowna, and aggressive

Penticton surely are not found often within a distance of seventy-three miles.

Vernon's soils, according to a Provincial agricultural expert, are admirable for grains and vegetables; Kelowna's for apples; Penticton's for soft fruits. And about it an area extending from the International Boundary, forty-five miles south, to twenty-five miles north does account for more than 90 per cent of British Columbia's soft fruit production.

Cherries, plums, pears, strawberries, loganberries, all kinds of berries, all kinds of vegetables—cover valley floor and lower slopes with an endless mosaic of blended greens. As the one region in all Canada where conditions are right for growing apricots commercially, quantities are produced here. Also apples. Above all, peaches!

Forty years ago, the extreme southern end of Canada's share of the Okanagan was a veritable desert of cactus, sagebrush, and rattlesnakes, shadowed by 6,500- to 8,500-foot mountains. Fur trappers and brigades following the Lower Columbia to the Okanagan River, to Okanagan Lake, to Kamloops, knew it best. Traces of that historic trail still can be seen there. It still boasts (?) the longest, hottest, driest summer in Canada.

After World War I, to establish a project for veterans, the Provincial government introduced irrigation and fruit culture. While waiting for their young trees to mature, veterans cultivated cucumbers and tomatoes. Today, this Oliver-Osoyoos area contributes a stream of cherries and other fruits and vegetables to Okanagan's cornucopia. One, the Osoyoos-grown zucca melon, is building a reputation once held for generations by a single family in Czechoslovakia. The monopoly was broken when a British Columbia-bound emigrant slipped a few of the closely guarded seeds across the Atlantic.

The stars that rule my destiny may have felt they had done enough in providing ideal weather at all but one of my many destinations. They took no thought for each community's Big Event. By a few days fore or aft, I *always* missed the salmon derbies, rodeos, stampedes, cattle shows, regattas. Now at Penticton, I had missed the 10-year-old August Peach Festival when visitors revel in tree-ripened Rochesters, Vadettes, Elbertas—all the nationally famous varieties—and, so inspired, square-dance in the streets.

Though the one orchard I had time to visit was dedicated to Delicious apples, fruit-culture-wise and historically it was of double-pronged interest. Behind an avenue of *olive* trees, its braced branches bear more than 2,000 bushels per acre of the spicy fruit in "good seasons," 1,000 in "poor." Since I had been told that so-so ranches harvest 200 to 250 bushels and the average yield for good ranches is 1,000, I naturally wanted to know the secret of its success.

"Good soil, plenty of sunshine, *and*," said the rancher, with a gleam in his eye, "*flume irrigation*." Sprinkler versus flume irrigation is an increasingly hot issue in the Okanagan. Severely singed several times from contact with it, I hastily asked if the ranch always had grown fruit. No, once it had been part of the Ellis Ranch.

The Ellis Ranch, founded in 1866 by Thomas Ellis, a dynamic Irishman, with a few cattle on a few acres and expanded to thirty thousand acres, dominated the region for thirty years. In 1892, when his ranch, his store, his steamer (the first on Okanagan Lake), and a small Catholic church were all there was to Penticton, he laid out two thousand acres as a townsite. But for so long had he intimidated incoming fruit-growers who thought to settle on the open ranges his cattle roamed that nothing happened. With little better luck, a land company some years later sank $150,000 in irrigating and subdividing part of the Ellis Estate for fruit ranches.

A rumor changed the picture. Penticton was to be made the western terminal of the Kettle Valley Railway!

More than a score of real estate firms rushed in to sell southern Okanagan lands for $2,000 to $3,000 an acre. By 1915, when the railway arrived, fruit ranches in their turn had put the cattle ranches to flight. Today every foot of land that can be irrigated is under orchard or farm.

And Penticton, with almost twelve thousand people, is both the metropolis of the Okanagan and, with boundaries since

1948 enclosing ten square miles, physically one of the largest municipalities in the Province. Ranchers whose orchards the new town limits embrace see clearly the advantages of municipal irrigation, electricity, fire protection, etc., but take a dim view of paying city taxes on agricultural lands.

Its own irrigation system is not Penticton's only original idea. Not by chance, its population is almost entirely of British descent. Though Indians work in the city, they live on the reservation outside. Unlike most Provincial cities, especially in the north where Chinese operate numerous restaurants, own much property, Penticton has but one. Most Provincial cities lack sufficient parks. Penticton has a score of parks and squares. And new citizens continue to bring original ideas with them.

Two young men from a Prairie Province, both under twenty-five, were telling the director of the Board of Trade when I dropped in that an uncle had offered to set them up in business anywhere in Canada. Hearing that Penticton was a prosperous, progressive town with a future, they had been looking it over! Now all that remained was to decide what business to buy. What would he advise?

"That would depend, wouldn't it," the director asked, "on how much you are prepared to invest?" Said one, "Oh, he promised us $50,000." Said the other, "Or $100,000 if we need it." Cautiously the director added, "And on your own training and experience." Blank looks answered him. Neither had any of either.

By the time I'd listened to Director Patton answer their questions and those of others on subjects ranging from anthropology to Indian beadwork I thought to risk the most difficult one of my own. Though Penticton is the peach capital of British Columbia, it was little better than Kelowna as far as getting my hands on a peach was concerned. So, when he turned to me, I asked, "Where can I get a ripe peach?" As he reached for his telephone, he said, "At my home. My wife's been trying to catch up with you for days."

Not only did I have huge, rosy, juicy peaches to hold, to eat, and to carry away. I had one more opportunity to enjoy the relaxed, informal hospitality characteristic of British Columbians and to marvel again at the cosmopolitanism of what Victoria and Vancouver call "the interior."

While travelling about the Province, I had grown accustomed to hearing host, hostess and chance acquaintance remark, "When we lived in Borneo"—or Papua, Indonesia, Paraguay, as well as better known corners of the world. Now the Pattons—and their home—were fascinating with tales and mementoes of their years in Abyssinia during the course of their odyssey, when first married, to teach their way around the globe.

Packing, canning, processing, shipping fruits and vegetables are, of course, Penticton's first industry. Outstanding is the Penticton Co-operative Growers' packing plant, owned by 234 local growers.

During the height of the picking season, its trucks collect 15,000 boxes of fruit a day from their orchards. In its huge workroom, expert women pack 10,000 boxes a day. The afternoon I was there, it was loading sixteen freight cars with 800 boxes each; can load twenty. Or, in refrigerated rooms, it can store 350,000 boxes, and does by the end of November when the apple crop is in, to remain until the fruit is ready for market, or vice versa.

Accessibility, climate, beautiful setting, numerous lakes and creamy beaches, good fishing and hunting, combine to make tourists Penticton's second major interest. Vancouver and Lower Mainland holiday makers swarm its streets, hotels, restaurants, en route to resorts and lake cottages. Others come from all parts of Canada and the American Pacific coast.

From Mt. Munson's lookout, just beyond the city, one sees more than an all-embracing view of foothills and lakes. Long freight yards, identify it as a CPR division point. Trucks streaming over the highways like ants from a disturbed hill indicate a trucking centre. Sawmills and light industries ring the outskirts.

And the stunning view, with constantly changing patterns

and colours of sun and shadow on hills and lakes, is only one
reason why Penticton also is the centre of a growing art colony.
The varied orchards and gardens, the Indian reservation bent
round Mt. Apex and the World War II veterans' housing
project, gay as a zinnia bed on Okanagan Lake's west bank, are
others. Here are many artists, among them Tony Only, whose
work is well known in Canada and the British Isles.

But what held the town together? All at once I realized that
everyone I'd met or listened in on, from great-grandmothers to
small fry, had been telling me. Vancouver goes mad over
professional football; Port Alberni, over basketball and its
champion team; Dawson Creek, over skating and its skating
stars. Every Provincial village, town and city has its favourite
sport. But language fails to describe Penticton's pride and joy
in hockey.

Though its team was organized in 1952 as a "two-bit local
outfit" and "never won a game until the last five minutes,"
it won them all. In two years, as Provincial and national
champion, it met and defeated Russia's top quintet, to bring
Penticton the world title.

Local fans glory in the fame it gives their home town in the
sports world. Businessmen value it as a forceful tourist attraction. Women with no knowledge of the game are thrilled by
its beauty and the courage and spirit of the players. On whatever else Pentictonians' views may clash, their interests compete, they are united in a strong community loyalty behind
their hockey team.

THE KOOTENAYS

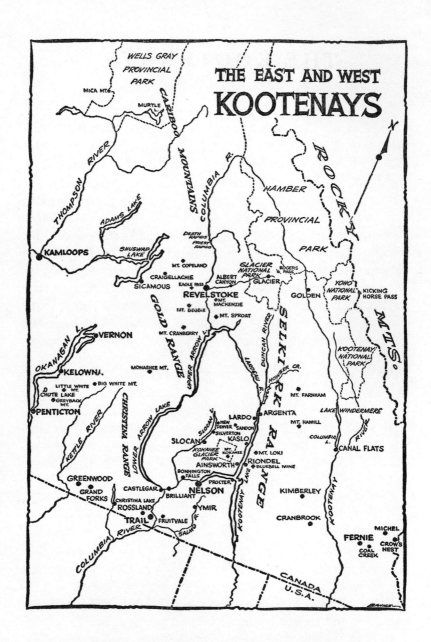

THE EAST AND WEST
KOOTENAYS

24

THE KOOTENAYS TAKE
SOME EXPLAINING

Explorers, fur traders and others did more than name the mountain ranges that stripe British Columbia north to south: Coast, Monashee, Selkirk, Rockies. They gave individual names —Purcell, Gold, Clachnacudain and many more—to subranges. The result is as involved as a Biblical chapter of begats.

Whatever their names, the ranges and sub-ranges make the Province in general, the Kootenays in particular, a delight for the traveller. To railroad builders, however, they are a chronic migraine headache. That headache became acute in 1858 when the Crown sent out the Palliser Expedition to lay out an all British-America route for a railway to the Pacific. Finding the Gold Range immediately west of the Columbia River impassable, the expedition reported that no continuous route north of the International Boundary existed.

Seven years later, while blazing a trail across that impassable barrier to enable Cariboo miners to reach the new gold strike in the Columbia's Big Bend, Walter Moberly paused to potshot a nest of eaglets with his revolver. But when their distraught parents flew away up a small valley, he followed—to discover a pass he named Eagle in their honour. Via Eagle Pass, in 1887, the Canadian Pacific Railway reached Vancouver.

One section of the Province took no part in the wild rejoicing. The CPR had entered British Columbia about two hundred miles north of the Boundary and on a gentle incline descended to Kamloops before turning south to follow the Thompson and Fraser Rivers to the Pacific. The area between the railroad's right of way and the Boundary—shaped, appropriately enough, like one of its own mountains—remained high, dry and transportationless.

In that mountain-shaped triangle three mountain-walled valleys ran north-south along outsized rivers and lakes. The

219

fertile Okanagan in central British Columbia. East of it, the Columbia and the Kootenay, known respectively as West and East Kootenay, rich in forests and minerals. True, surveys had been made across them, but one and all proved that construction of a railway through such a jungle of mountains was impossible. Worse still! Even if possible, these pioneer studies made plain, the thin economic future of such unlikely country never could warrant the formidable costs of building.

If, east and west, mountains isolated the three orphans from the world and one another, their rivers and lakes opened easy passage south. From the early 1860's, pack trains laden with gold, silver, lead and other ores and products from the Kootenays plodded two to four hundred miles to smelters, mining and logging camps in Montana, Idaho and Washington.

Sensitive to that sad sight, the Great Northern and allied American railroads based on Spokane, Washington, sped five branch lines across the Boundary and supplemented them with paddle-wheelers on lakes and rivers. For twenty years, 1890-1910, the Kootenays were as solidly a part of the vast Inland Empire revolving about Spokane as the American Northwest.

To cut off this lucrative trade, Dominion and Provincial governments urged the Canadian Pacific to construct a railway along the Boundary. In 1898, it did build a branch line from Lethbridge, Alberta, through Crow's Nest Pass, to an empty spot in East Kootenay known as Joseph's Prairie. Thereupon, the American lines lowered their rates, added more trackage, bigger and better stern-wheelers. Well pleased, most of the Kootenays' trade continued to funnel south.

The Great Northern's survey of still another branch line from Spokane to Penticton to assist the young fruit industry to reach a market was one of the very last straws. Under pressure, the Canadian Pacific extended its Crow's Nest Pass line across West Kootenay and the Okanagan to join the transcontinental line to Vancouver. But it had so little confidence in the new addition's future that, to dissociate it from the great main line, it named its unwanted offspring, Kettle Valley Railway.

The American railroads continued their solicitude until the

Kootenays' mines began to wear out in the nineteen-twenties and -thirties. By that time the Okanagan could stand on its own feet. But the Kootenays were a stormy sea of Monashees and Selkirks, topped by icefields and snow-capped peaks.

One hundred miles of that stormy sea lay between the two railroads. The fleets of stern-wheelers on their lakes and rivers shrank to one or two. Only a few small and widely separated areas were arable and level enough for orchard or field. And now that most of their mines were dead or dying, Victoria and Vancouver had no more concern for them than they once had had for the coastal prima donnas.

The Kootenays thus became British Columbia's "unknown country." With the exception of a few towns and mines, little is known of them today. The post-World War II boom which has rolled right up to the Yukon border only now is knocking at their doors.

With Eagle Pass, the Kootenays' mountain ranges extended Canada's western boundary to the Pacific. But as history makers they run a poor second to the Kootenays' two great rivers. More than a century before, the Columbia, aided and abetted by the Kootenay, had determined the settlement and partition of the whole Pacific Northwest.

The Columbia, rising at Canal Flat in Rocky Mountain Trench, about seventy-five miles north of the Boundary, runs north. The Kootenay, rising sixty miles north of Canal Flat, starts south. For a time, moving in opposite directions, they parallel one another. At one point, less than a mile apart, they could have saved themselves, British Columbia—and me!—considerable stress and strain if they had joined forces then and there. But the Kootenay, already well grown, upstaged its puny, younger neighbour to continue south.

A hard-headed young realist with ideas about getting rich quick, the Columbia continued north almost 175 miles before swerving round the last spur of the Selkirks and turning south in a Big Bend. Boiling out of one loud canyon into another in a succession of chutes and death-dealing rapids, it pockets a succession of rivers and streams fed by eternal snows and glaciers on the mountains. Fat and prosperous, it then expands into two long, handsome lakes, handsomely framed in glitter-peaked Monashees and Selkirks before it resumes river proportions and turns east.

The footless type that leaps before it looks, the 406-mile Kootenay explores western Montana and eastern Idaho, a bony land devoid of glaciers and nourishing rivers. So thin and jittery that its course looks accordion-pleated, it wriggles back into East Kootenay to drink long and deeply of an immense lake imprisoned in the Selkirks. Sleek again but no wiser, it bursts out of the lake that now bears its name to return south on a westerly course.

To end this anthropomorphism, before someone becomes ill, the westerly flowing Kootenay meets the east-flowing Columbia about forty miles north of the Boundary. Together, as the Columbia, they turn south to flow through Washington and Oregon for 745 miles before reaching their final destination in the Pacific at Astoria, Oregon. There they occupied themselves with building an immense sandbar across their exit.

What they did or where they went didn't matter until the white man came along with a headful of ideas about possessions, nationality and horsepower. But ever since Captain Vancouver sighted the Columbia's wide mouth in 1792, it has been winding in and out of Canadian and American history.

Like Spanish and Russian navigators before him, Vancouver thought the sandbar across its mouth impassable and sailed on. Less than a month later, the American captain, Robert Gray, sighted the mouth and sailed in. After exploring the river for fifteen miles and naming it Columbia for his ship, he sailed out. And that was that for almost twenty years.

In 1807, David Thompson, then head of a North West Company trading post in the Rockies, discovered the source of the Columbia. Believing it to be the Great River of the West that would lead to the Western Sea and so to the Orient, he longed to trace it to its mouth. But the fur trade, hostile Indians, and the shenanigans of the Columbia itself delayed his arrival there until July 15, 1811.

He was three and a half months too late. On March 29, the first contingent of John Jacob Astor's Pacific Fur Company had arrived by way of Cape Horn and was busy erecting Fort Astoria.

Thereafter, while Britain and the United States carried on the so-so War of 1812 on the east coast, the two British and American fur companies carried on a no-holds-barred war on the west for possession of the Columbia's mouth. (A free-handed if obscure procedure that somehow signified possession of a river's valley.)

Each won alternate rounds until 1814, when by what the Nor'Westers considered a legitimate purchase and the Americans didn't, Astoria changed hands. No sooner had this been done than the British war sloop *Raccoon* slipped into the river, its Captain William Black on fire with expectation that an Astor trading post would be a fabulous prize of war.

Though the fort was a collection of log huts his guns could reduce to matches, the captain was enraged to learn that now, as a British property, it was not subject to seizure. To have something to show for his long voyage he required it to surrender anyway, then renamed it Fort George.

That was that, also, until by the treaty of peace ending the War of 1812 all territories seized by British or American forces had to be returned. Mr. Astor then asked a question. Had Astoria been "captured" by purchase or as a prize of war? Thanks to the terrible-tempered Captain Black, the Peace Commission ruled "prize of war." In 1818, Astoria and all it represented again became American territory.

For Mr. Astor it was a Pyrrhic victory. First North West Company, then Hudson's Bay remained in control of the Columbia until the 1840's, when thousands of Americans followed the 2,020-mile Oregon Trail into its lower valley. The result, in 1846, was the International Boundary agreement.

Known only to fur traders, British Columbia's share of the Columbia continued to gather up its tributaries and, as it swung round its Big Bend, to enclose Selkirks so grand that Canada has established two National Parks—Glacier and Mt.

Revelstoke—within it. Later miners, loggers and, on its lakes, steamboat crews, knew it. After 1940, when a 193-mile highway was completed round it, motorists knew it.

And that was all until, suddenly, as of today—

During its 1,210-mile journey from Canal Flat to the Pacific, the Columbia, with its tributaries, does more than drain 250,000 square miles. Dropping 2,500 feet, through mountains most of the time, it holds the North American record as a source of hydroelectric energy. If and when fully developed, it is estimated that the Columbia system can generate 50 million horsepower or one-third of the total power all the rivers on the continent can produce.

Though only 465 miles of its course drain 37,500 square miles in Canada, they are most strategic miles. In themselves they could generate 4.5 million horsepower. But, more important still, as the headwaters of the Columbia they are under Canada's control.

Until the post-war boom stimulated industrial expansion on a Province-wide scale, all this was of academic interest to British Columbia. Except for five dams generating 700,000 h.p. on the Kootenay River, she made no use of the Columbia's energy. Now, with every community avid for industrial electricity, a power famine is foreshadowed within a decade. In the Columbia's waters that shadow can be washed away.

British Columbia now sees them as a force capable of revolutionizing not only her own economy but western Canada's. To attain that goal, however, she must do more than develop the power in her own share of the Columbia. She must obtain as much as possible of the potential power as yet unused in the freshet waters which every summer pour down from snowfields and glaciers into the Upper Columbia's tributaries.

South of the Boundary, meantime, the Americans of the Pacific Northwest, by a different route, have reached the same conclusion. With an investment of some $2 billion in the erection of eight dams, one of them the Grand Coulee, they have tapped the river for almost nine million horsepower. To meet their own spiralling industrial demands, they now are prepared to double that investment to obtain as much as possible of the potential power in those same unused freshet waters.

To both Canada and the United States the Columbia's power thus has become of paramount significance, economically and politically. Neither country, of course, questions the other's right to develop its own share of the river. Nor does the United States question Canada's control of the headwaters. The issue between them is concerned solely with the floodwaters that flow, unused, to the Pacific.

How to use them to the greatest advantage of each country is the key to the whole explosive question of power development on Canadian-American Boundary rivers. Now in the hands of a joint, high-level ministerial committee, the problem centres about a plan by which a dam on the Upper Columbia, in collaboration with those on the Lower, would generate electricity for the industries of both British Columbia and the American Northwest.

One feature of this plan would divert the waters of the Kootenay into the Columbia at Canal Flat, where the two rivers are less than a mile apart. Another is the 600-foot-high dam to rise on Mica Creek, one of the tributaries which empty into the upper river. Mica Dam then could create an 85-mile-long reservoir in which the freshet waters would be gathered, stored in slack seasons, and fed as required to the American plants on the lower river. In return for the benefits they derive from use of the floodwaters, the Americans would pay the Province in electricity.

This plan slims down the issue to one of the oldest and simplest questions in the world. How much? The question may be simple, but with both sides of the Boundary under heavy pressure to obtain the greatest possible benefits from the same waters, the search for the answer is both involved and prolonged. To the layman it appears to be a cosmic chess game in which the contestants, after various feints to remake the face of the Northwest to the disadvantage of the other, retreat into long, Olympic silences.

But so the game goes. And so goes time. Even when the answer is found, one to two years must pass before Mica Dam can be engineered, seven to ten before it can be completed.

As hosts to this great hydroelectric project, the Kootenays see not only expansion for their own industry but growth and development for every phase of their life—*if* and *when* Mica Dam finally is assured.

25

THE RANGER HAD A WORD FOR IT

With the building of the first railroad in North America, it became an established custom for eager beavers to rush ahead of the rails to take up land at strategic points. On the surveyed route of the Canadian Pacific through British Columbia, what point could be more strategic than the entrance to Eagle Pass?

Long before the rails reached that broad, level bench seventy feet above the Columbia, it was known as Second Crossing because there the trains would cross the river for the second time. After 1883, it took the name of Farwell for the young surveyor who laid out the townsite. After November 7, 1885, when the last spike was driven at Craigellachie in Eagle Pass, the Canadian Pacific renamed it Revelstoke, in gratitude to the English banker whose timely loan made possible the line's completion, and gave it purpose as headquarters of its Mountain Division.

A railroad town it is today, despite its scenically strategic location. Mountains, seventy-five hundred to ten thousand feet, circle it. Through them the Columbia hurtles down from the north in Death Rapids ("Graveyard of the Columbia") and Priest Rapids. From Glacier Park, the Illecillewaet, the river with the most melodic name in Canada, charges through dramatic canyons to join it. From mountain slopes, streams and waterfalls—Begbie, Sutherland, Silvertip, many more—crash into it. Suddenly it quiets, to flow decorously between rocky walls at Revelstoke's feet.

Within a few miles, lovely, blue Williamson and other lakes and streams are alive with trout; mountain forests and crags shelter moose, caribou, mountain goat, bear. In winter Revelstoke is a fairyland for winter sports and camera addicts.

Because the Kootenays' two railroads here are a hundred miles apart, I visited this northern gateway to West Kootenay

227

from Sicamous before going to the Okanagan. Though little more than a 35-mile journey, thanks to passengers and scene, I arrived in a slightly dazed condition.

The conversation of two world-weary young gallants, separated by half a car length, started my head rolling. As I found a seat, one of them yelled, "She told me she weeps and longs for you all the time. You engaged to her?" To which the other yelled back, "Not me, brother, not me!" "Well," persisted the first, "she's engaged to someone." And the second replied, "Thank God!"

If their amours were easy to follow, the antics of small, mad Eagle River were not. Incessantly we crossed and recrossed it as we twisted through mountains smothered in Douglas fir, lodgepole and yellow pine, into wilder mountains. Over them loomed blue peaks, patched with snow.

Kay Falls, a graceful fan of white water, flashed by. Then one immense lake after another spread over the widening valley floor. But when I spoke of them to the conductor, he first was puzzled, then scornful. "Lakes! Those aren't lakes. Just runoff from melting snow and rains on the mountains." As a token of the freshet waters going to waste in the Pacific, these made limpidly clear why the entire Pacific Northwest now considers them so important to its industrial development.

Mountains crowding together brought the lakes to an end. On the west, the Gold Range, as a sub-range of the Monashees, was a solid, 7,000-foot wall. To the east, snow-topped Selkirks rose to nine thousand feet against the blue-taffeta sky.

Abruptly we left them to run out on a long bridge over the wide, polished-platinum Columbia. High on its east bank, Revelstoke was a splash of brilliant lawns and gardens. Behind it, Mt. Revelstoke, rising grandly, diminished the level streets of homes and buildings to a tiny town of toys.

I stepped off the train to see more than a hundred men lounging elbow to elbow against the long platform's iron railing. Others clustered about the station. A four-headed tiger could have prowled unnoticed about their feet. Every eye was fixed on the train.

"Busman's holiday," said the conductor. "Sunday morning kibitzers. More than half this town's connected with the CPR. Walk down that line and all you'll hear is railroad shop talk." I did. And it was.

Kamloops, Penticton and other Provincial towns which serve as division points for CPR, CNR, or both, absorb railroad activities in their diversified economies. But except for a little logging and farming round about and, in summer, tourists, Revelstoke's economic weather rises and falls by the barometer of the CPR. In autumn, when prairie wheat rolls in waves across the mountains to Vancouver, the payroll runs high and the town lives high. During slack seasons or when layoffs or strikes threaten, it battens down its hatches and buttons up its wallets.

The psychological effect is even more apparent. Railroad personnel for the most part live as close as possible to station and yards. Non-railroad residents live as far away as possible. Because the "railroaders" so often are moved from point to point, they have little interest in the local social or civic life, no feeling of "belonging" to town or province. Yet, though they keep themselves to themselves, they move in two different circles. One revolves about the conductor-brakeman set; the other, about the engineer-fireman.

Railroad wives are responsible for the last word in dress, home furnishings, foods and other merchandise in Revelstoke's display windows. Because they travel on passes, can take off at will for Calgary, Vancouver, Spokane, Seattle, they always know—and demand—the latest.

But the railroaders account for only 50 per cent of the town's apathy toward Mica Dam. Though its proposed location is but eighty-two miles north and, as the only town in the region, Revelstoke undoubtedly will play a leading role in its construction and later, non-railroaders also refuse to become excited. "We've seen too many great possibilities unfulfilled. Now our motto *always* is, 'We'll believe it when we see it.' "

Not *always*. Loath as they are to admit it, they do entertain occasional tingles of anticipation for 1960, when the Trans-

Canada Highway across British Columbia will be completed. Then an 88-mile short cut across the Selkirks within the Columbia's Big Bend will give the Kootenays quicker and easier access to one another and to all Canada. From Golden in East Kootenay, by way of Rogers Pass, the highway will run through Glacier National Park to Revelstoke to open to motorists for the first time some of the most magnificent scenery in the Western Hemisphere. Revelstokians vision their tourist trade multiplying by leaps and bounds.

Engineers who know Rogers Pass compare it with the eighty-two miles of the Trans-Canada Highway through Yoho National Park. There it enters British Columbia in Kicking Horse Pass. About this narrow, 4,500-foot-high natural bridge, Rockies rise to such heights that many never lose their snow and glacier crowns. And they tread so closely on one another that to gain a mere ninety-five feet in altitude the Canadian Pacific had to spiral two 3,000-foot-long tunnels through the hearts of two of them. Lakes are glacial-blue reflectors. Waterfalls sometimes seem to drop from the sky.

At times this Yoho section of the highway had to be carved out of solid rock cliffs. Silt, sand and rock had to be packed 250 feet deep to fill river gorges, reduce inclines, and an old glacier melted away. The average cost of construction per mile was $300,000, with some miles ranging from three-quarters to a million dollars.

Rogers Pass promises "even tougher going," greater engineering feats. Snow-crowned Selkirks, 10,000 to 11,500 feet high, crowd 500-square-mile Glacier Park. Icefields and glaciers caused by the height of the mountains and an annual snowfall of more than seventy feet crowd their upper basins and shoulders. Illecillewaet Glacier, the largest, has a fall of thirty-five hundred feet from crest to snout. Deep valleys dense with forest; alpine meadows above the treelines; mysterious Nakimu Caves; foaming streams, lakes, waterfalls, hitherto known only to the hardiest mountaineers—add up, as one described it, to "an untouched beauty the long-sung Alps cannot offer."

But I hadn't come to Revelstoke solely to see the town and

look up at mountains. After months of doing nothing else, I wanted to look *at* them, face to face. And Mt. Revelstoke, as Canada's westernmost National Park, is surrounded by a hundred square miles of Monashees and Selkirks. I lost no time finding a taxi to carry me up the Royal Highway to its summit.

So named because many members of the Royal Family have travelled it, the 18-mile highway spirals through forests of melancholy-winged cedar, aromatic balsam, the whole family of conifers. Every turn reveals wider views of immediate mountains and of new ranges piling up behind them. Of the foam-white Illecillewaet and small, silver rivers wriggling through massed forests. Of Eagle Pass. Of the great twist of the Columbia. Of the town, now a mural painted on a floor. Together, they build to a climax of views on the 6,530-foot summit.

The summit itself is a climax. From mid-July to mid-September its alpine meadows, beginning with white anemones and slide lilies, range through every colour and kind of mountain flower. Now, at the close of the season, they were white with heather, scarlet with Indian paintbrush. In the midst of them, Heather Lake, blue as the sky in its tiny bowl of evergreens, mirrored rocky or snow-clad peaks miles away.

There I got my wish with a vengeance. Monarchs of the two great mountain families encircled me. Behind them others rose higher and higher, to merge their blue silhouettes with the sky, their hoary heads with mountainous cumulus clouds.

To north, east and south, Selkirks patterned the horizon. Behind Mt. La Forme (7,500), and Mt. Dickey (8,000), the Clachnacudains were a nightmare of sheer rock peaks, precipices, basins, in all shades of grey, scarred with yellow. In the clear sunlight, Gordon Glacier was a dazzle beside Mt. Harry (8,985) and the two snow-and-ice Alberts—North (9,560) and South (10,000). Handsomest of all, the southern trio—Cartier (8,600), Tilley (8,065) and McKenzie (7,720)—had the authority and elegance of thoroughbreds. North and west, the Monashees' Mt. Copeland (7,550), Mt. McPherson (7,965) and Mt. Begbie (8,965) with its glacier, ignored both the bluish blurs of forest fires thickening about their knees and their own Gold Range.

Though the shy young ranger on duty bemoaned my arrival at "the very worst time," when old snows were vanishing, fresh snows still to come, I gazed and gazed. Only a genius, simpleton or child, however, can remain long in the presence of grandeur without feeling ridiculously impertinent. Yet how can one who is neither turn away without a word of appreciation for all they represent in beauty, time and continuity? While I stood numb and dumb, the ranger, by a devious route, supplied the word.

Still excited over the day he had noticed "red snow dancing" below Begbie's peak, he said, "I thought it was insects and wouldn't believe it when somebody told me it was red algae. So I just ran over to see for myself." Misreading my astonishment that to descend Mt. Revelstoke, cross the Columbia and climb seven to eight thousand feet up trackless Begbie could come under the head of "running over," he added, "Of course, I don't go over to *any* of those peaks on days tourists are likely to come up here."

To perish that thought, he dutifully told me of the summit's popularity in summer with artists, including Revelstoke's own well-known Sophie Atkinson. Of the Nels Nelson Ski Jump, one of the two ski runs in North America approved by the *Fédération Internationale de Ski*, where world champions train and many world records have been set. And of the thrills local skiers know.

"To be up here on a night when the snow's so deep the Lodge is buried and every inch of every mountain—every tree —every *thing* as far as you can see—the whole world—is brand new—and white—and so still—and the full moon maybe's shining on the snow—or Northern Lights is throwing colours around like crazy—" Helplessly entangled in sentence and memories, he plunged into a silence in search of adequate words, came out of it with an awed and gusty "Gee!"

I took one long, last look round the encircling peaks and said to them gratefully in my mind, "Gee!"

26

BRITISH COLUMBIA RIDES A STAR

Under dimmed street lights, Penticton was a shadowy forest the morning I boarded the eastbound train at the ungodly hour of 4:30 for Castlegar and Trail in southern West Kootenay. Okanagan Lake, a well of night. The Monashee foothills blurs against an ebony sky frosted with acid-clear stars.

After half an hour of climbing, while the foothills became an irregular wave pattern against soft delft sky, golden sequins clustered on a bluish belt of lake below. Penticton and Summerland. Climbing, climbing, more and more slowly, while thinning darkness revealed a savage gorge below, lights again glittered into view on a long, satin-grey lake. Penticton and Summerland! Still we climbed, through jagged rock cuts beneath towering crests, to see high against milky-blue mountains and a white sky, a wild, wild world of pine tops, gigantic rocks, and precipices that dropped into inky crevasses. And far, far below—more lights. Summerland again! And Penticton! Not only on the wrong side of the train but on the wrong side of Lake Okanagan.

This is what comes of less than two hours' sleep and no breakfast, I was telling myself when the conductor came along. Neither Penticton nor Summerland had moved an inch, said he. Didn't I know I was on the Kettle Valley Railway?

From Penticton at 1,120 feet altitude to Chute Lake at 3,907 is fifteen miles. But so massed are the Monashees that to travel that distance the train had to crawl thirty miles round and round and up one mountain, always at a grade more than double the usual one per cent.

To construct this section of the railway, the engineers were confronted with terrain that required its rails to climb up for 115 miles, down for sixty-nine and up and down for sixty. Thousand-foot gorges had to be spanned with wooden trestles,

233

sometimes a hundred feet high and two to four times that long. In one area that can be seen at a glance, nineteen of them were necessary. For each beam in each trestle, a huge tree was felled and hewed to exact measurements. To secure the million feet of lumber each trestle required, sawmills were set up on the spot.

If the railroad builders proved the impossible possible, passengers on the first sketchy trains found their gymnastics impossible to take with equanimity. Especially those trestles! Women fainted or prayed. Men, including train porters, threw themselves face down in the aisles. Many were nauseated

Steel trestles or land-fills replace most of them today. Other hazards have been tamed. But the journey from Penticton to Castlegar still offers all the thrills—and more!—of a 233-mile roller coaster through mountain, river and lake country so varied it looks improbable.

When we stopped for the first time four hours later at a box station and a sawmill, I was as limp as a boat flag trailing in the wash of a launch. In those four hours we had travelled more than ninety miles to attain at Beaverdell, almost due east of Penticton, a crow-flight distance of twenty-five!

The train had climbed that first mountain to Chute Lake, a pond webbed with waterlilies, merely to take a leaf out of the Columbia's book. Turning north there, it followed Okanagan Lake almost to Kelowna before swinging round a spur of Monashees in a big bend to head south.

At first glance one never would suppose the round-topped, anthill-smooth Monashees as black as early surveyors painted them. But here they are as high or higher than most of the Coast Mountains. To the east they roll up to heights like Mt. Cranberry's 9,410 feet and Hallam's 10,560. Within the bend I saw again Little White and Greyback Mountains. To the north-east, the summits of Mt. Moore (7,118) and Big White (7,603) were bright with morning sun.

True, most of the Monashees lack cragged peaks and in summer, because of their distance from the moisture-laden Pacific winds, snowcaps. Few rocks or ravines break the living tapestry of greens that ripples down their slopes from summit to base. What each does have—for lack of a better word—is knees, as numerous and widespread as a seated centipede's. Rank after rank of them suggest a convention of centipedes, so crowded together that it is difficult to tell which knees are whose.

Between those knees, the gorges drop sharply to crevices through which creeks, large enough for small fish, if they swim Indian file, find their way to Okanagan Lake, three to four thousand feet below. To look down these long, shadowed funnels to a sunlit pigeon's-feather sail drifting about the lake is to appreciate that Monashee dimensions are much greater than they appear.

Each knee is a small range of hills in itself. The train follows round and up and down each rim before taking off over a trestle to the rim of the next. As unadorned as an angleworm (and against those ponderous slopes, seeming no wider), the first trestle, with the train suspended in mid-air over an abyss, does give one pause. The beauty of mountains and gorges, however, soon overshadows all else.

After two startling glimpses of Kelowna, we turned east, to witness a cosmic battle between sun and fog. From every gorge except one, white billows boiled high to blot out all but a far patch of blue sky. From that one, the billows were midnight black. The sun, a chalky, frightened moon-face, every ray absorbed, fought them valiantly, sometimes victoriously, only to go down to defeat before reinforcements boiling up from the next gorge.

Leaving the arena in mid-bout, we turned south into a new and brilliantly sunlit scene. While we continued to circle knees, cross gorges, beneath slopes that grew taller as we descended, an opposite rank of Monashees, slopeless, kneeless, rose sheer and purple behind undulating scarves of fog. Between us widened a small valley so parklike that a few men in a few days could transform it into a city park.

For whom? A barbed-wire fence, a house or two, white arrows indicating empty sidings? A silent sawmill here, a second miles beyond? Herefords grazing in a wild pasture?

Below us, an irrepressible brook—Westkettle River—tumbled down from the mountains over a stony bed several sizes too large for it, to join even more irrepressible Kettle River. Narrow or wide, deceptively placid or dizzy with eddies, it cavorted through sculptured clay and sand banks or eroded hills to the village of Kettle River. There it settled down to water a valley golden with hay and stubble fields, green with alfalfa. But for its frame of fuzzy, Teddy-bear hills, it might have been Evangeline's Acadia.

Midway, a hamlet of unpainted frame homes, barns, shops, lay in a V of mountains from which more green and golden fields flowed down every draw. There an official-looking gentleman, either sympathetic to my pleasure or concerned for the lounge car's picture windows, asked, "How would you like to ride the diesel for a while?"

He little recked that, given an ell, I'll take a hundred miles. When abetted, that is, by tall, lean, dark "C.F.," the engineer, and Fred, the fireman, fair and square. Two of that delightful kind who talk about what they know and know what they are talking about, they quietly brimmed with fun, interest and generosity for all the world. Thereafter, an open window beside me, a great wrap-around window in front, I enjoyed a ringside seat on the ever-changing panorama.

At Midway, Kettle River left us to cross the International Boundary and break into the falls which David Thompson named for the woven baskets, or "kettles," in which the local Indians caught fish. We climbed to Greenwood. A village now, but less than sixty years ago the Las Vegas of these parts, it had twenty-six mining companies, and twenty-five hundred people exploiting adjacent mineral deposits.

A few miles beyond rose the hill on which the Phoenix Mine in 1906 attained distinction as "the richest copper deposit in the world." Now, after almost a half century as a "ghost," it has reopened to recover the estimated three hundred thousand tons of copper ore remaining.

Hundreds of feet below, the Kettle Valley, though riverless

and walled by those Teddy-bear hills, every moment more closely resembled a Thanksgiving painting of abundance. Sleek cattle and sheep dozed in its sun-hot pastures. In its golden hay and stubble fields, aluminum irrigation pipes and a fingerling brook shimmered like the ballad's silver threads.

In vain Fred searched the hills for at least one of the scores of deer (when snow is deep, hundreds) that come down to feed along the right of way. "Hunting season opened two days ago," C.F. reminded him. "Must be, they're too far back in the hills by this time for any hunter to follow. They're not dumb about that—"

"Hunting season! So early?" I asked. "Not so early," said he. "Opened September eighteenth." Quickly I threw my head out the window lest they see that it was empty. Somehow, somewhere, I had mislaid three weeks! After almost five months of radiant summer, British Columbia had become for me a continuous August, an Avalon

> Where falls not hail or rain or any snow,
> Nor ever wind blows loudly!

And nothing about this day hinted that I was mistaken.

In a temperature that felt like the 106 degrees it sometimes attains, Grand Forks, a trading centre of about two thousand people, encircled by mountains, smouldered under heavy shade trees. Not much more than the upper storey of a handsome new, stream-lined school could be seen, and the old round-house that now, with the advent of the diesel, houses the Associated Growers. Thereby hangs a tale. When it became impossible during the war to import vegetable seeds from Holland, local farmers undertook to supply the demand. They were so successful that today they enjoy an established national reputation.

Among the important growers are members of the Doukhobor colony whose small, unpainted homes and barns, surrounded by meticulously kept fields and orchards, huddle at the foot of hills on the outskirts. Having broken with the sect's communal way of life, if not with its faith, they live and work as independent Canadian citizens. Here, too, is a small group of the intransigent Sons of Freedom.

Changes of scene now were bewildering. The Kettle River returned from its quick, body-building swing about northern Washington, to blast its way through obdurate granite formations and plunge from basin to basin beneath cumulus clouds of foam before resuming responsibility for its valley. To the south, Cascade Mountains, rose-red with sumac, dark blue with cloud shadows, outlined the International Boundary.

Almost at their feet we at last turned east, to climb up and down to 12-mile-long Christina Lake. From my open window, I looked straight down a thousand feet of shining evergreens to watch her graceful deep-blue waters emerge from dark-blue mountains, wind round rose and green mountains, into the slate blue of the Christina Range.

So help me, if we didn't turn north again, to run into an enormous gorge between stark, hot, red slopes where jagged, limbless trunks and charred stumps pointed accusingly skyward. One wall had been burned over twenty years ago; the other, less than five. But "mere earth, desperate and done with," nothing grows on either any more. Nothing restrains the snowslides that in winter bury the railroad's right of way thirty to forty feet deep. "What do you do then?" I asked C.F. As though that were an intelligent question, he answered, "Wait for the snowplows."

The next spate of mountains, brutal, mindless oafs, six thousand feet and over, ragged with bush, rough with rocks, I could have done without. Not C.F. and Fred. They were on first-name terms with every trout in every creek; with every aspen-felling beaver. "Yep," Fred announced after expert appraisal of a tree with an hourglass cuff above its ankle, "the boys'll have it down tonight."

They weren't the only ones to whom this bleak, mineralized country appealed. A small black square just below snowline, with a rickrack trail leading steeply to it, was the recently abandoned shack of a lone miner who had worked its poor ore for years. Widely separated points far back in the bush represented other shacks where miners of fifty years ago were hidden away. Some months before, "the government" had caught up with one such 87-year-old recluse and placed him in a home where he'd be cared for. "They won't have to care for him long. The bush was his life."

Blue peaks, one or two showing snow-filled basins through their haze, appeared beyond gaps in these dark mountains. Shortly, between two slopes, bright blue water flashed and was gone. "Arrow Lakes coming up," said C.F.

In 1830, a party of westbound fur traders, entering the Columbia Valley, made camp on the shore of a long lake, really two long lakes linked by a narrow 18-mile throat. One hundred feet above in the face of a sheer cliff, their guide spotted three small caves filled with arrows and brought down showers of them by gunshot. Later explorers, finding them among the shore rocks, named the lakes Arrow.

Generations before the white man left footprints on their shores, Plains Indians, Marines, Salish, many more, had hunted and fished about them. But the arrows are believed to have been shot into the caves some hundred and fifty years ago when Okanagan warriors celebrated their victory over the Kootenay in a winner-take-all battle for possession of the lakes.

Upper Arrow is forty-three miles long; at its widest, three miles. Crescent-shaped Lower Arrow is sixty miles long and, at times, one and a half miles wide. Together they give British Columbia one of the largest bodies of water in the interior and more than a hundred miles of alpine beauty.

Actually they are not lakes at all. About thirty miles south of Revelstoke, the Columbia comes upon a narrow trench between two mountain ranges. The western, less precipitous range is the Monashee; the eastern, sudden with tremendous rock cliffs and promontories, the Selkirk. In this splendid company, the Columbia expands into the Arrows before turning east to meet the Kootenay.

The mountain-locked Upper Arrow begins at the foot of 8,024-foot Mt. Sproat and runs south between densely ever-greened capes, headlands, canyons and slopes which rise to snow-crested 9,000- to 10,000-foot peaks. With the narrows, the white crests end. Forested slopes are less dense. Many park-like spaces open. The Lower Arrow is less rugged, with more parklike spaces, some so open and level they are cultivated as fields and orchards.

Someday one of the scenic highways of North America must make accessible this entire spectacular from Revelstoke to Castlegar. As yet, it only can be seen by an involved combination of gravelled roads and ferries. The railway follows the southern curve of Lower Arrow's crescent but, unless one has a very high saturation point, that is about all one can take at a time. Or so I found it on an afternoon that had become a preview of Indian Summer's most halcyon days.

One to two thousand feet below, the waters rippled delicately from deepest sapphire to turquoise, to aquamarine, to purest jade green. All about, immediate mountains were red with sumac and sandstone or other colourful rock, green gold with sunlit conifers, blue with massed clusters of Oregon grape and cloud shadow. Above them, to the north, others rolled across the sky in a single grey wave which from time to time broke in whitecaps as distant peaks lifted snow crowns above them.

For miles, no one spoke. After that, we didn't need to. Drawing a deep breath, big, quiet Fred released it on a sigh, said softly, perhaps to himself, "B.C. sure rides a star."

27

GIANTS IN THE EARTH

At the junction of the Columbia and Kootenay Rivers, long a favourite Indian camping ground, Castlegar is a railway division point, bus and ferry transfer centre. But tomorrow, as the driver of the bus to Trail was the first to tell me, it will "grow up." Celgar, Ltd., is erecting there the first $30 million unit of a pulp, newsprint and building materials plant that may become a $75 million investment. "Going to be a great thing for West Kootenay," he said.

To my eyes, filled with Monashees, Kettle Valley and Arrow Lakes, it didn't seem possible that anything could be. On one side, a raw, wild flat, dark with tangled scrub, lifted to raw, wild hills, made darker still by ominously gathering clouds. On the other, across a deep, wide, stony bed, the Columbia, not yet up to par after its holiday in the Arrow Lakes, smoothed snow-white sandbars. Beyond it, more hills were a darker wall of shadow.

But a sudden splash of colour *was* a great thing and a promise of more to come. Kinnaird, a row of fresh, bright ranch houses and bungalows facing over the highway to the river, had devised a unique floral plan. The wide border about each home's lawn featured only one flower: brilliant dahlias, rioting petunias, shaggy asters—no two alike. "Hard work, though," the driver commented. "Only ten-twelve years ago, all this was solid bush. Another ten, and this whole highway—eighteen miles—'ll be thick with them all the way to Trail."

Trail! That was one destination my imagination was fired to see. While I watched for Parthenon-like buildings to rise against the sky ahead, I wondered again why Provincial writers find so much romance in the well-worn fur trade, gold rush, cattle country; none in the industrial giants in the earth of these metallic hills.

241

Prospectors roamed them for years before a "guy called Joe" and another, Oliver, in 1890 followed a seven-mile creek from the Columbia to Red Mountain or Rossland. Though uncertain of the quality of the outcroppings they found there, they staked claims to two mines, War Eagle and Centre Star. Then with samples of the ore, but hardly a dollar in their pockets, they trekked fifty miles to Nelson to consult the Department of Mines' deputy recorder. When he thought the ores promising, they offered him an extension of Centre Star if he would pay their filing fees.

Having prospected those hills himself before taking that bread-and-butter job, "Colonel" Eugene Topping did not accept their offer until he had trekked back to Rossland to examine the ores on location. For a 50-mile hike and a $12.50 filing fee, he thus became the owner of the Le Roi, a mine that produced over $21 million in copper, gold and silver.

After organizing nine Spokane shareholders into the Le Roi Mining and Smelting Company, Topping sent his first shipment of ores by muleback, paddle wheeler and rail to the Butte, Montana, smelter. There they caught the eye of the smelter's owner, Fritz Heinze, a 21-year-old genius who had made most of Montana his private mining empire. That he was interested enough to send scouts to Rossland set off a rush of miners to these West Kootenay hills.

The scouts' reports, added to what he knew of East Kootenay's mines, inspired Heinze with ambition to gain control over both Kootenays also. To this end in 1890 he bought Topping's Le Roi. Six years later in the new townsite of Trail he built a smelter. Between mine and smelter he built a tramway to bring down the ores.

Heinze's expanding activities in West Kootenay in turn caught the eye of Canadian Pacific officials. Under pressure, they had built the Crow's Nest Pass line into East Kootenay. Farther they would not go unless some large and steady source of income could be found to offset the prohibitive costs of building and maintaining a railroad across West Kootenay.

In Heinze's smelter they found the source. Heinze did not

want to sell, but complications in his Montana empire prevented him from challenging the Canadian Pacific's entrance
to the Kootenay he had seen first. He therefore set a price on
both smelter and tramway of $2 million.

Heinze was an American. So was Canadian Pacific's President Shaughnessy. And he knew a third, a young Colorado
engineer who, as a college classmate of Heinze's, understood
something of how his mind worked. Shortly a young engineer
was moving about Rossland, artlessly secretive about the new
smelter he was to build there for the Canadian Pacific. True
to form, Heinze whittled his price down to less than a million.

But when the Canadian Pacific enlarged the smelter and
converted the tramway into a standard-gauge railway, a trigger-
tempered galaxy leaped into the act. Dissatisfied with Canadian
Pacific methods, the shareholders of the Le Roi Mining and
Smelting Company built a bigger, rival smelter at Northport,
Washington.

Though the Le Roi continued to pay them huge dividends,
they could not agree on their own methods either. So they
sold a major share of the mine to London's Whittaker Wright,
the Croesus of the British investment world, then refused to
give him control of either the head office in Spokane or of the
Northport Smelter. This brought on a long, bitter, international legal battle, which Wright won.

To keep the plot boiling, the Le Roi, War Eagle, and other
Rossland miners joined American miners in a strike for the
eight-hour day. Strikebreakers arrived. Bloodshed and rioting
followed. Convinced that Wright was behind the use of strikebreakers, the Rossland miners appealed to the Le Roi's shareholders to demand an audit of the mine's books.

The audit turned up glaring irregularities. Wright swallowed
cyanide. Rossland miners won the eight-hour day. Heinze
gambled the near-million he received from the Canadian
Pacific and forty-nine more in Wall Street—lost every dollar
overnight. And to ensure production for its smelter the Canadian Pacific began to buy or to consolidate with all the leading
mines in both Kootenays. It also consolidated with Rossland's

Power and Light Company, to expand its two small dams on the Kootenay into the five which today generate the 700,000 h.p. British Columbia uses from the Columbia system.

In 1906, mines, smelter and dams, operating together under the name of the Consolidated Mining and Smelting Company of Canada, Ltd., were on their way to realizing control of the Kootenays. Today, "Cominco," as it is popularly known, with assets of almost $200 million, is not only British Columbia's premier mining undertaking. It is one of the Dominion's greatest industries and exporters, and operator of one of the largest nonferrous smelters in the world.

To Tadanac, its main plant on the high bench above the Columbia, come Provincial ores, the Yukon's, the Province of Quebec's, and those of many distant points. From it go half of Canada's silver, eight per cent of the world's lead and zinc, and so on through antimony, bismuth, cadmium . . .

As Tadanac expanded, so did Trail. Across one section of its main streets, in fact, the two occupy the same spot at the same time to raise the question as to whether the land beneath the pavement may not be more valuable than what is above. Until 1911, this area was a marsh which traffic crossed on wooden trestles. Then Tadanac gave mountains of slag to fill and firm the bog for paving. Modern ore-refining processes now could recover a fortune, it is said, from the once-worthless fill.

Better still, as Cominco expanded its control over the Kootenays, Tadanac employed more and more thousands of highly skilled young men. And Trail's economy grew more and more stable. Today, the Market Index for this small, isolated city is more than 40 per cent higher than the national average.

Even the Great Depression did not affect it seriously. Neither did the Canadian Pacific strike in 1956 which threatened to tie the Dominion's economy into a knot. As industry after industry closed down, gloom and fear spread across the country. Not in Trail! Cominco's seventy-five hundred employees welcomed it as an exciting change from the monotony of security.

Only about eight hundred were lucky enough to enjoy layoffs—on unemployment insurance. Before the turn of the expectant majority came round, the strike ended. "Why couldn't it have gone on at least another week?" they lamented. "The wife and I were going to Calgary [Las Vegas, Spokane, fishing, hunting]. Now everything's back to ordinary."

Colonel Topping, the "Father of Trail," built better than he knew when he sold his Le Roi to pre-empt the land about the mouth of Seven-Mile Creek for a townsite. There he and a blacksmith friend tossed up a log cabin "hotel" to provide a roof for prospectors arriving by Columbia River paddle-wheeler or Dewdney Trail to hike to Rossland.

With Telegraph Creek Trail in northern British Columbia and the Cariboo in central, the Dewdney in the south wrote a colourful and important chapter in the Crown Colony's history. Though built by Edgar Dewdney, from the Pacific to Wild Horse Creek in East Kootenay, it was the brainchild of Governor Douglas. He foresaw streams of gold and other western wealth moving east, streams of settlers moving west *if* an all British-America road could be laid between the Pacific and Red River Settlement (Winnipeg).

Cariboo miners, however, prevented the trail from leaving the Fraser until gold was discovered on the Wild Horse in 1864. Then it was continued to Fort Shepherd, a Hudson's Bay post at the junction of the Columbia and Pend d'Oreille Rivers, a few miles east of the city of Trail. When Chinese construction crews walked out on it there to dig for gold themselves, white men continued it to the Wild Horse.

The town named for the trail really started from scratch in 1894. Then the Columbia, rising in flood, washed away the log hotel and the few huts thrown up about it. Fritz Heinze bought one-third of the townsite for his smelter, started surveys for his tramway. Topping and partner built a bona fide hotel. Hordes of prospectors rushed in. Within three years, Trail had sixteen hotels and all other features, in duplicate or triplicate, of a city. By 1906, with Cominco steadily expanding, the rest of the way for Topping's town was up.

Search the sky as I would, however, for tall towers appropriate to such a well-endowed municipality, only more, larger and darker hills appeared. Through them we followed the

Columbia into the very heart of the city and could have followed it right out again. The river's entrance and exit are the only real breaks in the circle of metallic crests.

Trail is their prisoner. Streets crisscross every foot of the levelled basin at their feet, mount high on their slopes. Buildings, dark with more than age, and wall to wall, crowd every street. And not a Parthenon among them. Not even a Piccadilly Circus.

But when the bus stopped I stepped down onto a network of railway tracks to come face to face with a most extraordinary structure or structures. A huge, skewgee, red-and-black Rube Goldberg conception, patched here and there with tin or zinc, it sprawled one way with a seedy, aimless, out-of-focus air. In every other direction, arthritic pipes, large and small, writhed and coiled. Behind them, the tracks, lumpy with dingy freight cars, ran off into acres of assorted industrial roofs. Above them stalwart chimneys pointed cloudward like charred trunks of fire-swept forest giants, one or two still smoking.

"For Heaven's sake, what's *that?*" I gasped. And a startled passer-by answered, "That? Why, that's Tadanac—the main plant of Cominco."

Technically Trail is not a "company town" but, with personnel and structural evidence of Cominco everywhere, it definitely is company minded. No matter what event in Trail's history entered a conversation, someone was sure to date it from some decade of the company's expansion:

1920's—When, though the great Sullivan Mine at Kimberley in East Kootenay was discovered in 1892, acquired by Cominco in 1910, a method finally was developed to separate the different gold, silver, lead, zinc and other ores.

1930's—When Cominco, after paying $300,000 in damages to Americans south of the Boundary for trees and other plants destroyed by Tadanac's smoke fumes, devised formulas for recovering and using commercially the poisonous sulphur dioxide in the smoke. Followed the construction of Warfield, its giant chemical and fertilizer plant high on the hill behind Tadanac.

1940's—When Cominco production did more than reach an all-time high because of the lead, zinc and chemicals it poured out for the Allies. Warfield played a strategic role in a hush-hush project that, the war over, turned out to have been the production of heavy water, a vital link in atomic research.

1950's—When Cominco began a $64 million expansion program—

Up Cominco's ladder, Trail climbed until its confined townsite overflowed. Residential districts crept up the hills to the limit that city services could follow. Others crossed the Columbia to open and fill new "residentials" on the east bank within three years. Forced outside the wall of hills, still others dot neighbouring valleys in a 20-mile radius.

Metropolitan Trail, including Tadanac and Warfield, estimates its population at fifteen thousand. Perhaps two or three times as many more whose livelihood depends on Cominco commute from these outlying suburbs. Of these, Rossland, high on Red Mountain, its mines long closed, is the star. In summer, its four thousand residents enjoy clear, cool air and a sweeping view, while Trail steams at the feet of its hot hills and smoke-belching chimneys. In winter, it enjoys one of the finest ski jumps in Canada.

As a community of vigorous young men—and women—Trail is sports minded. In this, the imposing $1,250,000 Memorial Centre, with its splendidly equipped gymnasium, arena, rinks and other facilities plays a leading part. As in Penticton, hockey is the favourite. Trail's "Smoke-Eaters" have brought home not only a world championship but seven Provincial championships in a row, and other honours.

Curling is not far behind. Memorial Centre's seldom-idle eight sheets for adults, four for children, have developed and are developing curlers known wherever sportsmen wield a broom. Skiing at Rossland, golf on one of the few championship courses in the Province, cruising, swimming, fishing in the Columbia or at Christina and the Arrow Lakes, hunting deer, elk, bear, in almost any direction, baseball, cricket—Oh, let's talk about things that begin with W.

When the bus driver placed my bags beside me on the tracks, the startled passer-by startled me by picking them up and saying briskly, "The Crown Point Hotel's just a step. I'll walk you over." During that step, he found time to say, "By the way, the Business and Professional Women's Club is meeting for dinner tomorrow night. If you'd like to speak for them, I think I can arrange it." As we entered the hotel, the desk clerk, at the phone, looked round, then handed me the receiver. "Is it all arranged?" a woman's voice asked. "Will you speak for us tomorrow night?" I agreed, but I wanted to reword Priscilla a little and say in return, "Why didn't you ask me yourself, Joan?"

This custom of the men speaking for the women in British Columbia was an ever-recurring phenomenon to me. According to its 1956 census, the population is composed of 687,000 men and 667,000 women. Only in the Lower Mainland, specifically in and about Vancouver, do women outnumber the men. Perhaps this numerical superiority encourages the men to nourish the quaint nineteenth-century notion—and to go to considerable trouble and inconvenience to do so—that women must be spared from assuming responsibility.

In a province which takes well-justified pride in its use of the latest and best ideas, materials and techniques, this is very curious. Lack of trained and experienced administrators, executives, technicians, frequently has proved a serious handicap to its surging present. Yet—

No woman holds an important post in any Provincial or municipal government. No woman holds an official position in any communication or transportation system. No woman heads a city or town department store, bank, hotel, or any other large-scale business. Women do fill the teaching, library, nursing, social welfare and clerical fields, but no woman heads a large elementary school or high school, library, hospital, welfare agency or management post.

If a dozen, or six, or three women were to be found in highly responsible places, I might have assumed—despite the evidence of my own eyes—that British Columbia was doing the best it could with what it had. But none! One day, in the calibre of its women, it may discover that the waters of the Columbia are not the only invaluable resource it has permitted to run to waste.

Weather-wise, Trail produced an unexpected phenomenon. Rain! From shortly after I entered the hotel until I left it to take a bus to Nelson, thick sheets of the unfamiliar stuff fell and fell. Umbrella, raincoat and such long since discarded, I hesitated to venture out until I saw Trailites splashing happily about without them. Splashing, too, then, I was astonished to be congratulated on the timing of my arrival. "When it rains, the air is clean and cool," said one. "But when it's hot and smoky, strangers usually have a word for it." Another added, "And, by coincidence, it's always the same one."

When the rain prevented me from taking the morning bus along the "old" highway through the Kootenay River Valley to Nelson, I also had a word for it. Not because, though it must be heresy or worse to admit it, I missed seeing Cominco's five dams on the river. One, above Bonnington Falls, is described as "spectacular." The valley held another interest.

Here the first Doukhobor colonies to settle in British Columbia transformed a wilderness into an abundant farming community. All about rise the large, identical, frame or brick communal houses in which several families lived together. At Brilliant, their largest settlement, is the old home of Peter Verigin, the leader who, with Tolstoi, was responsible for bringing thousands of Doukhobors to Canada.

A martyr to the bombs of the Sons of Freedom, he is buried at the junction of the Kootenay and Columbia, just above the site where the Doukhobors every summer held their huge religious gatherings. An elaborate monument placed above his grave as a shrine, only to be destroyed by the Sons, recently has been restored.

28

SANTA CLAUS—UP THE NEXT CREEK

Half a dozen miles east of Trail, the Columbia and its narrow valley of dark, rocky, thinly treed slopes turned south for the International Boundary. The new highway through Salmo River's little valley turned north into another of British Columbia's lightning scene changes. Wedged into crowding hills, its soil is so fertile that anything will grow in it. And forests, fields, gardens were doing just that on every slope and every foot of the valley not pre-empted by the curlicue river.

Small villages, too, were growing visibly. Montrose was a cluster of two- and three-toned cottages and gardens, largely owned by war veterans now employed by Cominco. In brave defiance of the native fir, pine, lacy tamarack and poplars everywhere else, Fruitvale was deep in elm, weeping willow, and birch. Its name dates back to 1901, when a company of optimists bought up square miles on which to grow grapes and establish a winery. When late springs and early fall frosts wrote a quick period to that idea, they sold the land to small farmers and vegetable growers.

Yet this was mining country! The hills are veined with lead and zinc, gold and other minerals. But not until we reached Salmo, a village on the bank of the river, where mills of the Emerald Tungsten Mine cover a nearby slope, was there sign or word of mines or minerals. In the fact that the Great Northern Railroad, which runs through the valley from Spokane to Nelson, was replacing its 90-pound rails with 110-pounders, the bus driver saw coming expansion. "They wouldn't do that just for something to do," he reasoned.

At that point the little girl in front of me turned round to say with stars in her eyes and voice, "I got to go to a school! But I like my own better." Her mother explained, "We live in a lighthouse on an island off the north coast. So Nancy's had to get her education for the past three years by correspondence. While visiting my mother, we also visited a school. But now that we're on our way home, she can't wait to start work as a fourth-grader—by mail."

Nancy is just one of eighteen hundred elementary students on remote ranches, farms and float villages, in logging and mining camps and lighthouses, who attend classes by mail. More than seven thousand high school students also are enrolled in the Provincial Department of Education's Instruction Courses. Many of them attend rural high schools where not all subjects necessary for college matriculation are offered. These they acquire by way of British Columbia's postal service. In both groups are youngsters homebound with chronic illnesses or physical handicaps and children of missionary families serving in foreign fields from the wilds of French West Africa to Formosa. All this has grown from a farmer's insistence in 1919 that his children, though living in a far corner of the interior, had the same right to an education as any other child in the Province.

As the hills ahead began to assume mountainous outlines and the vegetation thinned, Nancy and I tried to pick out Silver King Mountain, where by the thinnest of chances the first West Kootenay mines were found. To a little creek running down its slope, a luckless prospecting party followed the Salmo in the late summer of 1896. Making camp, they agreed to try their luck for one more day; if nothing turned up, to return to their homes in Colville, Washington.

Still unlucky by midafternoon, they sent two young boys with the party up the mountain to bring down straying horses. On the way the boys filled their pockets with bits of copper pyrite they thought to be gold. Tiring of that idea, the younger boy used his bits to flush grouse. The other carried his back to camp.

The next morning the whole party climbed the mountain to find the now famous Kootenay outcroppings. But as the odds were a thousand to one against other prospectors finding their way in here so late in the season, they turned their backs on the millions of dollars in exposed ore and went home anyway. In the spring, their samples analyzed as silver, they hurried back to stake four claims—Silver King, Kootenay Bonanza, American Flag and Kohinoor. Others rushed in then to plant stakes on or about the mountain. Late arrivals pushed on into the far-reaching hills until registered claims mounted into the hundreds.

No Silver King could we recognize, but black spots high on immediate slopes indicated mines, operating or closed. "Lots of 'em in these hills," said the driver. "They open and shut like doors, depending on whether the price goes up or down." Ymir, once the site of several gold mines, was a collection of miners' cottages, a sawmill, and a wild plum tree rosy with fruit.

Climbing into higher hills whose crests were dusted with the first fresh snow, we descended through a sunless pass into another open valley aglow with Indian Summer. And there was Silver King Mountain and, at its base, the city of Nelson. Its setting was a carbon copy of Trail's, with a 100 per cent difference.

The hills—foothills of the Selkirks—which girdle it were handsome, generous, good-natured giants, green with conifers to their summits. At its feet, the Kootenay River, so lakelike that some call it the West Arm of Kootenay Lake, flowed between shallow banks to join the Columbia at Castlegar. From waterfalls high on Silver King, two lively creeks tumbled down through residential and commercial districts.

Streets solid with clean, freshly painted buildings or homes covered the valley floor, climbed the slope as high as city services profitably could follow. Fortunately, just as the population was about to reach the limit of expansion, a suspension bridge replaced the ferries across the Kootenay. Now residentials are developing on the west bank, spreading into surrounding valleys.

As a taxi carried me to the Hume Hotel between walls of other hotels, I wondered aloud why a town of eight thousand people needed so many. "That's the Census for you!" the driver scoffed. "There's twelve thousand people within a mile and a half of our post office and more than seventy thousand in Nelson's trading area. But these hotels—twenty-three of them —all go back before 1900, when hundreds of mines were going great guns all around here and anybody who wanted to go anywhere had to come here first. Used to come up the Columbia and Kootenay on paddle-wheelers.

"Great times they had here in those days. To get this street, they filled in a gulch and pushed its creek through culverts to the river. Maybe you'll hear it tonight. Runs right under your hotel. They used to have horse races and foot races on it then —wasn't paved, of course. And all these hotels were covered with porches where people cheered them on. And dances! We don't see anything so fancy here these days, I can tell you. Held most of 'em in the big hotels, but on moonlight nights, on the boats. Had an Opera House, too, and a Spokane Company that played old tear-jerkers like *East Lynne*."

If I'd had any doubts that Nelson's past was purple, they were laid to rest when I saw the enormous, columned, mirrored and hardwood-floored lounges of the hotel and learned a little more. Within two years after the discovery of the Silver King mines, three to four thousand miners were camped along the gulch that is now Baker Street. Ten more, and Nelson was an incorporated, wide-open frontier town of a thousand people, lubricated by twenty-three bars in the twenty-three hotels, six saloons, four wholesale liquor houses.

Now, edging sixty, it makes a valiant effort to act its age. It points with pride to the fact that with two railroads, two airports, and highways it is the main transportation and distribution centre between Calgary and Vancouver. And, with numerous Federal and Provincial departments represented here, it is an administrative and judicial centre. With the million-dollar mill of the Kootenay Forest Products Company and smaller wood-processing and matchblock factories, it is the centre of an important logging industry. The oddly located but impressive glass-and-brick structure I thought an office building was identified as the Canadian Pacific's million-dollar diesel roundhouse. New public and commercial buildings, representing millions of dollars, were in various stages of construction.

But behind this estimable façade I caught the vibrations of the traditional prospector's eternal expectancy that Santa Claus is waiting up the next creek. And when I met an honest man, he confessed, "We like to say our industries are so diversified that, come boom or bust, we can maintain our economic composure. But if the price of gold ever again hits a decent level, I tremble for it. There's so much gold in these hills that overnight Baker Street would be solid with tents. And we'd all be right back where we started.

"Take the discovery of uranium three or four years ago in the rugged timber and brush country up near Slocan Lake. Even tourists who came to fish bought Geiger counters. Even the recorder of mines, though the poor fellow was so busy recording claims he never had time to use it. Not since the bonanza days around 1900 have so many claims been staked. Notice I *said* tourists! You wouldn't believe how many townspeople suddenly had a reason for driving up the narrow, twisting, pockholed road to the lake and breaking through the bush, Geiger counters in their hot little hands. *Mining's not only our first industry. Secretly, it's our first love.*"

Small wonder, with hundreds if not thousands of mines, fifty to sixty of them on an average always active, in a 40-mile radius. On West Arm, or Kootenay River, alone, commercially sized deposits of rare industrial metals—gypsum, cyanite, lithium, asbestos, tantalum, many more—wait for a persuasive price.

Like Trail, Nelson has a huge Civic Centre, equipped with rinks, gymnasium, courts and, in addition, a theatre and library. Its full year-round card of indoor and outdoor sports includes an annual Midsummer Bonspiel. No other place in the world can make that statement! Rinks from various parts of Canada and the United States compete. Thousands of tourists come to watch and enjoy summer sports in 80-degree temperatures.

Nelson's invigorating climate must receive some credit for the boundless vitality of its people. But much credit also is due to the stimulus of many nationalities reacting on one another.

The majority are of British descent, but Americans, Chinese, Germans, Italians, Japanese, Yugoslavs, are present in large or small numbers. Here, too, are many Doukhobors, who as business and professional men live and work as independent Canadian citizens.

Though short, the story of British Columbia's Doukhobor colonies really is two stories—that of the six to seven thousand members of the orthodox cults, and that of the two to three thousand Sons of Freedom. So many Doukhobors have married "outsiders" and broken all ties with the original communal settlements established in the Kootenay Valley between 1908 and 1915 that all figures are estimates.

After meeting Fred, the Doukhobor fireman on the Kettle Valley Railway, I was not surprised to hear Nelsonites speak of them as honest, hard-working, good people. It is only a matter of time, they believe, until the orthodox Doukhobors adapt themselves to life and living as Canadians.

Since 1940, their standards of living steadily have risen. The majority maintain the average standards of the Canadian farmers about them. Though most of them still remain on their community lands, no Doukhobor now lives on a self-sustaining communal. Almost everyone farms his own land, conducts his own business or profession, or works for hire as a semi-skilled or unskilled labourer. The exceptions depend on the workers for support or on government welfare aid.

The majority now speak English. Many speak both English and Russian, and not only are willing but desire, for themselves and their children, to be literate in English. Their intense religious beliefs, economy, food, dress, social life, recreation and magnificent singing do set them apart. But the men are as susceptible to bright, fast cars, to radio, movies and other features of modern life as their neighbours. Small fry are as susceptible to chewing gum and comics. Because they have less contact with the world, the women are the last and fewest to succumb to these "corrupting influences."

The Sons of Freedom profess to want all the freedoms from religious, educational, economic and political government control that the original Doukhobor emigrants sought when they left Russia in the late nineteenth century for Canada. Above all, they demand freedom from military service. Of all the Doukhobors, they are the least capable of submitting to direction or sharing. Nevertheless, they also want the communal with all its religious direction and economic sharing re-established.

Their general idea is to react violently against any process designed to adjust them to Canadian life. One point of view holds that they burn schoolhouses, dynamite railroads and bridges, stage nude parades to register their wholehearted disapproval of the Doukhobors who have adjusted. Another declares that, whatever their age, the Sons are publicity-mad adolescents. The proof of that pudding may lie in the outcome of their current headline-capturing campaign to return to Russia. If that land of all the freedoms agrees to accept them, will they go?

Undoubtedly still another reason for Nelson's vitality stems from the stamina and tenacity its pioneers had to demonstrate to survive its beginnings as a mining camp. More than sixty of them remain to tell the lurid tale. Those I met reminded me of lone pines near the snowlines of many peaks that had sunk their roots so deep into rocky clefts not all the rigours of nature could break or fell them. A notable example was Mr. Reuben Randolph McCandless.

"You must meet him," a friend said. "He's almost eighty now, and a living history of this country." But the afternoon I went down to the hotel lounge at the appointed four o'clock, none of the grizzled gentlemen drowsing behind newspapers answered to the name of McCandless. As I turned away, a slender, dapper, shrewd and alert-eyed banker type hurried up to apologize for being late. Mr. McCandless!

He and three other old-timers, the youngest, sixty-nine, at the wheel, had had to drive to Kaslo that morning, a trip I'd been warned not to take unless in a "jeep with wings." Said Mr. McCandless, "We'd have been back by two if a brainless

256

whippersnapper hadn't sideswiped us. Threw us all into a ditch and completely wrecked our car. Fortunately, an RCMP car got us back in time to attend the funeral of an old friend."

With that, he led the way on brisk, accustomed feet up the long, steep stairway to the ladies' beer lounge and began to talk, with never a word about himself. "In the early days we had laws and Mounties and officials here to enforce them. So we escaped the physical battles, burnings, outlaws and general mayhem the Americans knew in their wild and woolly West. But we had an equivalent more subtle and perhaps more lasting in effect in the blank-check bribes, stolen patents, and total disregard for the health and safety of the miners."

Just one of many events in the controversial life of John Houston, Nelson's first mayor, sets the scene. As a "boomer," or tramp printer, he gave the town its first newspaper. As the mayor, he used it to fight the powerful mining interests to gain ownership for Nelson of its own water rights. Finding himself in a losing battle, he set out for Victoria to place Nelson's case before the Provincial government. On the train to Vancouver, a smooth young man sat down beside him, placed an envelope on his lap. In the envelope was a blank certified check.

"Forget about Nelson's water rights," the smoothie suggested, "and fill that out to suit yourself." Houston handed back the check and went on to Victoria, to win his battle. As owner of its own water rights and power, Nelson today is one of the best financed cities in the Dominion.

Working conditions in the first mines were so bad that lead poisoning "killed more men than World War I." But mineowners did nothing to improve them until Canada passed laws making lead poisoning a "compensable disease." One mine was so tough that its first crews, all English and American, walked out. The owners then brought in Scandinavians. When they walked out, the owners imported Finns. When the Finns walked out, they closed the mine on the ground that "If the Finns can't take it, no man can."

In that kinship with fortitude, Nelsonites have carried on.

One was Frederick Niven, whose *Mine Inheritance, Mrs. Barry, Triumph,* and other novels and books made him one of Canada's outstanding writers. Though his scenes were laid in various parts of the British Isles and Canada, he chose Nelson as the ideal place to live. At a dinner party, his wife told me a characteristic instance of his dedication to his writing.

On Sunday afternoon, December 7, 1941, she was listening to the New York Symphony on the radio when an announcer broke in to report that the Japanese were bombing Pearl Harbor. Much upset, she rushed into the room where her husband was at work on a new novel to tell him the shocking news. "Yes?" he said, and went on working. Reassured by his lack of concern, she returned to the radio. But when the symphony was interrupted again with word that the Japanese now were attacking Midway, she again rushed in to tell her husband. "Yes?" he said, and went on working.

Two hours later he appeared beside her to say, "Our planes must have stopped those Japs at Midway. If they'd got through to Trail, we should be able to hear them now, shouldn't we?" Unable to believe her ears, she demanded, "Do you mean to say that, thinking the Japs were bombing *Midway, British Columbia,* you still went on working?" "Why, yes," said he. "I knew if they were that close, it would be a long time before I could start a new chapter, so I wanted to be sure I finished this one."

29

THROUGH THE LOOKING-GLASS
TO SHANGRI-LA

As the train ascended the Kootenay, the silver river, pale-
blue sky, and evergreen walls of the gorge suddenly framed a
magnificent sunset. For minutes, the high, luminous, primrose
glow, with three rosy-white cloud cones shining above and
through it, hung in the dusty-gold light of the early autumn
evening. Then, as we rounded a curve, it vanished.

No sign of its promise of another Indian Summer day remained when the brakeman jumped me down beside a watertank at Proctor, a hamlet of less than a hundred people scattered over a hillside. Picking my way across a tangle of tracks
and up a path to the lighted door of Holiday Inn, I entered
directly into a huge, warm kitchen and a bedlam of trilling
canaries.

The owners had just finished dinner but, not at all disturbed,
Mrs. B. laid a place for me and beside it a frying pan containing the remains of a fried chicken. After cashing a check for
a neighbour, Mr. B. wandered over to say, "Ever since I let a
guy who flashed a checkbook a foot square have fifty dollars,
I've hated to cash the things. I thought a man with a checkbook that size would be good for any amount, but I've never
seen a nickel of it since."

Advising me not to be alarmed if I heard loud voices, he
left to open the inn's beer parlour. His wife explained that
their weekend customers drive in from miles away "to whoop
it up where nobody knows them. Proctor is a quiet place of
elderly people mostly, living on small incomes."

It also is a place where new ideas are brewing. For one, a
monster diesel slid up and down the tangle of level tracks to
prove, in a manner not clear to me, its ability to revolutionize
freight hauling over mountains. Another was in the head of

Alec Garner, an artist whose modern oils and watercolours are winning increasing recognition.

Proctor, in short, capsuled the old and the new, the slow, dreamy pace and the swift, the stationary and the fluid life of the Kootenay Lake country. But I was too interested in the S.S. *Moyie* to realize it. The last of the stern-wheelers that once as "floating palaces" delighted miners and their ladies and tourists from all the continent, she waited at the foot of the inn's long lawns to make her weekly Saturday trip round the northern two-thirds of the lake.

In the pitiless light of the full moon she looked all of her sixty years. But on the dot of eight next morning, when the wooden blades of her paddle-wheel churned the green waters of Kootenay River into a white boil, she chugged off to a steady samba beat. The oak steering wheel's six-foot diameter almost filled her tiny sun-flooded bridge. From it depended two brass chains, one to ring a bell in the engine room below, the other a gong. A battered brass funnel pushed through the floor served as a speaking tube.

This would be one of the old stern-wheeler's last voyages, the captain told me. As soon as the highway round the northwest shore of the lake is completed, a tug that can handle ore-hauling railroad barges better and cheaper will replace her. But she never will know the ignominy of her sister ships, now rotting on the lake bottom, demoted to ferry or some landlubber's summer cottage. The Kootenay Historical Society will anchor her at a lake port to carry on as a museum.

Listening to the babble of voices below, he said ruefully, "She's still good for twenty years. We could have saved her if we'd had passenger lists like this every trip. Now it's too late, they come from all over Canada and the western States, even from the south. But that's the way life goes. The first boat on the lake was the *Midge*, a small, Norwegian screw steamer, in 1884. To get out of paying customs duties, they brought her in as an agricultural implement. The Indians were so crazy about her whistle that, just to be allowed to blow it, they supplied cordwood free for her fires. But when the railroads came in around 1892, stern-wheelers like the *Moyie* pushed the screw steamers off the lake."

As he talked, we left the river to turn at right angles into Kootenay Lake and I knew the sensations of a leaf floating at the bottom of a deep well. Cragged or snow-peaked Selkirks, 7,500 to 11,500 feet high, thrusting up from far below the surface, cribbed, cabined and confined every foot. And there to the northeast was my sunset of the previous evening! Above a high primrose line of shore mountains loomed three pink-white cones of snow.

Long before the Rockies were a gleam in nature's eye, the Selkirks reared their serrated, snow-capped heads above the prehistoric sea. Now subordinated by the upthrust of those brash, younger mountains, they occupy the 300-mile-long area, almost as large as England, within the great loop of the Columbia and Kootenay Rivers.

David Thompson first saw, mapped and named them Nelsons (for the British Admiral) in 1813-14. After the merger of North West and Hudson's Bay Companies in 1821, they were renamed to honour Lord Selkirk, founder of Red River Settlement, now Winnipeg. Why or for whom John Palliser, while leading his 1858 expedition across them, named the single range along the lake's west shore Purcell seems to be a mystery. Under any name, they remained practically unknown until the first prospectors paddled up the Kootenay River in 1865.

Though older than the Rockies, the Selkirks here have the knife-edged spires and ridges of youth. Except for a few stunted pines and firs, many are solid rock and so irregular that a ten-foot-square level is rare. Under the searching sun, these myriad planes run the gamut of colours, but it is sandstone and a pink-flowering plant that give them their warm rosy hue. Even when forests soften their slopes, they roll in rhythmic folds, and each fold ripples to its own rhythm. What they lack in the height, breadth and depth of the Rockies they more than make up in the grand manner, plus an individual style and *élan* all their own.

Rivalling them in beauty is Kootenay Lake. An imprisoned sea of dark, clear, jade-green waters, about sixty-five miles long, one to four wide, and frequently more than a thousand feet deep, it is fed by streams and waterfalls.

The Arrow Lakes had their own distinctive beauty. But to come on the Kootenay in its stunning frame of Selkirks less than sixty miles distant was almost too much. To learn that midway between them lay still another—Slocan Lake—*was*. No wonder the Kootenays boast four national and five Provincial parks!

So absorbed, I didn't know we were passing beneath the world's longest suspension span until a newcomer to the bridge recalled me. Swung between two 500-foot-high steel towers, the 10,656-foot span carries the wires of Cominco's power line from Trail to Kimberley in East Kootenay. Cominco also controls the water rights to the lake, he was adding when, high above the shore Purcells, the sun flashed on ice. Thanks to the brilliant clarity of the day, we caught a seldom-seen view of Kokanee Glacier, a seven-mile-square icefield just beneath Mt. Kokanee's 9,100-foot family of peaks.

As we began a weaving course back and forth across the lake to stop at mining camps, hunting lodges and villages, day and scene became more dreamlike. In motion, only the throb of the engines broke the stillness; in port, even that sound ceased. At times not a soul was to be seen on shore. Crewmen left freight on fixed or floating docks, and we were on our way. Occasionally we took aboard a few passengers, all male, who disappeared into some accustomed recess on the freight deck. "Kaslo shoppers," said the young helmsman, with a wink.

Ainsworth, where the first prospectors on the lake camped, and using Kootenay Indians as Geiger counters, located silver and lead mines, is still a mining centre. It is also a small spa whose health-giving hot springs boil out of rocky caves to provide the baths and a large, outdoor swimming pool.

Riondel hides behind the ridge which joins mainland and a small island to form a tiny, sheltered harbour. Round it and for some distance under the lake run the workings of the famous

Bluebell Mine, now a Cominco operation. Since 1800 or before, as a dark-brown stain on a bluebell-massed cliff, the mine was known to Indians and fur traders as a source of lead for bulletmaking. But, as the cause and scene of the "Bluebell Murder," its fame dates from 1885.

Three years earlier, Robert Sproule and two companions staked claims to the ledge of silver-bearing lead ore. But by the dubious procedures of the times, Thomas Hamill, with the gold commissioner at his side, was able to jump them while Sproule was on his way to register them in the gold commissioner's office 240 miles away. Today a memorial cairn marks the spot where Hamill was shot from ambush by misfortune-crazed Sproule.

Rocking north toward always grander mountains, we passed miles of slopes unmarred by man except where the new highway scratched a ragged grey line or a trail led up a draw to mines, hunting lodges, and on to Slocan Lake. Thus, unwarned, we rounded a headland into Kaslo's small, hidden harbour.

A village on two levels, its setting even in pioneer days was known as the "Lucerne of North America." Tall white peaks shelter it on the north; Mt. Kokanee on the west. Directly across the lake rose my sunset ridge and, above it, the three white cones of Mt. Loki (9,120), Hooker (8,055) and Kaslo (7,700). Beyond and above them loomed Mt. Findlay (10,-780).

Kaslo's history also shows peaks. Founded in 1891 as the outlet for British Columbia's most important silver, lead and zinc district, one year later it counted twelve hotels, churches, newspapers, school—all the "trappings of civilization." Over them towered a three-storey theatre, with a saloon on each floor, a revolving stage on which a branch of Spokane's notorious Comique Variety Show entertained nightly, and "80 box-rustler girls."

The population had reached five thousand when, out of the blue, burst the Great Depression of 1893. Everything stopped. Everyone who could get away did. Less than a thousand remained when fire destroyed half the town and a flood washed away the rest.

Two years later, the "Great Boom" rebuilt it. Mines and population bloomed again. Between it and the Slocan district, where camps sprouted into Slocan City, Silverton, Sandon, New Denver and others, the Great Northern laid a bizarre 22-mile railroad. Its narrow-gauge rails ran round stumps and boulders too large to move. One grasshopper trestle jumped it across a 1,100-foot gulch. Snowslides buried it. Floods undermined it. But, because of the tremendous tonnage in ores it carried, nothing was permitted to stop it until the boom collapsed in 1900. The Great Northern then abandoned it to rot and rust. And the Slocan's burgeoning towns faded into British Columbia's largest collection of ghosts.

Just in time to save Kaslo from the same fate, the soil proved right for fruitgrowing. As the fame of its apples and, especially, Bing cherries spread, orchards replaced miles of forest all round the northern end of the lake. Now that fruit culture is waning, logging is the main industry, with tourism impatient to replace it. (A novel tourist attraction is the aisle of Bing cherry trees shading each street, the fruit free for the picking.) But returning high prices for lead and zinc would start the town scrambling up another peak.

Meantime, in the miners the *Moyie* brings in every Saturday, Kaslo finds rich ore. When we picked up our "shoppers" later in the afternoon, they walked aboard with a jaunty air, their bottled purchases only thinly disguised.

At Kaslo, we entered the "Lardeau country," which, ever since Revelstoke, people had been assuring me was the real reason why Canada moved heaven and earth to move the Canadian Pacific to the Pacific Ocean and so induce British Columbia to remain in the Confederation. Of the thousands of California forty-niners who headed for the Cariboo goldfields, many could not afford to come by sea. Following a land route through Idaho into the mountains between Kaslo and Lardo, they struck gold. Soon they were shipping so much gold south of the Boundary that the Dominion government at last took action.

What we saw on the lower benches of those mountains were small new farms whose stubble fields floated like golden patches of Sargasso Sea on waves of pine and fir. Below them, along the route of the coming highway, new homes were rising. And around another headland, the little logging village of Lardo curved about another hidden harbour.

Lying at the foot of a horseshoe of white-capped Purcells, Lardo looked across harbour and lake to Mts. Wilamot and Vena (8,000). Just north of them, a great white crescent of Selkirks rose behind low, rounded green hills to bring the tapering lake to an end. Among them, Mts. Hamill (10,640) and Tony, just three feet lower, appeared to merge their miles of glaciers. As distant dazzles, Mt. Jumbo (11,217) to the north and to the northeast Mt. Farnham (11,342) soared above rippling white crests.

At any time, the Selkirks are not easy to describe. Here on Kootenay Lake, as in Glacier Park, some extra dimension, not physical, tunes the heart to a song without words.

Convinced that I must spend the rest of my life in this Lardeau country, but unable to decide where, I consulted the captain. Waving a hand to include miles of Shangri-las, he said, "Help yourself. Four dollars an acre."

Between that high crescent and the rounded hills lies Howser Lake. Into it the Duncan River runs down from the northeast to open a pass to country so reminiscent of England that it early was named Windermere. And from the northwest the Lardeau River runs down to open another to the Arrow Lakes.

There, practically inaccessible as yet, lives one of the most original collection of characters to be found in a province whose unpeopled coastlines, islands and bush beyond lakes and rivers have been sought by "loners" since fur-trade days. Veterans of the 1895-1900 mining boom, they resent the approach of the highway as an unwarranted invasion of their private domain.

In well-to-do, travelled and gallant "Mr. Barrow," Kootenay

265

Lake also knew a most unusual solitude seeker. Off and on for fifty years he lived in a remote spot on the northeast shore. When in residence he always was to be seen somewhere on the evenings the *Moyie* passed. When desire for the bright lights of Proctor or Nelson overtook him, he'd bring cot and blankets down to the shore and, if she delayed beyond his bedtime, retire. Crewmen then carried him aboard, sound asleep and sometimes covered with snow, to wake the next morning in Proctor.

"If you come along twice and don't see me," he told the captain, "come ashore. I'll be dead, but everything's ready." The day the captain did stop to see him, everything was ready, even to the casket hung out of the way against the ceiling.

Argenta, our last port, was a surprise. New trucks and farm machinery stood about its brand-new dock. Men and women in shorts, jeans and sports shirts, the first I'd seen on the lake, laughed and talked as they eyed the *Moyie* for mail and freight. Down the hill hurried a belated pair, the man pushing a metal wheelbarrow in which a woman rode at ease. (A modern adaptation of an old boom-days custom when women with their full skirts and high-heeled, pointed shoes had no other way of getting about.)

"American Quakers," a passenger said. "Seven families came in here three or four years ago to start farming from scratch on the old covered-wagon principle. From California chiefly, where as conscientious objectors and pacifists they found hard going during the war. Can't be much smoother here, physically at least. Argenta's been a ghost town for more than half a century." But in the minute I had ashore, one of Argenta's new pioneers added, "We're here as settlers who want to devote the rest of our lives to farming, peace of mind and integrity in a Quaker community."

From Argenta the *Moyie* turned south through a dreamy, iridescent afternoon. The lake was peaceful as a painting; the air, dry as a good sauterne. The mountains, green, rose and white beside us, deepened to blues ahead. Mountains, water, sky, nothing more. Not even a bird.

For the second time the passengers opened their generous picnic baskets to have tea on the bare tables in a huge dining salon that had known velvet draperies, napery to the floor, phalanxes of silver, and white-coated stewards earning "college money." Most interesting to me were the members of the Women's Institute of Balfour and Queen's Bay, who were enjoying a last outing "before the rains."

In Fort St. John I had admired the Provincial president and superintendent of British Columbia's 237 Institutes. Though they had been speaking for various groups on their way north from Vancouver, they appeared fresh as dew for their scheduled sessions with Peace River groups next day. Later in the Cariboo, I learned I hadn't admired them enough.

Caught there by a cloudburst which washed out a bridge, they had not waited with other marooned travellers for the rains to end and transportation to be resumed. To keep their Fort St. John appointment, they had climbed down a steep, improvised ladder to a rowboat, crossed the swollen river to what remained of the bridge, climbed another ladder, and walked ashore to catch a northbound bus.

At that time I had wondered if such risk and effort were necessary. Now I learned that theirs had been a characteristic demonstration of the spirit and methods which have made the Institutes a national and international force in less than sixty years. The idea was born when a small boy in an Ontario village died from drinking impure milk. Resolved that women in rural areas should know how to feed their families well and safely, the boy's mother organized a small club. Similar clubs—later Institutes—spread rapidly across Canada. By 1914, British Columbia had forty-seven, and their program was widening to include improvement of every phase of homemaking and life in rural communities.

Incorporating then under the new Agricultural Act, they became a sub-department of the Provincial Department of Agriculture, which, in appreciation of their work, supplies and finances their executive offices and staff in Victoria. In 1919, they joined all the Canadian groups in the Federated Women's

Institutes. Fifteen years later, with the organization of the Associated Countrywomen of the World, they became affiliated with kindred groups that now circle the globe.

Under daylight saving time, British Columbia enjoys summer days until ten, in the north until eleven, o'clock. Not on the Kootenay! When I returned to the bridge about 4:30, the sun already was sinking behind the western peaks.

While the Selkirks deepened to silhouettes, the full white moon climbed slowly up the southeast sky to burnish peaks and glaciers with a pearly lustre. As we moved down that jewelled, ebony canyon, the *Moyie's* engines throbbed to the rhythm of "The test of beauty is the measure of the pleasure it gives." By that measure, the Selkirks about Kootenay Lake added themselves to the Grand Tetons and to the Himalayas, seen from West China, as my choices of the most beautiful mountains in all the world.

30

THE ROCKIES KNEW BETTER

One summer day in 1893, Father Coccola looked about his 17-year-old Mission of St. Eugene near the junction of the Kootenay River and St. Mary's Creek in East Kootenay. Then he looked at the quantities of gold and silver ornaments worn by the Kootenay Indians crowding the ramshackle little building. Reminded by the glitter that Indians first had known many of the fabulous mines like Rossland, Silver King, Kimberley, operating all about, he did not preach his usual sermon. He talked instead about minerals and how to find and recognize them. In conclusion, he made two promises. To any parishioner who located a new deposit, he would give a big present. All money he received from the discovery would be used to build a fine new mission.

A few days later, Father Coccola and an experienced miner named Cronin followed wizened "Old Pete" to a mountain. For more than a mile up its slope ran an enormously wide outcropping of silver-bearing lead ore, the best Cronin ever had seen. Priest and miner staked two claims—the St. Eugene and the Peter.

The St. Eugene developed into the greatest silver and lead producer of the time in Canada. To the company Cronin formed to develop both mines, Father Coccola sold his claim for $12,000 and built a fine new mission. Cronin sold his share for $500,000 and was seen no more. Old Pete's present was $300 and a big, one-room, frame house, with doors, windows, chimney, heater, and bright yellow paint.

At the presentation ceremony all but one of the Kootenay Indians attending were impressed. When everyone had gone, Old Pete dragged his tepee inside, set it up in the middle of the floor, and built a fire. As the fire burned through and dropped to the ground beneath, dense smoke filled the room.

Axe in hand, Old Pete climbed to the roof and completed construction of his new home by cutting a fine new smoke vent beside the chimney.

The St. Eugene was not the first mine discovered in East Kootenay, but its history is typical of one of the zaniest rushes in British Columbia's large collection. The first mines came to light in 1864 when, at word of gold in the Kootenays, a horde of California, Montana and Idaho miners stampeded across the Boundary. About forty miles north of it, one party sighted wild horses grazing along a creek and, thus assured of good forage for their own animals, camped for the night.

Automatically but unexpectantly, they panned the creek. Finding gold, they went no farther. Within a year, in two rival centres, Tonyville and Fisherville, Wild Horse Creek counted a thousand miners, storekeepers, labourers, from all the continent.

As their numbers swelled to more thousands, a sawmill provided lumber for hotels, saloons, dance halls, brewery, jails and stores. Everything else had to be packed in over a 450-mile trail from Walla Walla, Washington. To simplify life for themselves and their customers, the storekeepers sold all suplies for the flat price of seventy-five cents a pound and seventy-five cents per drink.

Ethics on the Wild Horse were equally simple. By writing their names on their pokes, the miners "banked" their gold with Walla Walla's storekeeper. When his safe, the only one in the Northwest, could hold no more, he tossed the rest into an open keg. No receipts were asked for or given; no poke lost or stolen.

On the other hand, though the Wild Horse yielded a steady production of gold from 1864 to 1902, punctuated by periods of gold-rush proportions, no man can say how many millions of dollars were taken from its sands and gravels. For every ounce registered with the gold commissioner, more than ten were slipped across the Boundary, gambled or drunk away. The $16,000 the commissioner collected in one six-week period lay around safely in an old travelling bag.

Among the leading spirits was Dave Griffiths, who ran three barrels of whisky into a small fortune. He also was one of the few who had no reason to hide his identity behind such names as Kansas Johnny, Galloping Kid, Dead-Shot or Bull's Eye Petes and Bills. The ladies, too, were reticent. Axe-Handle Bertha, Wildcat Jenny, Gunpowder Sue were formidable characters. But so was Little Lou. She could pilfer pokes, render home-and-mother songs, play poker, and deliver powerful camp-meeting sermons with equal facility.

When at last the mines began to wear out, Tonyville was almost a memory. Fisherville had been burned down to get at the gravels. Pack trains then brought in British Columbia's first hydraulic machinery to work the canyon walls thoroughly. Thousands of patient Chinese cleaned up what gold remained.

Meantime, a few miles south of both the old St. Eugene Mission and Wild Horse Creek, a sweep of wild hay known as Joseph's Prairie continued to be a favourite Kootenay camping ground. To it never penetrated the whistles of Canadian Pacific trains passing 150 miles north or those of the Northern Pacific 150 miles south. But in faraway Victoria, Colonel James Baker was learning more and more about the branch line the Canadian Pacific was under pressure to build through Crow's Nest Pass into the southern Kootenays.

What could be a more obvious choice for division point or terminal than Joseph's Prairie? Lying in the Rocky Mountain Trench, less than thirty miles north of the Boundary, it was one of the few level spots in the Kootenays' sea of mountains.

Just west of the Kootenay River, in the lee of a mountain that now bears his name, the colonel in 1892 laid out a townsite on 160 acres, named it Cranbrook for his birthplace in England, and planted it to oats. In oats and hay the prairie remained for five years. Then a group of merchants celebrated the completion of Fort Steele at the junction of the Kootenay and Wild Horse as the coming choice for the railway terminal. They underestimated the colonel.

Among the oats on his townsite, he marked the sites of depot, stores, hotels and built Cranbrook House as the first of them. Next he offered the Canadian Pacific a "fat slice" of his rapidly developing town. Soon construction crews arrived to throw up colonies of tents and shacks in advance of the railway. Miners from the Wild Horse joined them. Pack trains poured in from Bonners Ferry, Idaho, with supplies and seas of liquor. So did the usual assortment of gamblers and other birds of prey who followed advancing frontiers all over the continent.

They came over roads "too awful for stagecoaches," hardly less unbearable for horse-drawn wagons and sleighs. They came up the Kootenay from Nelson on stern-wheelers so constantly in danger of dashing against shore rocks that men with ropes ran along both banks to hold them steady in midstream. And when the first trains chugged in, in 1898, they came in aged boxcars fitted with slatted wooden seats.

Passengers arriving from Nelson to travel those trains east then faced a new ordeal. To reach the trains, they first had to climb a 50-foot ridge, then hop, crawl and pray themselves across a thread of unguarded trestle whose loosely irregular ties seemed bent on tossing them into the swamp below.

Nevertheless, Cranbrook became the Crow's Nest Pass line terminal. When Fort Steele's merchants and Provincial government officials recovered from that devastating blow, they moved down. Sawmills swarmed into the surrounding untapped forests. In 1901, a branch line was built to Kimberley, twenty miles north, to handle the ores of the Sullivan Mine. All that remained to ensure law, order, fire protection and other features of a town permanently fixed on a map was incorporation.

This the two hundred independent-minded pioneer residents refused to consider until fire almost destroyed the neighbouring village of Fernie and the Canadian Pacific threatened to move its terminal elsewhere. In 1905, they incorporated. Cranbrook began to grow.

Such tales of its robust beginnings in British Columbia's wild and woolly east naturally excited my interest in the town of five thousand people that now is East Kootenay's metropolis and trade centre. The hours before darkness curtained the wide lounge-car windows on the journey from Proctor did nothing to dampen my expectations. Like still waters, superb Selkirk silhouettes in profoundest blues and purples flowed by. At their feet, Kootenay Lake mirrored their reflections and those of distant settlements and fishermen's lights winking on and off like fireflies. High above, the moon, now golden, haloed everything.

But when the train stopped at Cranbrook I stepped down into a midnight so black that the station lights made no impression on it. While cold hit me between the eyes like a vengeful fist, a whistling north wind snatched my breath away. To the castanet beat of my teeth, the rescuing taxi driver said, "Lady, the altitude here's 3,018 feet. But this cold ain't *our* cold. It's the Arctic's. The Trench brings it down like a flue. You'll see how in the morning."

In the morning I did see. Just across the wide, paved main street—Baker Street, of course—lay Joseph's Prairie. Though only a fraction of the 1,000-mile Rocky Mountain Trench, its low dark shrubs, stunted trees and sweep of browning wild hay offered no protection from even the morning's eccentric breeze.

Hugging the prairie east of Baker Street, Cranbrook was as rugged as its midnight weather. But, to my surprise, mining now has to compete with railroading to hold second place in its economy. Though various mines do operate in the region, they are overshadowed by the Sullivan Mine and, to the east in Crow's Nest Pass, by Coal Creek and Michel, main sites of British Columbia's most productive coal mines.

Coal Creek, I said, *Coal Creek*! Later, while I was drinking coffee in historic Cranbrook House, another coffee fan asked, "You the lady that's writing the book about B.C.?" Remembering all the writers I'd met and heard about in the Province, I qualified, "A book."

"That's all right," he said largely. "I just want to tell you one thing *not* to say. Don't call Fernie a coal-mining town. The coal mines is at Coal Creek seven miles away, and at Michel and on east. Fernie's the administrative centre for

Crow's Nest Pass. And a lumber town. And if the oil companies prowling around the pass have any luck, one day we'll be a big oil centre. We get tourists, too—fishermen, hunters, skiers. Wouldn't get them if Fernie wasn't a nice, clean little town."

With ten major lumber operations making their headquarters in Cranbrook, logging is its main industry. The lumberjack, not the miner, "built the town—with his broad axe, peavey, cant hook, and tendency to spend his money as fast as he earns it."

Back in the early days between 1897 and 1907, sawmills could be set up anywhere. Unbroken timber assured them of an ample supply of logs. Cranbrook citizens snapped up every board as fast as it was cut. When the forests, like the mines, were depleted, many millowners retired on their profits. Others have continued by keeping up with the new methods.

During the Great Depression, however, the large mills closed down, not to reopen until the late thirties. But the small ones devised a method of their own which proved a boon then and ever since. They invented the "portable mill." Smaller still and inexpensive, it could travel anywhere on skids. With it, they survived by filling Canadian Pacific orders for millions of railroad ties.

Again when World War II created an insatiable demand for lumber, any kind of lumber, the "portables" obliged by cutting, selling and shipping rough boards still damp and warm from the saw. The war over, many dropped out. Others carry on today as planers for the large mills. But the idea carries on in other parts of the Province. In isolated fjords, on float villages in island or coastal bay, in new areas opening for settlement in the interior, the cries of the portables are loud and welcome.

Cranbrook waits only for adequate highways and roads to welcome an industry that may rival mining, railroading, even logging. Because of its location, halfway between Banff and Spokane, it is a natural tourist centre. In the fall, big-game parties make it their point of departure for the mountain retreats of black bear, brown bear, and the fast-disappearing grizzly; for moose, elk, white-tailed deer; for mountain goat and sheep.

From pioneers who still remember the mining, railroad building and early logging era to its famous Girls' Band, Cranbrook has many facets of interest. But the only words I heard clearly concerned the weather. For months I'd been looking forward to Cranbrook as the climax, scenically and historically, of all I'd seen and heard in British Columbia.

From there I would travel the Rocky Mountain Trench north between snow-capped and glaciered Selkirks on the west, snow-capped and glaciered Rockies on the east. I would ascend the Kootenay to its source and the Columbia from its source at Canal Flat through the lovely Columbia and Windermere Lake country. See Kootenay National Park's five hundred square miles of Rockies, celebrated Radium Hot Springs, marble canyons, "paint pots," iceberg lake, and other natural wonders. Visit sites, like Boat Encampment, fixed in Provincial history by David Thompson and the fur brigades.

October, however, with its promise of rains or snows that would make such a journey witless, had just turned the corner. And that morning as I left my hotel I had seen more than Joseph's Prairie.

To the north, beyond low, rippling green hills, rose the Rockies. Mile after mile of rocky peaks, rather. Welded together at the shoulders in one great wind-blown wave of crests, basins, ridges, they rolled up the pale-blue sky. Not a tree or blade of grass dared to grow on them. Not a flake of snow appeared to soften that mighty mass of solid, battleship-grey rock.

Never one of their admirers while viewing them in close-up from train, car or mountain lodge, I remained fixed to the sidewalk before their grandeur in perspective. Sudden gusts of dust swirled about me. Pedestrians walked round me. Still I stood, fascinated, while a scroll-like grey cloud, exactly as long as that wave of rock was wide, formed above them.

For minutes perhaps it hung motionless. Then with the finality of a proscenium curtain when the stars of a play have taken their last bow, it began to unroll. Slowly, deliberately, it covered the peaks, then the ridges and basins. At last it dropped behind the low green hills and the upper edge folded down to erase from the now cloudless sky every sign that the Rockies ever had been there.

"When the songs are over, the clock runs down" repeated itself in my mind as I watched. Once that had seemed a pretty Chinese verse that made no sense. Now it had a definite and personal meaning. I knew at that moment in Cranbrook that my British Columbia safari had come to an end.

I couldn't believe it, wouldn't believe it. Against that conviction, I piled the assurances of everyone I met in Cranbrook. To a man—and a woman—they declared that these clear, warm, sunny days would continue for another two weeks. In vain.

The next morning as the Kettle Valley Railway sped me back to Vancouver, I spent a miserable twenty minutes watching bright sunshine make a golden glory of the poplars against the sombre greens of the conifers. Suddenly, and with the fury of the monsoons, the rains came.

THE LOWER FRASER VALLEY

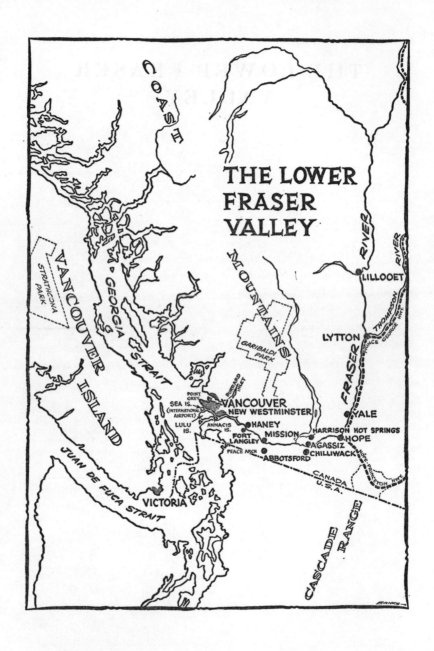

THE LOWER
FRASER
VALLEY

31

THE GEOLOGIC BONUS THAT
WAGS THE PROVINCE

The silt-laden Fraser's gallantry at Lytton in permitting the Thompson to flow south beside it, clear and undefiled, does not —cannot—last long. No sooner do they meet than the eastern ranks of the granite-hearted Coast Mountains mass across their way.

Through 6,000 to 7,000-foot peaks, the Fraser has carved a 72-mile canyon, avoided others whose white crests rise to 9,500 feet and over. Naked granite, sheer or jagged, walls it. Above those walls, the mountains rear back, banded or patched with weathered granite, talus, sand, and conifers so thinly scattered they stand out like hair on a mad cat.

Continuing its attack on those narrowing walls, the Fraser chews and claws. Swirls in grinding eddies about mid-channel rocks and rocky islets. Batters down or over others in turbulent rapids. Unable to stand the brutal pace, the Thompson breaks up; after some thirty miles, gives up.

Granite walls, a hundred feet high and less than two hundred feet apart, here form a veritable Hell's Gate. With a crash that echoes round the mountains, the Fraser rushes into it, twenty to a hundred feet deep, depending on the season, digs down, piles up in a foaming melee. Drab as ever, if a trifle paler, it emerges in the Devil's Wash Basin below as a spinning whirl-pool, gathers momentum, boils on.

The toll in human life that this fearsomely beautiful canyon has taken is reflected in man's consistent respect for it. Before a European ever saw it, death in its snarling waters had taught the Indians to discard canoes for crude tree-trunk-and-vine ladders and spans fixed precariously to its walls. Fearless, tire-less Simon Fraser and his party cached their equipment at the centuries-old Indian encampment on Lytton's ridge and took

279

to the ladders and spans. After working one day on the trail Hudson's Bay traders tried to break through the canyon, one man committed suicide rather than work another. Early miners bypassed its gold-riddled sandbars to cut the Cariboo Trail through the mountains to Lillooet on the upper river. In the 1880's, Canadian Pacific engineers waited until two seamen who had learned their trade on sailing ships strung ropes from rock to rock or tree before, barefoot and clinging to those supports, they ventured to lay out the work for the first construction crews.

"Men were tougher in those days," the lounge steward told me. As proof, he pointed to a smoke smudge on the façade of sand and gravel above and below a Canadian National tunnel overlooking Hell's Gate. From the highway far above, a truck had fallen down on the track and burst into flame just minutes before a train roared through. Thrown out and wrapped round a tree, the truck driver escaped both flames and train. "But," said the steward disgustedly, "from the way he yelled for help, you'd think he'd been killed."

Hell's Gate is the key to the migration and survival of Fraser River salmon, according to the International Pacific Salmon Fisheries Commission. During the years the Canadian Pacific and Canadian National were blasting out their roadbeds on either side, falling rock all but sealed this narrow passage. Trying to conquer that blockade to reach their spawning grounds above, sockeye died in such thousands each season that by 1921 the end of their migrations could be foreseen.

To save them, the commission built two concrete fish ladders below the Gate. Three storeys high, one five hundred feet long, the other two hundred fifty, they appear, to the human eye, to be Band-Aids applied to the water-black and -bruised rocks, but to the sockeye they were lifesavers. While salmon production on other river systems declined, the Fraser's expanded into one of the Province's most interesting and important industries.

Other inhabitants of this lonely, tumultuous world are the Indians who come to fish in summer. Beneath arbours high on rocky ridges, their split salmon dry on crossbars in the sun.

But their fishpoles and stripped branches hang like bits of driftwood from rock or sandbar just above the water. Only a crescent of small, bobbing corks below betrays the nets.

Time was, says a Salish legend, when the Fraser was so crystal clear that the ancestors of these canny fishermen waited in vain for salmon or sturgeon to come within range of their spears and poles. Facing starvation, they appealed to Q'als, the Great Transformer. He turned the waters dark.

After almost sixty of these terrifying miles, the Fraser, though still dangerous, quiets enough for Yale, on another ridge, to become one of British Columbia's oldest sites. From the Indian camp here, Simon Fraser stole a canoe, kidnapped a guide, and went on to sight the river's exit in the Gulf of Georgia and, to his keen disappointment, learn it was not the Columbia. Here, in 1848, Hudson's Bay erected a trading post, only to have it overrun eight years later when the first gold was found on Hill's Bar, a mile and a half below.

As the richest sandbar on the river and the longest worked, Hill's Bar made Yale the most important town on the Mainland, and the gayest north of San Francisco. The 400-mile Cariboo Road began here. Though the first small steamers were tough and their captains tougher, navigation of the Fraser ended here.

Only the little Church of St. John the Divine remains to remind the dwindling village of its heyday. No, the mountains remain. Through an enormous gap to the south, three snow-covered peaks promised a sensational climax to the canyon. Not so! Beyond them others rose until, at the very least, I expected the Fraser to celebrate its victory with a Niagara or Victoria Falls. I should have known better! The tawny river ran out into a parklike valley, to fall flat on its face.

At this "foot" of Fraser Canyon, Hope, once a trading post and now a peaceful logging and tourist centre, bills itself as the "Gateway to the Interior." As a stop on the Trans-Canada Highway and head of the new Hope-Princeton Highway across the Coast Mountains, it may be right. But for me it was the gateway to the Lower Mainland, which bills *itself* as "the most important area in British Columbia."

Once upon a time between this point and the Pacific an enormous icesheet, so deep that only the highest peaks rose out of it, ground its incalculable weight over the extreme southwest corner of the Province. As it withdrew, glacier after glacier moved down from surrounding crests to crush and pack mountain shards into a more or less rolling, funnel-shaped bed which powerful sea tides further packed and levelled.

To the southbound Fraser, this long-necked, west-facing funnel offered not only a short cut to the sea but almost a hundred miles of tidal flats where for the first time in its long course it could rid itself of its burden of silt. For millions of years it did just that until the larger and larger islands it thus created merged to gag it with its own debris.

Forced back into its old routine, it cut a deeper and deeper channel through the upper valley, various channels through the lower. Today it leaves Hope as a river seven hundred to a thousand feet wide and forty deep. Expanding steadily until it sights the sea, it forks then in a triple-mouthed delta to join the Pacific via the Gulf of Georgia.

But for icesheet, glaciers and Fraser, there would be no Lower Mainland. Vancouver, if anything, would be an Estevan Point or isolated fishing village. Stranger still to contemplate is the fact that, despite the Fraser's assorted mouths pouring dark waters into the gulf, this most accessible section of the British Columbia coast was one of the last to be "discovered."

Not that it hadn't been seen! In 1790, Eliza, the Spanish navigator, passed the delta while searching the Mainland for an entrance to Northwest Passage. Suspecting a river ran there, he named it *Florida Blanca*, but sailed on without verifying his suspicion. Two years later, two small Spanish ships tried to find it. Failing, they had anchored off Point Grey, just a few miles north, when Captain Vancouver came along. He not only had sighted two mouths of the Fraser. He had "condemned" them, says Howay, as mouths of the Columbia. So when the Spaniards asked if he had seen the *Florida Blanca*, he declared no such river existed.

Salish Indians living in the delta first heard of the white man when fellow tribesmen from Vancouver Island told them of the weirdly dressed, pale-faced Sky People in "white-winged canoes" who had visited their shores in 1792. But the Mainlanders had to wait until 1808 to see samples. What they saw was bronzed and buckskinned Simon Fraser and his men descending their river from the interior. They were not impressed.

Twenty more years passed before the white man came to stay. In 1827, Hudson's Bay Company erected a small Fort Langley at the Fraser's mouth. That site proving too dangerous, it built a bigger, better and "permanent" Fort Langley some thirty miles up-river.

Icesheet, glaciers and Fraser shaped the Lower Mainland's fifteen hundred square miles as a natural geographic unit. Coast Mountains on the north, Cascades on the south, and on the west the gulf reshaped it as a ragged autumn leaf and natural scenic unit. As crown colony and province, British Columbia developed it as a natural economic unit.

Here is Vancouver, Canada's largest Pacific port, manufacturing and commercial centre. Here about 60 per cent of the population is concentrated. Here is the "Larder of the Coast."

Fish in the river, game in the forests, wild berries, nuts, edible roots and fertile soil already had proved it a larder for the Salish and for prehistoric peoples before them. The plethora of salmon established a reputation with the first Fort Langley which the second rapidly amplified. "Brine-cured" salmon and oolichan flowed from its saltery; grains and potatoes, cattle and pigs, butter and cheeses, from its fields, pastures, dairy. In addition, it built up a good fur trade.

Because of its bounty, Langley assumed key importance in the 1840's when the 49th Parallel appeared the probable choice as International Boundary. Replacing Fort Vancouver on the Lower Columbia, it served as terminal for all Mainland fur brigades and supply base for the trading posts until that gold strike at Hill's Bar.

In order—and disorder—Victoria, Langley, Hope and Yale went down before the inrush of miners. When the Indians deserted their traps to work for the mines' high wages, the entire fur trade was demoralized. But, though reduced to a mere port of call, Fort Langley still had one more date with history. Within its cedar-log stockade, on November 19, 1858, Governor Douglas officially proclaimed the Crown Colony of British Columbia.

Nine days later, in the townsite of Derby, laid out nearby for the new colony's capital, lots offered at $100 sold like popcorn for $750. All seemed set for an auspicious future when the site was declared unsuitable for a port and for defence.

An unbroken stretch of forest rippling over low hills along the north bank of the Fraser, about fifteen miles from its mouth, proved a truly capital setting. The river supplied a fine fresh-water harbour. Round the horizon curved the great crescent of Coast-Cascade Mountains.

Within a few years, New Westminster, as Queen Victoria named it, no longer was a capital. But as a booming frontier town of sawmills and fisheries, it laid the foundation for the "Royal City" of today's thirty-three thousand people. From a commercial core on the first terrace above the river, its residential districts rise more than two hundred feet or spread along the highways almost to merge with neighbouring municipalities. On the west, it shares borders with Burnaby, which borders Vancouver.

One of the few Canadian cities almost completely industrialized, New Westminster does stand next to Vancouver as the Province's largest processing centre for lumber, fish and beef products. Log booms for its giant mills line the Fraser for miles. To its harbour annually come more than four hundred deep-sea vessels, countless coastal boats, barges, tugs, fishboats, to bring or carry away more than four million tons of foreign and domestic trade. While other cities vie to attract new industries, its problem is to find ways to expand what it has.

Meantime, farms spread over the thousand square miles which the Fraser had buried under its fertile silts. Along both river and tributaries, logging camps and small mills with picturesque sugar-loaf waste-burners exploited the forests. Fishing

284

villages, picturesque also with drying nets and fleets of fish-boats, dotted the riverbanks or climbed steep headlands about the beautiful bays scalloping the coast below the delta. When the Provincial government drained away Sumas Lake, something new was added—Canada's leading hopgrowing area, tobacco fields, vineyards and cherry orchards. Until World War II, as nostalgic old-timers describe it, the Lower Mainland was a Garden of Eden.

About ten thousand farms, representing 40 per cent of all Provincial farms, still remain. Among them they yield two-thirds of British Columbia's total production of dairy and poultry products. All manner of small acreages produce fruits, berries, vegetables, seeds, and specialties from bulbs to mushrooms to (filbert) nuts. Horticultural farms and fur farms do their share to give the valley one of the most diversified economies on the continent.

But today these products of the land do not even rate among the Lower Mainland's basic industries. And tomorrow lumber and fish may be demoted from first and third places to third and fourth. Manufacturing, as a more stable and profitable industry, rapidly is forging to the top. Shipping and transcontinental transportation press closely on its heels.

On these contenders, Lower Mainlanders base Great Expectations for the future of their little geologic bonus. British Columbia always has been a land of raw products. Now it is ripening like an Okanagan peach for industry. This ripening coincides with the development of new technological methods, to widen the field for both primary and secondary industries.

Fraser sockeye, trawl and tuna fishing and oyster production are increasing. Many fish by-products once considered waste now can be processed. As vast new timber areas suitable for pulp open, all kinds of textile, cellophane, paper and allied manufactures can be added to the plywood and veneer mills. Kitimat's aluminum promises to attract secondary industries making everything from house numbers to machinery frames.

Now that oil and gas have been piped down from northern British Columbia and Alberta, other metals can be treated, brick and ceramic manufactures developed. Geologists and oil-men recently ranked the Lower Mainland next to Peace River country, Fernie, and the Queen Charlotte Islands as fourth among the seven Provincial regions where the possibilities of striking oil, gas or both are greatest. And so on. And on.

Unlike the rest of the Province, the Lower Mainland has sufficient hydroelectric power. By the early 1960's, when the British Columbia Electric Company's $200 million plant at Port Moody is completed, it will have thermal power. Vancouver and New Westminster now have established industrial cores. Shipping and transportation, already well developed, are capable of tremendous expansion.

Vancouver and New Westminster, with the largest and best-equipped sea and fresh-water harbours in the Province, can work together as a unit. Two transcontinental railways, one Provincial, and the American Great Northern Railroad from Seattle link it with every corner of North America. All west-bound Provincial and Canadian highways eventually funnel into Lytton and Hope and so through the Lower Mainland to Vancouver.

At the Peace Arch on the Boundary, the Prince George Highway from Vancouver connects with U.S. Highway 99 and all main American highways. Sea Island, one of the delta group, as the Province's International Airport, is a frenzied chambered nautilus, enlarging and enlarging but never large enough. Smaller airports serve the valley and Vancouver when fog or rains "sock in" Sea Island.

All this and more add up to the Lower Mainland's two great Great Expectations. Location, raw materials and transportation facilities naturally make it the market for the developing trade of all western Canada and Alaska. As Canada's "Gateway to the Pacific," it anticipates a practically unlimited foreign trade with the Far East. The year 2000, if not before, will see a population of a million and a half flourishing within its Coast-Cascade and Gulf of Georgia boundaries.

Such heady prospects have inspired a land rush not unlike the gold rush of a century ago. Thousands of Canadians are flocking in to overrun rooted villages or plant new ones along the main highways. Their motels, restaurants, oil stations, garages, antique and woollen shops, souvenir stands, used-car lots, lumberyards and real estate offices run together in a sprawl of temporary structures about which the less said the better right now. Doubtless with the years they will emerge as cities appropriate to their beautiful setting.

Annacis Island, recently a sandbank in the Fraser's mouth, now is an ultra-modern industrial park. Lulu Island, a marsh drained years ago to become a pastoral of farms and commercial gardens, rapidly is vanishing under new industries and housing developments. Banks of the Fraser are being washed down, its bed dredged up to create new industrial sites.

Elsewhere and everywhere residentials sprout like cabbage fields, their homes as precisely rowed, as varied as cabbages are varied. About them the one-time farming, lumbering and particularly the fishing villages cling like frayed and fading fringe.

To glimpse the Garden of Eden of pre-war memories, one must leave the highways for the byways. Against the blue and white walls of Coast and Cascade Mountains, fields, orchards and flawless commercial gardens ripen in the sun; dairy herds are sleek in green pastures.

But to the dismay of Vancouverites, who long have dreamed of the day when they can retire to a few of these fertile acres "with a view," the current owners have eaten heavily of the fruit of knowledge. Their acres, few or many, are for sale—but not to private individuals. No matter how far they may be from the highways, *they* confidently dream of the day when opportunity must knock at their doors. And there, checkbook in hand, will be the purchasing agent for a new industry or a de luxe housing development!

After extensive motoring with one pair or another of frustrated Vancouver dreamers, I read with interest the recommendations of the Lower Mainland Regional Planning Board. The Lower Mainland has the industrial sites to support a million and a half population if they can be conserved for that purpose. Other sites must be reserved for recreation, military or social purposes. Arable acres must be preserved for agriculture. Residentials must be guided into the less valuable upland areas. The size of its cities must be limited. Future industries must be located in small, dispersed towns in decentralized areas.

They can dream, too, can't they?

32

MEET THE JONESES

This is destined to be a great city, perhaps the greatest in Canada. We must see that it has a name commensurate with its dignity and importance. Vancouver it shall be if I have the ultimate decision.

Sir William Van Horne, the dynamo then driving the rails of the Canadian Pacific over five hundred miles of mountains, made that prophecy in 1884 about a collection of log and frame structures strung along the south shore of Burrard Inlet. In the twenty-two years since John Morton felled the first trees for a cabin, early comers had run through such names as Gastown, Liverpool, Hastings, currently were considering Granville.

Sir William was not the first prophet. Ninety-two years before, Captain Vancouver himself had forecast for the area about the inlet he named for Sir Harry Burrard of the British Navy:

· The serenity of the climate, the innumerable pleasing landscapes, and abundant fertility . . . require only to be enriched by the industry of man . . . to render it the most lovely country that could be imagined.

Shaped and dormant as a sloth that has provided against the need for all future effort, the 45-square-mile hump between inlet and Fraser River that is Vancouver proper slept away seventy-three of the years between prophets. The Gulf of Georgia pillowed its blunt snout. Burrard Inlet cushioned one curled forepaw. The North Arm of the Fraser smoothed its long back. Fraser silt and rain forest 150 to 200 feet deep covered it. Wooded islands in the gulf and a rampart of Coast Mountains along the inlet's north shore sheltered it from arctic gales and temperatures.

Another century had to near its end before the history of the city that replaced the forest revealed a pattern. If graphed, it would resemble the peaks and valleys of those North Shore Mountains in evening silhouette. Its deduction is as clear. When in a valley, Vancouver need not wait with Mr. Micawber for "something to turn up." Somewhere an event is in the making to carry her to a new peak.

This good fortune may be by grace of the beautiful and virtuous twin daughters of a great chief who thousands of years ago made peace among the warring coastal tribes. Impressed, the Great Spirit immortalized them as the twin peaks of the North Shore Mountains "to guard this sunset coast" forever. Thereafter, the Indians knew them as the Twin Sisters or Chief's Daughters; the realistic pioneers, as Twin Peaks and Sheba's Breasts. About 1886, they were renamed The Lions for the sculptured beasts about Lord Nelson's Column in Trafalgar Square and their duties restated as "Guardians of Vancouver."

Two events of 1865 seeded Vancouver's location. The erection of the Hastings Saw Mill on the inlet's south shore. And, in the Selkirks, Moberly's discovery of Eagle Pass. An Atlantic-to-Pacific railway over an all-British route now a certainty, a group of "frontier busters" felled but did not clear a 20-acre "CPR townsite."

There, one autumn morning, Lauchlan Hamilton, "Godfather of Vancouver," named the three sides of the square palisaded by unbroken forest Cambie, Hastings, and Carrall Streets; the fourth, along the inlet's beach, Water. Nineteen years later, in April, 1886, as a village of six hundred to a thousand frame and log structures and other properties worth more than one million dollars, Vancouver incorporated.

Before the year ended, two disasters toppled it off that first low peak. Ignoring its townsite, the Canadian Pacific stopped its rails at the head of the inlet to make Port Moody its western terminal. In November, fire reduced Vancouver to ashes.

One year later, the Canadian Pacific entered a Vancouver of twenty-five hundred people and properties worth more than $5 million. So did the first cargo ship from London. Within five years the town had new industries, a Customs House, waterworks, streetcars and fifteen thousand residents. Arrival of the Empress ships to inaugurate trans-Pacific shipping established her reputation as transportation centre and seaport.

In 1893 came depression, the severest winter ever recorded, and floods that washed out Lower Mainland farms. While ruined farmers and unemployed loggers flocked in to her soup kitchens, masses of her own citizens departed. Three years later, gold was discovered in the Klondike! Outfitting the maddened hordes and building ships to carry them and mountains of freight north put Vancouver back on her feet as export and foreign trade centre. By 1905, cable connections with Australia completed, her trade, commerce and boundaries expanding in all directions, she embarked on a spectacular real estate boom.

At its peak in 1911 depression struck again. Following on its heels, World War I drained away her young men for military service and working population for the war industries in the east. In 1920, the Panama Canal opened! Now she could compete for Atlantic as well as Pacific trade. Now grain from the Prairie Provinces could be shipped more cheaply from Burrard Inlet, via the Canal, than by the eastern routes. The million tons she shipped in 1921 multiplied 105 times within ten years.

The Great Depression that rocked the east coast in 1929 did not seriously disturb the west until the 1930's. Millions of dollars poured into Vancouver tills by North Americans unable to afford European or world tours were an important factor in helping Vancouver to weather that crisis until the outbreak of World War II. *This* time, war industries and war workers came to her, and thousands of young men and women in uniform. When the war ended, some thirty thousand remained or returned to become permanent residents. By 1946, the post-war boom was under way. By 1947, British Columbia was Canada's fastest growing province, and Vancouver—

Next to Montreal and Toronto, Vancouver is Canada's largest city. With more than 366,000 of the Province's total 1.4 million population, she is British Columbia's metropolis.

As Metropolitan Vancouver, she almost doubles that number. True, the vigorous and independent neighbours mushrooming over the lower slopes of the North Shore Mountains, along the Fraser and across the Lower Mainland are reluctant to make that title official. But the handwriting of the Torontos and Chicagos of this continent is large and clear upon their walls.*

Enough surely has been said and written about the Coast Mountains, Gulf of Georgia, Burrard Inlet and Lower Fraser to suggest that, scenically, Vancouver can boast one of the most beautiful natural settings in the world.

Perhaps it is too beautiful. Residents and visitors alike are apt to entertain an illusion that the city equals its setting. In fact, on the radiant May morning I arrived from a seven-month winter east of the Rockies, I viewed all assurances to that effect as sheer understatement.

Not until I returned from travelling the Province did I begin to grasp the meaning of Fielding's baffling line, "Where beauties lie in ambush . . ." The ambush is that in spring, summer, fall, winter such halcyon days may continue for weeks. For permanent residents, of course, the cycle repeats itself, with variations, year after year. At such times the world and its headlines, next door or afar, are not easily remembered. One actually must struggle to escape the tentacles of complacency, to maintain an objective viewpoint.

Objective-minded citizens are struggling now against that complacency to replan and rebuild square miles in the heart of the city and to guide its future development toward a realization of Van Horne's and Vancouver's prophecies. Already, with such uniquely beautiful buildings as the British Columbia Electric Company's skyscraper projecting an impressive skyline, the city resembles Emily Carr's memorable painting "Old and New Forest," in which fresh young firs rise, tier on tier, as their aging elders lean to fall. Meantime—

With almost fourteen hundred deep-sea ships and thirty

*Burnaby—83,000; Coquitlam—21,000; Delta—9,000; New Westminster —33,000; North Vancouver—20,000; North Vancouver District—26,000; Richmond—26,000; Surrey—49,000; West Vancouver—20,000, and a number of small communities and areas.

thousand coastal vessels coming and going with almost twelve million tons of cargo each year, Vancouver is a world port. As a few of the latest available annual figures show, she is British Columbia's financial, trade, industrial and tourist centre:

	VANCOUVER	PROVINCE
Checks cleared against individual accounts.	.$12,579,751,243	$15,231,472,672
Construction value of building permits....	64,579,148	112,139,014
Selling value of factory shipments	750,277,091	1,659,527,000
Retail sales..........	680,460,000	1,563,921,000
Tourist trade........	50,000,000	90,000,000

As the focal point of all shipping, rail, air and bus lines, of telegraph, telephone, cable, and the major radio and television stations, she is the Province's transportation and communication centre. Medical centre. Sports centre. Arts centre. But for one small, two-year college in Victoria, she concentrates on the University of British Columbia campus all the opportunities for higher education in the Province. With the exception of the capital, she possesses or controls all phases of Provincial life.

Her population is as cosmopolitan. The great majority, naturally, are of British descent. Thousands of them have come not only from all parts of the Dominion but of the Commonwealth to round out their lives in a beautiful setting and a balmy climate. In this she shares honours with Victoria, to compile a statistic with provocative implications, economic and otherwise. Eleven per cent of Canada's sixteen million people are sixty years of age or older. Ten per cent of the eleven per cent live in British Columbia.

She is also the choice of more Italians, Germans, Scandinavians, Netherlanders and Ukrainians than make up the entire population of Kamloops or Trail. Some ten thousand Chinese provide her with a Chinatown second in size and interest only to San Francisco's. Japanese and Sikhs, Poles, Russians, Jews, and other Asiatic and European peoples merge their languages, customs and cultures with her own. Whatever their national origin and background, their three main interests are the harbour, sports or outdoor recreation, and gardens.

Burrard Inlet is indeed the most important, exciting and varied feature of the city's life. One of the world's great harbours, fifteen miles long, two and a quarter miles at its widest, with a hundred miles of water frontage, fifty square miles of deep-sea anchorages, it is also Canada's largest port for year-round navigation, second largest in deep-sea tonnage.

To relieve the congestion at wharves that now berth ninety-seven ships, a new dock is adding about two thousand feet. Transit sheds and refrigerated warehouses provide a cargo area of more than two million square feet. Seven grain elevators have a capacity of 18.7 millions bushels. One of them, Alberta's Wheat Pool, is among the largest in the world. Another is Saskatchewan's. Aluminum from Kitimat, her own and the Lower Mainland's incoming industries, the immense projects under way in the Province and western Canada, bright prospects for trade with the Orient, promise to double and treble them.

The stevedore and his wife whom I encountered enjoying a busman's holiday on the waterfront characteristically voiced the consensus of local opinion. Said Mr. Vancouver, "One day we're bound to be as big or bigger than San Francisco. One day we'll be the biggest port on the Pacific." Said Mrs. Vancouver, "Bigger, much bigger."

What makes it excitingly different from most world ports is not the ocean liners and cargo ships from the seven seas. It is the traffic, motley as the motorized traffic on Hastings Street, which moves among them in an urban version of Inside Passage's rural sea country. White ferries, ship-size and small, million-dollar dredges, halibut boats, seiners, gillnetters, barges, tugs towing everything from ore-laden barges and log booms to float houses, weave in and out of the inner harbour. Yachts, sailboats, cruisers, launches, outboarders, sculls, canoes, even the odd rowboat, dodge about to create much the same problems as pedestrians ashore.

Occasionally a Page One stranger appears—like the trim white ship with a bee-stung nose that had laid the longest line ever of 138,000-volt cable between the Mainland and Vancouver Island, to supply electricity to the lower Island. Revolutionary forerunners of tomorrow's gillnetters and log carriers may not be strangers long.

The first, a far, glad cry from the ungainly, cheerless fishboats now in use, equipped with radio-telephone, echo sounder, electric anchor, built-in bunks, galley and other devices and comforts, can do ten knots an hour. The second, a barge almost three hundred feet long and sixty wide, can carry a million board feet of logs from the Queen Charlotte Islands to Vancouver in half the time of the old carriers, dump its cargo in less than half an hour, and within minutes be ready to return for more.

As a composite of a floating community's city services, the omnipresent tug, *Brocton II*, chugs around with the authority of a police chief's car, to sweep the harbour clean of debris, repair marine property, warn or charge traffic violators, rescue boats in distress. A street of floating gas stations, fixed offshore, serves small boats as handily as their land equivalents serve automobiles.

If the inner harbour is Hastings Street, the outer, notably on weekends, is Stanley Park. As the curled paw of the sloth, the park itself juts into the inlet to create the First Narrows between the two harbours. This 1,000-acre vestige of primeval forest gives Everyman opportunity to share in harbour, sports and gardens, yet retains much of its wilderness quality. For good measure, it adds Malkin Bowl where TUTS—Theatre Under the Stars—to date has delighted more than four million spectators with its expertly presented musical comedies.

South and west of the park, within minutes of the city's centre, bathing beaches, picnic grounds and, after every tide, hunting grounds of local beachcombers ring the outer harbour. Sports fishermen in every sort of craft dot the waters; others, from small boy to octogenarian, dot the shore. When smelt are running, hundreds equip themselves with small nets or improvised containers to gather them in as ships plowing through the swimming millions in mid-channel drive them shoreward in waves. Here are the water skiers, speedboats, racers, yachts, red- and white-winged sailing regattas. Here wander the young in heart with moonbeams and appleblossoms in their eyes while the less fortunate sag in relaxed content about beach fires, fried fish in their hands.

From Point Grey, Vancouver's westernmost tip, the University's 996-acre campus commands the whole magnificent seascape of inlet, gulf, mountains and islands. Second largest university in Canada, with one of the highest scholastic ratings, it points with pride to a distinguished faculty cheerfully raided from other universities and eight thousand students. Among them are the three hundred students, faculty members and their wives from the forestry department of Hungary's Sopron University who escaped the 1956 revolution to continue their work here in freedom.

As the centre of one of the most intensively managed fish areas in the world UBC leads all other Dominion universities in attention to fish and fisheries. Logically, too, it houses the wireless station of British Columbia's far-flung search and rescue organization. From this nerve centre, expert operators maintain a 24-hour watch over the eight different wave lengths used in ship-to-shore communications to pick up distress signals and relay them to the Jericho co-ordination centre, from which the search and rescue operations go into immediate action.

Setting and climate join to inspire Vancouver's love of sports and outdoor life. After every session long or short of rains or fogs, young and old seek the sun as a starving man seeks food. They throng scenic highways running in all directions except west. They wind bumper to bumper round Stanley Park's highways overlooking the harbour, through more miles of forest. They fill its courts, courses, and playing fields for tennis, golf, soccer, cricket, bowling on the green, checkers, square dancing.

Then every younger, smaller park, square and playground comes to life. "Little Mountain," or Queen Elizabeth Park, crowning the city's highest point, swarms with sun worshippers enjoying the stunning sunken gardens about the foot of a waterfall and panorama of native trees and shrubs. Others find Cleveland Dam Park where, across the Capilano River's captive waters, The Lions dominate a mountain view more than reminiscent of Banff.

They take over the outer harbour for every kind of water sport; turn out by thousands to angle for a prize-winning entry in the fantastic salmon derbies of late summer. They seek Howe Sound and the gulf, or inland lakes, rivers, streams, for either salt- or fresh-water fishing, swimming, camping. As alpinists or hunters, they climb the mountains. From as early as September sometimes to as late as July, they keep three ski runs busy—Mt. Seymour, reached by car; Hollyburn and Grouse Mountain, by chair lift.

Or, as spectators, they enjoy superlative views of Coast and Cascade Mountains, of city and harbour, of the gulf and of Gulf and Vancouver Islands. From the summit of Grouse, they follow footpaths into aboriginal wilderness to stand at the feet of Douglas fir, five hundred to a thousand years old, hemlock and cedar only a little less tall.

They ride bicycles draped with skates and hockey sticks or towing toboggans to flooded squares or snowy park slopes. Spring is a gay procession of cars topped with boats or followed by boat trailers bound for summer moorage; autumn, a sad return. They ski in the morning, swim in the afternoon, picnic on a beach, and play tennis or square-dance under lights.

Not content with what nature offers, they go in heavily for spectator sports. Horse racing and boxing. Baseball and hockey. Above all, for that peculiar Canadian madness, professional football.

Port authorities may complain that many Vancouverites regard Burrard Inlet as a playground or "piece of scenery." Sports fanatics may deplore fellow citizens who can take sports or leave them alone. But no one can point to the man (or woman) with soul so dead who never to himself (or anyone else within range) has said, "*My garden . . .*"

From the first crocus to the last chrysanthemum and rose, the gardening passion flames openly. During the rest of the year, it is merely banked among seed catalogues, gardening books and peat moss. Every newspaper features a garden column. Almost every radio station rings nightly with a floral Voice of Authority. At any given moment during the open season, thousands can be observed kneeling before a flower bed, poised like a mountain goat on a knife-edged level of rock garden, or on tour with lawn or power mower.

Their fluency with Latin names of trees and flowers would confound Cicero. Their fey processes of acquiring and transmitting their knowledge frequently confounds others. As one obviously green-thumbed gardener informed me, "If an arbutus is a larch, that tree is an arbutus." The tree *was* an arbutus, but an arbutus is not a larch.

To Vancouverites themselves, roses are the queen of flowers. Grown since pioneer days, abloom almost the year round, they are guests in 80 per cent of the gardens. The Rose Show in June, when scores of top-flight "rosarians"—though amateurs —exhibit, is the big event of the year. To the visitor, however, the rock garden is Vancouver's triumph. Because of the rolling or hilly terrain, rocks come naturally or must be found for walls and embankments. The creative imagination and labour that transform them into mosaics of harmonious colour and design would build Lions Gate Bridge.

Fraser silt, centuries of leaf mould, a beneficent sun, and an annual rainfall that ranges from forty inches at Sea Island to 125 at Capilano, ten miles nearer the mountains, come with the lease. Professional landscapers and gardeners stylize the grounds of suburban showplaces. But it is the self-made gardeners, whose perennials, annuals, shrubs, flowering vines and flowering trees flow down mile after mile of residential streets in a changing pattern of forms and colours, who imprint the visitor's mind with the vision of a city that rivals its setting.

All in all, and in short, Vancouver has no need to keep up with the Joneses. For good, ill, and British Columbia, she *is* the Joneses.

BIBLIOGRAPHY

For two reasons, this Bibliography is brief and divided. Much of the information is too immediate to have made its way between book covers. Much of it was derived from conversations or interviews with men, women and children on the scene or by unabashed use of my own eyes.

To verify or amplify what I heard or saw, I relied on a few books and reports by British Columbia's own authorities, notably F. W. Howay, the Province's highly valued historian. Other books and articles came my way as I travelled about.

Reference Volumes

British Columbia Atlas of Resources. British Columbia Natural Resources Conference, 1956

British Columbia Natural Resources Conference, Report of Fifth, Victoria, Feb. 27-28, 1952

British Columbia, 1956, Summary of Business Activity in. Bureau of Economics and Statistics, Department of Trade and Industries, Victoria.

British Columbia, the Making of a Province. By F. W. Howay. Ryerson Press, Toronto, 1928.

British Columbia and the United States. By Howay, Sage, and Angus. Ryerson Press, Toronto, 1942.

Canadian Regions, a Geography of Canada. By Putnam, Brouillette, Kerr, and Robinson. J. M. Dent & Sons, Toronto-Vancouver, 1952.

Lower Mainland Looks Ahead, The. Report and Outline Plan of the Lower Mainland Regions of British Columbia. Prepared by Lower Mainland Regional Planning Board of British Columbia, New Westminster, 1952.

Queen Charlotte Islands. British Columbia Heritage Series II, Vol. I. Department of Education, Victoria, 1953.

Other Books and Articles

CARR, EMILY. *Growing Pains: The Autobiography of Emily Carr.* Oxford University Press, Toronto, 1946.

CRISP, WILLIAM G. *White Gold in the Cassiar.* J. M. Dent & Sons, Toronto-Vancouver, 1955.

DAWSON, WILL. *Ahoy There.* J. M. Dent & Sons, Vancouver, 1955.

DUNCAN, ERIC. *Fifty-Seven Years in Comox Valley*. Comox Argus Company, Courtenay,

EVANS, HUBERT. *Mist on the River* (Novel of Skeena River). Copp Clark Company, Toronto-Montreal, 1954.

HAIG-BROWN, RODERICK. *Return to the River*. William Morrow & Company, New York, 1941.

———. *The Western Angler*. William Morrow & Company, New York, 1941.

HAWTHORN, HARRY B. (ed.). *The Doukhobors of British Columbia*. University of British Columbia and J. M. Dent & Sons, Vancouver, 1955.

HUTCHINSON, BRUCE. *The Fraser*. Rinehart and Company, New York, 1955.

———. *The Unknown Country*. Coward McCann, New York, 1942.

JENNESS, DIAMOND. *Indians of Canada*. National Museum of Canada, Anthropological Series, No. 15. Third Edition, 1955.

JOHNSON, KATE. *Arrow Lake Country*. Nakusp, 1952.

KELSEY, VERA. *Red River Runs North!* Harper & Brothers, New York, 1951.

———. *Young Men so Daring*. The Bobbs-Merrill Company, Indianapolis, 1956.

LEACOCK, STEPHEN. *Canada; The Foundations of Its Future*. Privately Printed in Montreal, 1951.

LYONS, C. P. *Milestones in Ogopogo Land*. Evergreen Press, Vancouver, 1957.

MADISON, GRANT. *River for My Sidewalk*. J. M. Dent & Sons, Vancouver, 1957.

MUNDAY, DON. *The Unknown Mountain* (Mt. Waddington). Hodder and Stoughton, London, 1948.

PATTERSON, R. M. *The Dangerous River* (Liard River). Allan and Unwin, London, 1954.

RAVENHILL, ALICE. *Native Tribes of British Columbia*. Charles F. Banfield, Victoria, 1938.

ROBINSON, NOEL. *Blazing the Trail Through the Rockies* (Walter Moberly). *News-Advertiser*, Vancouver, n.d.

STEPHEN, PAMELA. *Winged Canoes at Nootka*. J. M. Dent & Sons, Vancouver, 1956.

WHEELER, A. O. *The Selkirk Range*. 2 vols. Government Printing Bureau, Ottawa, 1905.

BUCKLAND, F. M. *Co-operative Marketing in British Columbia*. Okanagan Historical Society Report, 1951.

Bibliography

MAGOR, JOHN F. *British Columbia's North Country, Prince Rupert Daily News*, Aug. 25 to Sept. 19, 1956.

MCBAIN, C. W. *Vancouver's Early Days*. Report of Proceedings of the 45th Annual General Meeting of the Corporation of British Columbia Land Surveyors.

MCKELVIE, B. A. *Fort Langley, The Province*, Vancouver, 1947.

———. *Vancouver and the Trail of '98, The Province*, Vancouver, May 18, 1957.

PORTER, MCKENZIE. *To Live on an Island in the Pacific* (Gulf Islands), *Maclean's Magazine*, Oct. 1, 1955.

SAGE, WALTER. *Vancouver: The Rise of a City. Dalhousie Review*, Vol. 17, April, 1937.

INDEX

Aberdeen, Lord, 199
Agriculture, 36, 56, 60, 67, 70, 77-78,
  82, 87, 109, 125, 133, 145, 180,
  183, 186, 188-189, 195, 200,
  237, 239, 266, 284-285
Alaska, 8, 11, 71, 97, 101
Alberta, 77, 86, 91, 294
Astor, John Jacob, 73, 190, 223
Astoria, 190, 222, 223

Baker, Colonel James, 271
Banff, 274
Bedaux, Charles Eugene, 73
Bennett Buggy, 70, 186
Bennett, R. B., Prime Minister, 70
Bering, Vitus, 34
Black, Captain William, 233
Britain, 12, 35, 108, 109, 121
British Columbia cities, towns, vil-
  lages:
  Ainsworth, 262
  Alberni, 141, 143, 145
  Alert Bay, 17
  Argenta, 266
  Ashcroft, 186, 187
  Atlin, 97, 102
  Bamfield, 164
  Barkerville, 174-178
  Beaverdell, 234
  Bella Bella, 22-23
  Boat Encampment, 275
  Bridge River, 172
  Brilliant, 249
  Britannia Beach, 169
  Burnaby, 284, 292
  Campbell River, 134-140
  Castlegar, 233, 234, 240, 241
  Chamiss Bay, 162
  Chemainus, 126
  Clinton, 185
  Clo-oose, 164
  Coal Creek, 273
  Coal Harbour, 164
  Coquitlam, 292
  Courtenay, 133
  Cowichan Bay, 126
  Craigellachie, 227
  Cranbrook, 271-276
  Dawson Creek, 70, 71, 75-84, 95,
    96, 180, 215

British Columbia cities, towns,
  villages—Continued
  Delta, 292
  East Pine, 69
  Esperanza, 161
  Esquimalt, 117
  Estevan Point, 150-151, 155, 156
  Fernie, 272, 273-274, 286
  Fort Nelson, 73, 96, 97
  Fort St. John, 71, 74, 85-94, 95,
    96, 267
  Fruitvale, 250
  Golden, 230
  Gold River, 157, 158
  Grand Forks, 237
  Greenwood, 236
  Hazelton, 55
  Hope, 281, 282, 283, 286
  Kamloops, 186, 187, 189-195,
    201, 204, 219, 293
  Kaslo, 256, 262, 263-264
  Kelowna, 202-208, 209, 210, 211,
    213, 234, 235
  Kemano, 24, 26, 27
  Kimberley, 246, 262, 272
  Kinnaird, 241
  Kitimat, 20, 25-34, 56, 102, 294
  Ladysmith, 126
  Lardo, 264, 265
  Lillooet, 173, 174, 182, 280
  Lytton, 179, 187, 279, 286
  Masset, 35-36
  Michel, 273
  Midway, 236, 258
  Montrose, 250
  Nanaimo, 126-131, 134, 141
  Nelson, 252-258, 272
  New Westminister, 117, 122, 284,
    286, 292
  North Vancouver, 292
  Ocean Falls, 24-25, 44, 145
  Oliver, 211
  Osoyoos, 211
  Oyster Bay, 134
  Parksville, 142
  Penticton, 204, 209, 210-215, 220,
    233, 234
  Port Alberni, 134, 143-148, 153,
    215
  Port Alice, 163

303

Index

Index

Index

Index

307

Index

Index

309

Mar 24	46	May 2			
May 14	SEP 27	Oct 8			
2994	NOV 1	Mav 20			
Jun 30	JAN. 3 1962	Apr 17			
672	JAN. 22 1962	May 8.			
Jul 12	FEB. 23 1962	Dec 28			
3501	APR. 5	Feb 10			
Aug 2	APR. 28	Hens			
616	Sep				
Aug 13					

PACI

RUPERT

BANKS.